Adolescent Psychotherap

Counsellors and psychotherapists are faced with ever-increasing complexity in their work with adolescents. In this book, Bronagh Starrs offers an understanding of developmental and therapeutic process from a relational-phenomenological Gestalt perspective.

Starrs shows how the adolescent's presenting symptom issues are statements of compromised lifespace integrity and demonstrates therapeutic sensibility to the adolescent's first-person experience. Throughout the book, the clinician is offered extensive relational and creative strategies to support integrity repair for the adolescent. The developmental impact of various lifespace contexts are discussed, including parental separation, complex family configuration, grief, adoption and emerging sexual orientation and gender experience. Therapeutic responses to common creative adjustments are explored, including anxiety, school refusal, depression, self-harm, suicide, eating disorders, alcohol and drug use and sexual trauma.

Adolescent Psychotherapy: A Radical Relational Approach will help counsellors and psychotherapists to develop deeper levels of competency in their work as adolescent psychotherapists, as they navigate the complex and fascinating experience of therapy with teenagers. This exceptional contribution is highly suitable for both experienced practitioners and students of counselling and psychotherapy.

Bronagh Starrs is Creator and Programme Director for the MSc Adolescent Psychotherapy at Dublin Counselling & Therapy Centre, Republic of Ireland and University of Northampton, UK. She is also Director of Blackfort Adolescent Gestalt Institute and maintains a private practice in Omagh, Northern Ireland, as a psychotherapist and clinical supervisor, specialising in working with adolescents and their parents.

"This practical and sensitive book should be in the hands of every adolescent psychotherapist. Bronagh Starrs brings both therapist and 'parenting adults' to hear the young person's often devastated *experience* – lost, confused, excluded, and so on. Then the disturbing behavior begins to make sense to everyone, and often to become less necessary. So well-written that it is hard to put down, this book is a humanistic treasure."

—Donna M. Orange, Ph.D., Psy.D., author, *The Suffering Stranger:*
Hermeneutics for Everyday Clinical Practice (Routledge, 2011) and
Nourishing the Inner Life of Clinicians and Humanitarians:
The Ethical Turn in Psychoanalysis (Routledge, 2015)

"Every committed teacher waits their career for that student who not only 'gets' what they are trying to teach, but gets it better than they do themselves, taking an insight or perspective to a new place, revealing entirely new implications and applications. For me, that student has been Bronagh Starrs. Over the years, I have watched her develop a brilliant vision and a fierce commitment to understanding and healing troubled adolescents. If you work with adolescents and their families, read this book; and then read it again. It will change the way you work."

—Mark McConville, Ph.D., author, *Adolescence:*
Psychotherapy and the Emergent Self

"Not since McConville's eminently readable and accessible book, *Adolescence*, have I read such an informative, readable, and humane book on therapy with suffering adolescents. In every chapter, her love and practical wisdom shine through her words. A trove of helpful inspiration and ideas, as well as theory to support your practice, for anyone who treats adolescents."

—Lynne Jacobs, Ph.D., co-founder of the Pacific Gestalt Institute, and
Training and Supervising analyst at the Institute of Contemporary
Psychoanalysis, Los Angeles

"I once saw an expert kayaker take only one precise paddle stroke before calmly navigating a terrifying rapid. This image was brought to mind while reading Bronagh Starrs' incisive reflections and advice about the best ways to help adolescents in the therapeutic context. She provides keen recommendations on how to help teens keep their own boats from rolling during tricky passages. She also makes clear how therapists can maintain, in her words, "robust composure during decidedly tense moments." All of us who either have teenagers or work with them will benefit from her expertise."

—Peter Mortola, Ph.D., Professor of Counseling and
School Psychology at Lewis and Clark College in Portland,
Oregon, and the author of *Windowframes: Learning the art of
Gestalt play therapy the Oaklander way*

"For years colleagues have raved to me about Bronagh Starrs' work with adolescents and their worlds; now I understand why. This book is essential reading not only for therapists, counselors, teachers, and others who work with adolescents (or with their parents), but also for the parents and families themselves, and others who live with adolescents, love them, are alternately charmed and frustrated by them (and frustrate them in their turn), find them at times uncommunicative, unpredictable, even maddening, (and of course drive their adolescent loved ones crazy as well) – and/or all of the above!

Starrs places the emphasis of her approach right where outcome research shows it should be: on the *therapeutic relationship itself*, that crucial contact space which precedes and underlies all the acronyms and 'how-to's' or ordinary models of other manuals. If this is a 'how-to' book, it's about how to build that "meaningful therapeutic relationship," on which everything else depends. The goal and result are not just the 'fixing' of a temporary symptom, but a restoration of healthy development and growth.

Each chapter offers rich, practical insights, grounded and unified by this clear relational perspective. I've been in practice for over 40 years, have raised six adolescents, and my foster son is now a high school principal in his later thirties. And in the chapter on Fostering, for example, I read insights that I wish I had had twenty years ago when he was in his turbulent years. Thank you, Bronagh Starrs, for this gift to all of us who live and work with the issues of this great inflection-stage of life, and through us to our clients, students, children, grandchildren and others."

—Gordon Wheeler, Ph.D., President and CEO,
Esalen Insititue, Big Sur, California, and
author of *Gestalt Therapy* in the APA book series
Major Methods in Psychotherapy, and co-editor
(with Mark McConville) of *The Heart of Development:
Gestalt Approaches to Children, Adolescents, and their
Worlds (Vol. I: Childhood; Vol. 2: Adolescence)*

Adolescent Psychotherapy

A Radical Relational Approach

Bronagh Starrs

Routledge
Taylor & Francis Group

LONDON AND NEW YORK

First published 2019
by Routledge
2 Park Square, Milton Park, Abingdon, Oxon OX14 4RN

and by Routledge
711 Third Avenue, New York, NY 10017

Routledge is an imprint of the Taylor & Francis Group, an informa business

© 2019 Bronagh Starrs

British Library Cataloguing-in-Publication Data
A catalogue record for this book is available from the British
Library

Library of Congress Cataloging-in-Publication Data
Names: Starrs, Bronagh, 1970– author.
Title: Adolescent psychotherapy : a radical relational
    approach / Bronagh Starrs.
Description: Milton Park, Abingdon, Oxon ; New York, NY :
    Routledge, 2019. | Includes bibliographical references and index.
Identifiers: LCCN 2018034621 (print) | LCCN 2018034958
    (ebook) | ISBN 9780429460746 (Master) | ISBN 9780429864636
    (Web PDF) | ISBN 9780429864629 (ePub) | ISBN
    9780429864612 (Mobipocket/Kindle) | ISBN 9781138624252
    (hardback : alk. paper) | ISBN 9781138624290 (pbk : alk.
    paper) | ISBN 9780429460746 (ebk)
Subjects: LCSH: Adolescent psychotherapy.
Classification: LCC RJ503 (ebook) | LCC RJ503 .S717 2019
    (print) | DDC 616.89/140835—dc23
LC record available at https://lccn.loc.gov/2018034621

ISBN: 978-1-138-62425-2 (hbk)
ISBN: 978-1-138-62429-0 (pbk)
ISBN: 978-0-429-46074-6 (ebk)

Typeset in Times New Roman
by Apex CoVantage, LLC

Printed and bound in Great Britain by
TJ International Ltd, Padstow, Cornwall

For Gráinne

Contents

Acknowledgements

This book is a synthesis of my understanding of the dynamics of development in adolescence and how psychotherapy can support the unfolding of this process. Without support and collaboration from others, this book would not have been possible. My special and foremost thanks and admiration goes to the many adolescents I have had the privilege of coming to know in therapy, especially those who gave permission for their stories and images to be represented throughout the book. My appreciation also to the parenting adults who have trusted me help navigate these young people through their developmental challenges. Identifying information has been altered to ensure anonymity for both adolescents and parenting adults.

As a critical influence in my evolution as an adolescent psychotherapist, I owe deep gratitude to Mark McConville for his wisdom, friendship and encouragement over the years. A sincere thank you also to Maeve Lewis and Pat Deery for their support and guidance through the years. For reading of chapters of this manuscript, I wish to thank Tim Hannon and Leslie Brown.

I owe a special and ongoing debt of gratitude to all faculty, staff and students at Dublin Counselling and Therapy Centre. In particular, Paul O'Donoghue, Brian Howlett, Jennifer Foran and Anne Randolph.

I wish to thank Joanne Forshaw, editor, and Charles Bath, senior editorial assistant, at Routledge, for their interest and support throughout the project. I would also like to acknowledge Sheri Sipka, production editor, and the production team at Routledge for their thoughtful attention to the manuscript.

Finally, I want to thank my family. My husband, Colin, for his unwavering encouragement and his graceful accommodation to my dedication to my work. I am grateful to him and to Edel, Anita, Stephen and Nicola for their boundless support and for the sense of belonging they bring to my life. And to Emily and Odhrán, my niece and nephew – two wonderful emerging adolescents who have my heart.

Introduction

The aim in writing this book is to offer an alternative to the typical treatment manuals which are available to clinicians who work with an adolescent client population. In the last number of years schools, counselling organisations and those in private practice have experienced a notable increase in both referrals and direct requests for therapeutic support for adolescents. Many professionals have undertaken either a child- or adult-oriented training and feel out of their depth with the complexity of the work with adolescent clients. What follows are my interpretations and conclusions, from my accumulated experience, regarding the dynamics of development and therapy with this age group, which have fascinated me from my earliest days as a therapist. This model is anchored in Gestalt therapy theory and in recent advances in the study of both neuroscience and developmental trauma.

Establishing relationally meaningful therapeutic alliances with both the adolescent and his parents and securing the adolescent's commitment to becoming a client in the first place require rich appreciation and close attention to nuanced contact episodes from the outset. Much of the literature is written from beyond this point, as if it is a given that the helping professional innately possesses the required contact skills to engage meaningfully with an adolescent. In my extensive experience as a trainer and supervisor, this is certainly not the general experience for professionals, irrespective of therapeutic orientation, who typically find themselves challenged by the frequently directionless and bewildering experience of therapy with a teenager. Many books are written from a cognitive and behavioural modification perspective and are focused on finding solutions for problems. Strategies are offered which relieve symptoms and outcome is evaluated on symptomatic amelioration in the short term.

This book is unique in that it offers a radical relational methodology which not only addresses symptoms, but also attends to the adolescent's wider developmental process. Therapeutic work with adolescents is approached from a relational-phenomenological perspective and offers strategic guidance to clinicians from the assessment process right through to specific clinical presentations (e.g. anxiety, eating disorders, suicide, etc.) and case management issues. Attention is afforded to a broad spectrum of clinical tasks, including formulation of a developmentally appropriate therapeutic plan, ongoing work with parents, development of a meaningful therapeutic alliance with the adolescent, ethical and legal issues and working within a multi-disciplinary context. A methodology is presented, which provides specific relational techniques for an array of presenting situations, all of which will be immediately translatable within the therapeutic space for any professional who reads the book.

The book's focus is on demonstrating to the reader the art of contact assessment and intervention. Exploration of therapeutic praxis includes detailed deconstruction and elucidation of contact process in the work with adolescents and their parents – demonstrating a relational approach to working with struggling adolescents. Emphasis is placed on development of the therapeutic relationship and commitment to the adolescent's first-person experience. This model of development and therapy has been created over 18 years of working as an adolescent psychotherapist. The first four chapters set out the methodology. Most of the remaining chapters deal with specific clinical presentations and case management issues. Rather than simply instructing the reader on *what to do*, this book also attempts to illustrate *how to do it* as I describe the detailed nuances of contact with the adolescent.

The opening chapter offers an exploration of how presenting symptom issues are understood from a relational perspective, drawing on and extending Gestalt therapy theory with regard to defining adolescent developmental process. Chapter 2 deals with assessment in adolescent psychotherapy and includes commentary on differences between counselling and psychotherapy in work with young people. Several principal difficulties encountered in psychotherapeutic work with adolescents are identified and management of these challenges is discussed.

Chapter 3 emphasises the art of supporting parents to develop deeper attunement to their adolescent children. Parenting strategy work is described, and instruction is offered on how to identify and manage family dynamics which may be influencing the adolescent and the therapeutic enterprise. This section includes discussion of how the complexity of confidentiality is managed in therapeutic work with adolescents.

Chapter 4, focusing on one-to-one engagement with adolescents, offers a deconstruction of the detailed nuances (both verbal and nonverbal) in contact with adolescent clients to extend the clinician's capacity to develop trusting and meaningful therapeutic relationships with this age group. The reader is offered an in-depth description of how to work with creative process to support contact, which includes an introduction to a creative therapeutic approach which I have developed and named *Sandspace*.

The structure of family systems has changed and very often these dynamics of family experience create additional challenge for the adolescent as she attempts to find a newly emerging sense of belonging and identity in the world. Chapter 5 explores the impact of separation and complex family configurations for the adolescent, paying particular attention to the adolescent's first-person experience. A clear relational framework for organising therapeutic intervention is presented, which includes intervention with parenting adults.

Adolescent development occurs within a lifespace context which is often complex and traumatic. The adopted or fostered child's personal biographical context creates additional layers of complexity as she rises to the developmental challenge of taking ownership of the self. And so, Chapter 6 will explore the complex lifespace dynamics which form self-experience for the adopted and fostered adolescent. Living with parental loss will also be explored. Content will include discussion of the core existential and phenomenological issues for these adolescents; appreciation of the challenge of identity integration relating to both domestic and international transracial adoption; exploring the meaning behind impulsive, anxious and insecure presentation. Strategies will be presented to support the adolescent to find language for and make meaning of his experience; and to explore family-field dynamics and find ways of supporting parent-adolescent relational connections.

The following three chapters focus on the most common presenting symptoms which are encountered in adolescent psychotherapy. Chapter 7 explores the dynamics of anxiety, depression, self-harm and suicide. The nature of anxiety, as a clinical presentation in adolescence, is explored from a phenomenological perspective and the multi-layers of context enquiry are demonstrated through a comprehensive case example. Emphasis is placed on fostering both curiosity and relational connection in the work, rather than employing specific techniques.

This chapter also explores a relational-phenomenological approach to working with adolescents whose presenting symptom issues include depression, self-harming behaviours and suicidal presentation. The symptom structure of these clinical presentations is examined and description is included of how contextually relevant dynamics influence the adolescent's self-experience. I outline how undersupported developmental process, transitional insecurity, the presence of trauma and wider environmental influences may be shaping the adolescent's lifespace, resulting in the manifestation of these symptoms. Relational methodology for working with depressed and self-harming adolescents is presented.

Chapter 8 offers an exploration of the phenomenological experience of the eating-disordered adolescent. Readers will be introduced to my specific manner of working with this client group, which includes an understanding of the deeper, developmental meaning of the eating disorder for the adolescent and interventions aimed at heightening the adolescent's self-concern and choicefulness. Chapter 9 focuses on the issue of impulse-driven behaviour with regard to substance use and its implications for the developing adolescent physically, psychologically and interpersonally. Strategies are presented which aim to support the adolescent in adopting greater choicefulness and ownership of his experience.

Chapters 10 and 11 address the area of sexual development in adolescence. The prevalence of sexual assault, sexually transmitted disease and unplanned pregnancy continues to increase, despite us being more open than ever before in dialogue with adolescents about sexual matters. It is evident that information alone is insufficient for the adolescent to support the adolescent's adoption of full and responsible ownership of his sexual identity, and so I present to the reader a metaphorical manner of supporting choiceful sexual decision-making and expression, which I have been successfully implementing with clients. Supporting and challenging the adolescent who has engaged in sexually maladaptive behaviour will also be discussed. In addition, strategies for supporting the adolescent who is exploring and embracing his sexual orientation and gender experience are also offered. Attention will also be given to therapeutic intervention with sexually traumatised adolescents, supporting their recovery from devastation to a more empowered and safe experience of lifespace identity. The many aspects of recovery and meaning-making are outlined.

Many adolescent clients have already acquired one or multiple diagnoses. Chapter 12 offers a phenomenological approach to understanding the adolescent by exploration of the adolescent's lifespace dynamics through the lens of diagnosis, his capacity to make contact and the manner in which he creatively adjusts in the world through this label. In it, I attempt to demonstrate how to depathologise the adolescent's self-experience through meaning-making and non-shaming integration of the diagnosis into overall experience, supporting movement away from a sense of the self as pathologised, to adopting greater ownership of experience and choicefulness in his life.

The final chapter addresses case management issues which the therapist is bound to navigate in the course of her work with adolescents. Therapeutic work with this age group is often situated within a wider multi-disciplinary context which can create anxiety for the practitioner who may be unclear and unconfident with regard to her and others' roles in situations where interprofessional collaboration is required. These anxieties can make it difficult to continue to hold the adolescent therapeutically. This chapter also defines the adolescent therapist's role and responsibilities with regard to child protection, therapeutic, ethical and legal issues with arise in the work with young people. Strategies will be presented which support clinicians to adopt greater competence within the wider professional arena. Broad guidance regarding case meetings, report writing and legal work will be included.

The focus of this book is to illuminate the transformative possibility of the therapeutic enterprise with adolescents. In it I offer the reader a weave of my understanding and case examples which, I hope, will render its contents clinically useful and immediately transferrable to the clinician's own therapeutic practice. My hope too is that it may contribute to the wider attempts at understanding how to intervene therapeutically to make a difference in the lives of adolescents who are struggling. It is an immense privilege to steward a lost, distressed adolescent, through the process of healing, towards the authoring of a personally meaningful future. I passionately believe that this is *always* possible *with sufficient support*. Unfortunately, however, not every troubled adolescent has access to the extent of support that he needs.

Chapter 1

Development, shame and lifespace integrity

Fourteen-year-old Daniel lives with his mother and two younger siblings. His parents separated during the fifth month of his pregnancy. His father, who was violent and alcoholic, punched his mother in the face and stomach as she sat in the passenger seat of their van. She opened the door and jumped out of the moving vehicle. This marked the end of their relationship. Daniel, the child in her womb, survived. His mother, who has been medicated for depression for over a decade, has been in several relationships since and is now pregnant with her fourth child. Her new partner, this child's father, has recently moved into the family home. Daniel spends much of his time playing his game console and hanging out with his friends. He was diagnosed with ADHD when he was 6 years old and has been in trouble often in school for disruptive and aggressive behaviour. He is verbally and sometimes physically abusive to his mother and siblings. The school principal has spoken to Daniel's mother, suggesting therapeutic support to help him manage his behaviour. Both she and the school are at a loss as to how to reach and influence him. The adolescent comes unwillingly to the initial session with his mother, having been promised a new pair of trainers in return for his attendance.

Sixteen-year-old Louise is the youngest of three girls. Her siblings are both studying medicine at college, and she lives at home with her parents. High achievement in academics and career has been a core family value and focus throughout the children's lives. Louise is a perfectionist, spending long hours studying and sometimes re-starting a homework assignment from scratch late on a school night, if she deems it sub-standard. She is top of her class across all subjects and has never received less than 92 percent in any examination. Louise is also involved in a number of extra-curricular activities, including music lessons, drama and football and is a keen member of the local athletics club. Recently Louise has been losing weight at a concerning rate and looks very thin, although she assures her mother that she is eating sufficiently. She has become vegetarian and has cut wheat and refined sugar from her diet. Louise's mother is becoming concerned. Her father is less so and feels that his wife's insistence on making an appointment to see a therapist is an overreaction. Louise feels strongly that there is no problem, though she obliges her parents by attending this one session.

As more and more adolescents find their way to therapy, practitioners are encountering increasingly complex clinical scenarios. Most of these young people, like Daniel and Louise, have been nominated by concerned adults as suitable candidates for psychotherapy. Some engage willingly, responding readily to dialogue and interventions. Others arrive sceptical and oppositional, resolved neither to say a word nor to come back a second time. The adolescent therapist is presented with some intriguing dilemmas: How does she create a rich and meaningful therapeutic relationship with someone who may not even want to show up? How does she recruit him as a client in the first instance? How does she engage with someone whose capacity for self-reflection will, in all likelihood, be limited? How does she understand what is happening, or trying to happen, developmentally in his life? What it is that he needs? How might she intervene to make a difference in the growth and development of this adolescent who has found a way into her office and her life? I have pondered these questions for years and in the process have attempted to grasp the dynamics of the adolescent journey and to appreciate the unique subtleties of therapeutic engagement with this age group.

When an adolescent is referred for psychotherapy, this is generally an indication that there is a lack of support for and momentum within his developmental process. This will often manifest in the emergence of symptoms. For example, the adolescent may present with an eating disorder or anxiety or may be engaging in high-risk or self-harming behaviours. There are three principal categories of referral:

Direct Issues: The adolescent is or is not doing, feeling or thinking something which is troubling him and/or others. Examples include anxiety, depression, substance misuse, low academic motivation, aggression, etc.

Indirect Issues: The adolescent's environment is creating complexity and strife for him. These issues include separation, trauma, grief, adoption, peer isolation, etc.

Overt Developmental Issues: The adolescent's 'attitude' and 'lack of respect' for parents, his 'treating this house like a hotel' or battling with parental control are seen as the problem.

Referral typically comes with expectation to eliminate these issues. Symptoms are regularly misinterpreted as instances of maladaptive behaviour and as problems to be solved. It is always advisable to look beyond presenting issues to understand the dynamics which are influencing an adolescent's experience in the world, as this will help orient the therapist with regard to intervention. Praxis with any adolescent client is predicated on the clinician's tentative assessment, which is not primarily attuned to symptoms or problem behaviours, but to the underlying, unfolding, developmental drama.

The concept of development

Human experience has always been the subject of fascination for psychotherapists, philosophers, psychologists, anthropologists, educationists and sociologists.

Theories of adolescence include biological, cultural, psychosocial and cognitive aspects of experience. Development is understood as the maturation of various functions, such as pathways of sexual energy (Freud and Strachey, 1949), structural cognitive schemes (Inhelder and Piaget, 2013), capacity for social learning (Bandura, 1962) and so on. Schools of psychotherapy have traditionally formulated developmental models as meta-psychological frameworks, often integrating these concepts into their theoretical constructs. These models contain each school's presumptions concerning what it means to be human and serve implicitly as theories of psychopathology. For example, an anxious adolescent's presentation might be understood as evidence of intrapsychic conflict, perhaps triggered by emergent adolescent libido; as evidence of family dissonance; or as maladaptive thoughts and behaviour which require modification. How meaning is made of the information presented, depending upon the psychotherapist's theoretical orientation, will shape therapeutic interventions.

My understanding of adolescent development has been influenced by Gestalt psychology and psychotherapy, specifically the work of Kurt Lewin (Lewin, 1939) and Mark McConville (McConville, 1995), who conceive of the essence of adolescent developmental process from a holistic, phenomenological perspective. Gestalt psychologist Kurt Lewin (1890–1947), in his theory of adolescence *Field Theory and Experiment in Social Psychology* (1939) asserted that adolescents do not develop in isolation, but that development is an integrative process of biological, psychological and social circumstance which shapes how we construct our experience and move forward in the world. Lewin created the term *lifespace* to describe this mutually influential ground of environmental and personal elements which comprise the adolescent's phenomenological and ever-expanding world of experience. It is a dynamically evolving and mutually influential process whose spatial and temporal dimensions are continuous. Perception is constructed and behaviour is shaped at every moment within this interactive *self-in-and-of-the-lifespace* phenomenon through reciprocal contact.

Our relationship to the lifespace resembles our relationship to oxygen: we are continually breathing in and out; we do this unconsciously, even when we sleep. We cannot see the oxygen and are mostly unaware that we are breathing at all, even though our very existence depends on it. Similarly, our lifespace is the framework within and around which we have our existence. It houses our body, mind, feelings and thoughts; our familial, social, cultural, political and geographical contexts; our biographical context, including pre- and perinatal experience. It shapes everything about us. Self cannot exist outside of this lifespace and is not separate from it. There is no such thing as self-development. There is only self-in-and-of-the-lifespace development. The adolescent's experience will *always* make sense when we situate the detail of his presentation within his wider lifespace context.

Contact, for Gestalt Therapy theory is the cornerstone of psychological functioning, referring essentially to the way an individual engages and interacts with the world and with himself. In the magnum opus of Gestalt Therapy, *Gestalt Therapy: Excitement And Growth In The Human Personality* (1951), the concept

of contact was postulated as the defining characteristic of the self, in sharp con-
tradistinction to the dominant intrapsychic psychoanalytic models of the day. The
authors spoke of the *contact boundary* as the concrete, experiential meeting place
of self and other. It is the evolution of this meeting place, its organisation and
functioning, that Mark McConville offers as the critical issue for understanding
adolescent development (McConville, 1995). His model tracks the evolution of
the contact boundary via recursive processes of differentiation of the adolescent
in the family field. He contends that as the adolescent develops, his sense of differentiation in and from his environment increases and he begins to feel somehow
different in terms of subjective experience of himself. These changes lead him to
engage his world in new ways.

Adolescence is universally described as a time of separation and individuation.
These terms are misguiding: human beings are neither separate nor individual.
We do not become separate from our families: we may live without them in our
day-to-day world, even managing to maintain rigid psychological boundaries
which prevent us thinking about them or feeling into memories from our childhood. However, like it or not, we are imprinted by and forever connected to our
formative relational experience. During adolescence *our relationship to these
relationships* evolves with ever-increasing sophistication. Characteristically during the teenage years, adolescents begin to create more definitive boundaries *in
relation to* their families, their peers and the wider adult world. The adolescent's
relationship to the world of other becomes progressively more differentiated as
she searches for balance between relational intimacy and personal agency. Development in adolescence is the defining of these contact boundaries (McConville,
1995). The adolescent's behaviour and experience begins to make greater sense
through appreciation of the growth of contact functions through adolescence.

Creative adjustment

As Gestalt therapy theory understands development as the evolution of contact
boundary process, the mechanism by which development takes places is concep-
tualised as *creative adjustment* (Perls, Hefferline and Goodman, 1951). The adolescent's lifespace is imprinted with the people and experiences he encounters.
This imprint shapes how he thinks of himself and of his world, as well as influencing his contact style within his lifespace. He is creatively adjusting to the conditions within his lifespace at every given moment: attempting to balance his needs
with given or perceived environmental conditions. If the lifespace is experienced
as generally supportive, then we can expect that the adolescent will come to trust
this support and will develop faith in himself and in his world. Similarly, a hostile
imprint within the lifespace engenders feelings of exposure and mistrust, creating
low expectation of being supported, very often translating into a self-statement of
inadequacy, where the adolescent finds himself lacking.

If we attend to an adolescent's phenomenological experience, we inevitably
discover developmental wisdom in any creative adjustment. However, the rigid

quality of thoughts and behaviours may have long since outlived their usefulness and may themselves pose the biggest threat to his integrity. For unsupported
adolescents these creative adjustments may become destructive and inflexible.
Feelings of shame naturally emerge in response to compromise within the adolescent's lifespace. Lee and Wheeler (2003) describe shame as the experience of
one's needs not being received, potentially resulting in a disconnect both from
others and from the need. This is a familiar experience, especially in adolescence,
where there is potential for shame at every turn. However, if an adolescent has
been persistently compromised and support is typically inadequate or absent, the
individual becomes saturated with *ground shame* (Lee and Wheeler, 2003). This
pervasive experience of shame becomes the lens through which he views himself
and his world.

There is no such thing as 'normal' development; there is only supported or
under-supported development. The Gestalt premise of adolescent development
as *contact boundary development* (McConville, 1995), encompassing biological,
psychosexual, cognitive and social development in a whole-field phenomenon,
together with the concept of creative adjustment as the process by which development unfolds, emphasises that development is neither linear nor pre-determined.
This developmental approach orients the clinician to understand an adolescent's
presenting issues not so much as symptoms of a diagnosable disorder but as the
manifestation of an under-supported developmental process and of a lifespace
situation infused with shame. Each adolescent lifespace experience is appreciated as a uniquely personal developmental narrative, and as such, this approach
offers an implicitly respectful, existential model of adolescent development. It
follows, then, that all therapeutic intervention emerges from the ground of this
appreciation. And so, this theoretical orientation directs the therapist to assess
the lifespace conditions that contextualise the symptomatic adolescent, becoming
curious about how the adolescent's presentation is experienced and responded
to – a response which includes his parents and also now his therapist. Rather than
being a technique-oriented methodology, it is, at its heart, a genuinely existential-
relational encounter which creates possibility to deepen and enrich contact – that
is to say, to support development.

Unsupported development and trauma

Over the past number of decades, considerable research has been undertaken as
we continue in our attempts to understand trauma and its impact on the experience of being human. Recent developments, particularly in the field of neuroscience, have contributed significantly to our understanding. The various modalities,
including Eye-Movement Desensitization and Reprocessing (Shapiro, 2001),
Dialectical Behavioural Therapy (Linehan, 2015), Cognitive-Behavioural Therapy (Beck, 2011), Sensorimotor Psychotherapy (Ogden et al., 2015) and Psycho-
dynamic Psychotherapy (Jung et al., 1983), have each developed approaches to
treat trauma survivors. Divergent methodologies include emphasis on cognitive

processing, behaviour modification and physiological experiencing, with varying degrees of appreciation of the complex nature of trauma.

I have long been fascinated in figuring out (phenomenologically at least) what precisely it is that becomes traumatised and how it is healed. My experience as a clinician over the years has taught me that the adolescent is motivated by three principal yearnings. These yearnings are for physiological, psychological and interpersonal integrity. By integrity I mean an experience of wellbeing, security and comfort which emerges when these yearnings are sufficiently supported. The adolescent has a fundamental yearning to inhabit a body which is healthy, able and safe; to have a sense of belonging with others who care for and appreciate him; and to experience himself and his world with benevolence. When I speak of trauma, I am describing an experience which creates considerable disruption and compromise for the adolescent within these physiological, psychological and interpersonal domains of experience. Trauma can be a single event, a cluster of events, or a chronic situation which is negotiated on a repeated basis. The experience falls outside the range of what is normative, and it is not possible for the adolescent to process the experience in the present moment; subsequently he enters a state of alarm and overwhelm. The aftermath of trauma for any adolescent typically includes a detrimental impact on sensory and affect regulation, self and world-concept and interpersonal relating (Van der Kolk, 2015).

The adolescent's level of distress is commensurate with both the gravity of the situation and the level of support available to him. So, for example, Shane is ambivalent about continuing to play soccer as he and his friends have recently formed a band. When he is not selected for the school team, this does not cause him much consternation. Support comes from his emerging identity as a rock guitarist, his newly forming music friendships and his waning interest in soccer. He shrugs it off, and there is no insult to his integrity. Conversely, when an adolescent is forced to tolerate serious compromise to his integrity without adequate support, he is traumatised by the experience and this contact episode begins to shape how he feels, thinks and behaves. An adolescent who is traumatised by an experience tends to have a vested interest in dumbing down contact and faces many more developmental challenges and vicissitudes than his more supported counterparts. For example, Karen, who has become accustomed over the years to hearing her father's footsteps ascend the staircase and enter her bedroom, knowing what is to follow, endures an ongoing and pervasive threat to all aspects of her integrity. Due to the years of molestation, Karen experiences her body as a grotesque and dangerous shell which encases her. She trusts nobody, and like many traumatised adolescents, prefers the company of animals to humans. The interpersonal world is threatening: *"people are idiots"*. Psychologically, there is a tightly held vitriol present in her feelings and thoughts about herself and her world. She despises herself and feels that life is pointless, wishing she had never been born. Karen has recently made several serious attempts to end her life. My young client has known neither body nor relational integrity, resulting in pronounced psychological anguish. Her lifespace has always been a hostile landscape which has not supported her yearnings for integrity. Sadly, for too many adolescents, trauma is the ground of their lived experience. Their trauma happens within the home; within parental relationships. Their legacy includes despair, self-experience saturated with shame and powerlessness and a deep-seated conviction that they are defective human beings. This adolescent's integrity has been devastated, though as we will see, this devastation is reversible, with adequate support.

Bessel van der Kolk, in his seminal text *The Body Keeps The Score* (Van der Kolk, 2015), explains the impact and legacy of trauma physiologically, psychologically and interpersonally; and thanks to continuing advances in neuroscience research (Porges, 2011), our understanding is becoming increasingly refined. In any traumatic situation, activation of the sympathetic nervous system occurs. This state of hyperarousal does not necessarily recede and may become a chronic physiological experience, which has a cascade effect on all levels of functioning. The psychological and interpersonal impacts potentially result in a lifespace infused with overwhelm, dissociation, mistrust and scepticism (Van der Kolk, 2015). The adolescent who endures pervasive trauma within his lifespace, due to chronic abuse or neglect, remains defensively prepared to negotiate an expanding lifespace which he expects will meet his yearnings with hostility. The imprint of an unsupported lifespace is difficult to disregard as he moves through adolescence, and so, the extreme stress of integrity compromise shapes his experience: shame, despair and meaninglessness begin to define his self-experience and expectations, as a result of the profound integrity loss he has suffered. A repertoire of feeling, thought and behaviour-level responses emerge as he adjusts to a compromised lifespace. His contact may be characterised by inertia, where he feels depressed, passive and despairing. Similarly, he may display aggressive and impulsive tendencies. Yet again, he may be determined to transcend his difficulties by finding ways to create more supportive conditions within his lifespace, as many adolescents do in a remarkably impressive manner. Though, for many, their creative adjustments have a tendency to generate adversity.

Restoration of integrity: an integrity model

As the adolescent creatively adjusts to the limitations of an inadequately supported expansion of his lifespace and capacity for contact, the aim of therapy is to steward him towards a life of integrity. The adolescent may be referred for psychotherapy, with the presenting symptom defined as a direct or indirect issue, an overt developmental dilemma or a combination of all three. The therapist is typically under considerable pressure to intervene at the creative adjustment level: to make the adolescent feel, think and behave more positively and productively. Those bringing him to therapy have a wish for the young person to feel happier, refrain from risky behaviour, stay alive, improve grades, obey rules and talk to family members and other adults with less attitude and more respect. And whilst the adolescent psychotherapist wishes all of these for the adolescent also, for they are the hallmarks of a supported adolescent lifespace, the principal focus for the therapist is the restoration of integrity within the young person's lifespace.

The psychotherapeutic steps I have identified in this process of integrity restoration involve responding to physiological, psychological and interpersonal integrity compromise; attending to the legacy of shame; and transforming creative adjustments within the lifespace. They are broadly outlined below and further developed throughout subsequent chapters:

Physiological: Attention is afforded to physiological experiencing to establish more grounded, embodied contact for the adolescent. This may happen indirectly through the diffusion of the therapist's grounded and embodied presence within the therapeutic space (it is amazing how subtleties in the depth of her own breath and physical presence are transformative for her client). Use of creative devices such as sideways contact and sandspace (see Chapter 4) which diffuse intensity and promote calmness in contact are also relevant interventions in therapy with the dysregulated adolescent. Similarly, focusing directly on the adolescent's somatic experience during sessions may be healing. However, the therapist's enthusiasm for initiating sensorimotor techniques can prove too intense for many clients, who are not so much affected by their somatic experience as by what is happening in the contact between client and therapist. Feelings of vulnerability and exposure during these exercises are common for even the most ostensibly cooperative adolescent. As a consequence, I employ these sorts of direct techniques sparingly.

Psychological: Development of perceptual, cognitive, affective and motivational potential supports an emerging capacity for meaning-making in adolescence. This is the time when human beings begin in earnest to assign personal meaning to significant lifespace experience. And so, a tremendous gift for the adolescent is to have a therapist support him to make sense of his lifespace experience in such a manner that his self-experience and his future are not shaped by the hostility he may have had to endure in his young life. The therapist's influence in the acknowledgement and validation of the mental and emotional effects of adverse lifespace situations enables the young person to understand and appreciate his experience through a less individualistic, self-critical lens.

Interpersonal: Integrity repair at this level of being is addressed through reflection on the adolescent's experience of the interpersonal dimensions of his lifespace, especially his relationships with parents, wider family, peers, educators and others whose influence has been significant. In addition, cultivation of a respectful and developmentally appropriate therapeutic space acts as a healing balm for any interpersonal violation he has experienced, as the therapist fosters mutuality and empowerment. The seeds of lifespace transformation are planted through the experiencing of therapeutic space integrity. The adolescent is supported to become increasingly choiceful in forming and maintaining relationships which are supportive and which validate his yearnings for authentic connection and belonging.

As shame is addressed and neutralised, the sense of self as defective, contaminated or accountable recedes. As this happens, it is important that the adolescent's unmet yearnings and the legacy of his loss is acknowledged and grieved. The therapist's active empathy guides the young person through this aspect of the work towards a sense of hope and belonging. Subsequently, momentum is created within the traumatised adolescent's lifespace. He begins to take himself seriously and finds his voice and his vision. Restoration of integrity and the generation of self-compassion, activated through acknowledgement of and grieving for what might have been, organically modulates creative adjustment responses to some degree. This is further supported by therapeutic interventions aimed at deepening the adolescent's inclination to live with integrity, as the therapist highlights discrepancies between creative adjustments which have begun to outlive their usefulness and the adolescent's emerging capacity for more authentic ownership of his experience.

The adolescent is healed when he no longer defines himself by the trauma he experienced, which is to say, when his capacity for contact is rich.

References

Bandura, A. (1962). *Social Learning Through Imitation*. Lincoln, NE: University of Nebraska Press.

Beck, J. S. (2011). *Cognitive Behavior Therapy, Second Edition: Basics and Beyond*. New York: Guilford Press.

Freud, S. and Strachey, J. (1949). *An Outline of Psychoanalsis*. New York: W. W Norton & Company, Inc.

Inhelder, B. and Piaget, J. (2013). *The Growth of Logical Thinking from Childhood to Adolescence*. London: Routledge.

Jung, C., Storr, A., Jung, C. and Jung, C. (1983). *The Essential Jung*. Princeton, NJ: Princeton University Press.

Lee, R. and Wheeler, G., eds. (2003). *The Voice of Shame*. Cambridge, MA: Gestalt Press.

Lewin, K. (1939). Field theory and experiment in social psychology: Concepts and methods. *American Journal of Sociology*, 44(6), pp. 868–896.

Linehan, M. (2015). *DBT Skills Training Manual*. New York: Guilford Press.

McConville, M. (1995). *Adolescence: Psychotherapy and the Emergent Self*. San Francisco: Jossey-Bass Inc.

Ogden, P., Fisher, J., Del Hierro, D. and Del Hierro, A. (2015). *Sensorimotor Psychotherapy*. New York: W. W. Norton & Company, Inc.

Perls, F., Goodman, P. and Hefferline, R. (1951). *Gestalt Therapy: Excitement and Growth in the Human Personality*. New York: Julian Press.

Porges, S. (2011). *The Polyvagal Theory*. New York: W. W. Norton & Company, Inc.

Shapiro, F. (2001). *Eye Movement Desensitization and Reprocessing*. New York: Guilford Press.

Van der Kolk, B. (2015). *The Body Keeps the Score*. New York: Penguin Books.

Chapter 2

Contact assessment

Content vs. contact assessment

Content assessment is primarily focused on the gathering of information for the sake of clinical evaluation and treatment planning. It commonly involves matching observable behaviours to lists of psychopathological symptoms to arrive at appropriately specific treatment techniques. The assessment process may take different forms, depending on the therapeutic setting. For example, in private practice, the therapist undertakes all aspects of the assessment herself. If the therapist is working in a counselling organisation or within a wider health care system, an appointed clinical assessor will often be the initial point of contact with the adolescent and/or parental figures. In either case, the process typically involves uncovering details of the presenting issue and family background. There are also practitioners who, somewhat alarmingly, elect to proceed with individual counselling work directly with the young person, by-passing any system of assessment. They frequently are working in places such as schools and youth clubs, although sometimes also in counselling organisations. In these instances, a concerned adult has identified the need for support for the adolescent, parental consent has been sought, some broad details about the presenting issue are shared with the counsellor, who then undertakes a limited number of sessions with the young person.

To complete an adequate assessment, it is important that the therapist is clear about precisely what she is assessing. She is certainly interested in determining information with regard to family configuration, developmental milestones, notable experiences and social interaction throughout childhood and adolescence thus far. And whilst this information is important to gather, there are several equally or even potentially more illuminating strands to assessment work with adolescents. Particularly revealing are relational themes and contact dynamics between the adolescent and parenting adults, as well his emerging personality dynamics within his lifespace. This type of assessment is referred to as *contact assessment* and is concerned with the therapist's attention to contact boundary dynamics, in addition to presenting issue information. To undertake this type of assessment, it is almost impossible to grasp the essential nuances of contact within the lifespace without involving parents in the assessment process to experience episodes of contact as they unfold in the live encounter.

Assessment in adolescent psychotherapy is one of the key components of the work. Incomplete assessment creates difficulty and frustration within the therapeutic space and inevitably the work moves into counselling mode (which is not to say the work will not be of value). However, if the therapist fails to challenge dynamics which pose threat to the integrity of the therapeutic process, she runs the risk of professional compromise.

Power struggles

There are four specific power struggles which are frequently encountered in the work as an adolescent psychotherapist. By this I mean that there are four scenarios where clinical work is being directed by someone other than the therapist. If the clinician finds herself caught in any one, or possibly all of these situations, then it is virtually a given that both therapeutic contact and her professionalism are compromised:

The Adolescent: The young person directs the work by being selective about topics for discussion, talking endlessly about interests, friendships and his social calendar. Whilst it is not unusual to dialogue about these things, the therapist understands implicitly that they cannot progress to more central issues which are shaping the adolescent's experience, as this will not be tolerated. There is a redundantly circling feeling to therapy; contact has a plastic quality to it; the therapist feels bored, undervalued and has a vague sense that nothing is happening in the encounter.

Adolescent-directed work also happens when the young person refuses to *give permission* to the therapist to engage with parents or is demanding a level of confidentiality which compromises the therapeutic space. For example, it is not uncommon to hear of an adolescent disclosing some information about his drug use or sexual activity which comes with an "*I'll kill myself if you tell my parents*" clause. This is not a useful dilemma for anyone.

The Parenting Adults: Over-engagement or lack of engagement with parents can present a challenge to the work. For example, a parenting adult may see his role in the therapeutic process as simply someone who delivers the young person to the door of the therapist's office and pays for the service, much like bringing one's car to a mechanic for repair. A question universally asked is, "How long will this take?" Elsewhere, marginal parents often feel estranged from and suspicious of the entire therapy process, and for the adolescent, his parents' tacit embarrassment and disapproval of therapy can be a huge impediment.

Contrastingly, the time-consuming parent may be very keen to make contact, telephoning, texting or emailing before and after every session, requesting progress updates – this is particularly prone to happen when there is anxiety in the field or when separation is an issue. In these cases, as much or perhaps even more time is spent in contact with parents outside sessions than with the adolescent himself, which feels draining and frustrating for the therapist, ultimately creating resentment. Parental expectation can be high in these situations and the question, "is there anything more *we* can be doing?" often translates as, "is there not more *you* should be doing?" Worse still, parents frequently show up at the beginning of sessions having pre-selected the themes for discussion between therapist and adolescent: "I'd like you to talk to him about his attitude around the house and also to get him motivated to study for his exams", essentially locating responsibility for how he interacts with family and his academic performance with the therapist. The concluding assumption is that, following the session, if the adolescent fails to come up to standard in either attitude or study, this is a statement of the therapist's incompetency. In all of the above scenarios, parents have not become genuine collaborators in the therapeutic process, which creates expectation and shame potential for the adolescent therapist.

The Organisation: Here, the organisational setting within which the work takes place imposes limitations. Often funding is an issue, and perhaps there is a finite number of sessions afforded to each client which, for some, equates to a drop in the ocean of support realistically required. For example, six individual therapy sessions for a traumatised adolescent whose lifespace is hostile is most likely not going to be adequate. The organisation may have a particular model of therapy which is adhered to, say a cognitive-behavioural or solution-focused manner of working, with the expectation that every therapist will treat every adolescent within an identical methodological framework. This would be effective . . . if only all adolescents, their developmental location and their lifespace contexts were alike.

Additionally, environmental conditions may not support the work, which makes the therapeutic space both unsafe and uncomfortable. School counsellors know this only too well: they regularly find themselves working in a cramped store room at the end of a long corridor, because space is at a premium. During the session, a teacher may interrupt the session, apologetically searching for French grammar books; a few minutes later a bell sounds to signal a lesson's end and dozens of students move past the makeshift counselling room in boisterous exchange. The following week, counselling is located in another equally small and unsatisfactory space, because someone else is using last week's allocated room today. We would never consider working under these conditions with adult clients, yet it perplexes me that they are somehow deemed acceptable spaces for our adolescent clients. The level of support and space afforded to the school counselling process is also usually commensurate with the extent to which the school principal values the service.

The Wider System: There are times when the work is situated within a wider system context, for example, a legal process may be concurrent. Correspondence is received, not so much requesting, as *demanding* disclosure of all details of therapeutic work, including clinical notes. This may happen following disclosure of say, a child protection issue such as sexual trauma. It is our ethical duty to collaborate *appropriately* with these requests. However, it is a different matter when these petitions are made by legal representatives of divorcing parents who are at war with one another and who wish to recruit the therapist into their drama, contaminating the therapeutic space for their already distressed child.

Returning to the scenario of sexual abuse disclosure, the therapist may be the only person to whom the adolescent is willing to talk, and very often, the dialogue is sparse because trauma and shame are so prevalent. Other professionals are, necessarily, keen to discover as much detail as possible. In these scenarios, social work departments, as part of the broader national health and care system, may attempt to influence the therapist to adopt more of an investigative, rather than therapeutic emphasis in the work. I know a number of therapists who have attended interprofessional meetings in which an agenda for ongoing therapeutic work was established by others in attendance. This is an example of failure to take ownership of our profession *par excellence*.

When the therapist is not the only professional involved in supporting an adolescent, as is the case when she is also attending a child and adolescent mental health service, under the care of a psychiatrist, cooperative collaboration is not always assured. Insistence on termination of the therapist's work is common, irrespective of how effectively the work is progressing or how therapist, adolescent and parents feel about this stipulation. Sometimes this call is appropriate, and at other times, it very definitely is not. In these instances, or when the case becomes 'interesting', an external decision to transfer therapeutic work to another professional within the system risks being dismissive of the adolescent's integrity, not to mention professionally insulting to the therapist.

Locating the dilemma

When external direction in any or all of these four scenarios is present, psychotherapeutic work and psychotherapy as a profession are undermined. Hence, it is important that the clinician works as much as possible *on her terms* for therapeutic work to proceed with integrity. Power struggles must be acknowledged and attended to, which is not to say that they will be eliminated. One cannot work under perfection conditions with every adolescent. The presence of power struggles does not suggest that the work will be of little benefit; often therapy under these conditions makes all the difference in the world to the adolescent. My point is that unless power struggles are addressed, disempowerment will infuse the therapeutic space and the therapist's professional identity. This disempowerment manifests in therapy sessions being tediously hard work; in the therapist adopting personal responsibility for how the work is progressing, shaming herself when progress is not evident; and in holding herself accountable to adolescents, parents, organisations and systems who have their own ideas about how the process should be unfolding.

I compare this to an orthodontist who fits a brace for a patient whose teeth are slightly crooked and who desires a 'Hollywood smile'. The orthodontist informs his patient that it will take approximately 12 months for her teeth to straighten. However, the patient dislikes wearing the brace, choosing to disregard it most of the time. At the end of the year, the patient is, naturally, frustrated at the disappointing result. Both patient and orthodontist hold the latter personally responsible for the failure. He begins to doubt his competence: perhaps the braces were ill-fitting, or maybe he's just losing his touch and wonders if now might be a good time to change occupation or retire altogether. Of course, this is a ridiculous scenario: he would never consider these possibilities. However, deflections and power struggles are much more frequent and challenging in adolescent psychotherapy than in orthodontia. The art of holding one's ground develops with experience and support.

And so, if an adolescent is unwilling to talk; if parents cannot or will not engage; if there are only a limited number of sessions; if the office setting is less than ideal; or if there are other professionals involved who are making decisions which directly impact the work, it is vital that the therapist places the dilemma of professional ownership with those external directors, rather than internalising the situational shame and making a statement about her lack of competence. Yet still, inadequate practice may also be at play.

Expressing to others, in a composed, dispassionate, non-shaming manner, the dilemma that the work will be compromised at best under these conditions, ensures a more realistic perspective for all. If the dilemma remains rigidly defended against, this is the point where it may be advisable to disengage. The orthodontist cannot make his patient wear the brace. Similarly, the psychotherapist cannot enforce collaborative alliances or magically cure symptoms.

Attachment and contact

I use the term 'parenting adult' to indicate any adult who has adopted, either by choice or default, a parenting role in the young person's life. This includes biological, step and adoptive parents; temporary foster carers; parenting relatives from the wider family field, for example, grandparents, aunts and uncles; staff from residential settings which have been home to the adolescent at points in his life, and so on. Some adolescents may have at most two parenting adults in their life, whilst others will have had multiple parenting adults. It is important that assessment of each of these relational connections is made for both adolescent and therapist to fully appreciate the influence of interpersonal dynamics on his sense of self and wider developmental narrative.

Attachment theory has given us one valuable mode of understanding human experience and motivation (Ainsworth and Bowlby, 1991). The attachment lens, however, may not provide us with a sufficiently clear and accurate description of the evolution of contact which occurs as adolescence gets underway. Whilst the research indicates that the more secure the attachment, the more likely the adolescent is to navigate the adolescent years with greater success and less inclination towards mental health problems and the risks associated with impulsivity (Allen and Land, 1999), nevertheless, the rapid and radical transformation which is undergone within the parent-child relationship is not necessarily reflected in an experience-near manner through the description of its attachment security status. For example, 6-year-old Mary and her mother enjoy a close and loving bond; there is an ease in their relating and their connection bears the hallmarks of a secure attachment. Fast-forward ten years: Mary is a feisty 16-year-old adolescent. Communication between them almost inevitably results in tension and contempt, although Mary can be charming and responsible – usually when she wants something. The adolescent believes that her mother's agenda in the world is to make her daughter's life a misery; her mother feels that Mary's 'attitude' and new-found friends are the problem and laments the loss of her lovely little girl. In a few short years, there is a good chance that Mary and her mother will experience an easier, more companionable relatedness. Attachment and contact are different phenomena; and whilst Mary and her mother might well continue to have a fundamentally secure attachment – by adolescence, the quality of their contact certainly has undergone dramatic change. So what happens to the child-parent connection during adolescence that can create such fraught and shaming interaction? Surely we cannot put it down merely to hormones.

The parenting space

The nature and influence of the connection between adolescents and the parenting adults in their worlds has considerable potential for support, and equally for adversity, as the young person journeys towards existential selfhood. For the adolescent, his principal environmental context is his parents. This relational context, which is referred to as the *parenting space*, is a continuous interplay between the intrapsychic and interpersonal worlds of experience, with mutual influence and ongoing co-creation of self-experience occurring in the encounter between self and other. There are varying degrees of receptivity within the parenting space which impact the adolescent's emerging sense of self and manner of engaging with her environment. There are three general grades of receptivity which can be experienced in the parent-adolescent dyad. These include *receptive, non-receptive* and *hostile* parenting. These descriptions are organised according to a parenting adult's capacity to manage the transitioning contact boundary in an appropriately supportive, non-shaming manner, according to the developing adolescent's needs. These are not rigid categories of parenting experience: rather, one of these qualities of receptivity will usually emerge as the dominant style of contact within the dyadic encounter. The parenting space is a dynamic, fluctuating experience for the parent-adolescent dyad.

The receptive parenting space

The adolescent's emerging experience of 'self' is, in every moment, exposed to the environment in a dynamic process of living. To be wholly received by his environment means that the adolescent experiences a consistent, attentive, supportive and responsive interpersonal world. This experience of being received, in turn, nurtures and encourages the construction and development of a rich lifespace experience. He grows by experimenting with and exploring his environment – hopefully finding that his experimentation and exploration is received and affirmed by that environment. This support and validation promotes ownership of experience and the emergence of a firmly grounded sense of self and connection to others. Life is meaningful, interesting, rich with possibility; life is worth living.

Receptive parenting is the capacity to attend to the relational needs as well as to the more practical, functional needs in the adolescent's developmental journey. The parent ideally relates to his son in a manner which cultivates a sense of being cared for, of mattering, and creates the expectation of being received and supported by her environment. Throughout childhood, the parent has hopefully received and encouraged the development and expression of his child's inner world, which in turn supports the emergence of a strong, grounded sense of self for the child. During adolescence, the parent intuitively understands that the young person's inner world of private experience, which is deepening and expanding, is becoming more and more the adolescent's business. The parent's role now is to continue to influence his son by holding him accountable for actions and decisions in a way which is affirming and non-shaming of the adolescent's attempt to define who he is in the world. This is a developmentally healthy posture for parents of adolescents, though not always sustainable – particularly when he rolls in at 2.00 a.m., smelling of cigarettes and cider.

Non-receptive parenting

An ongoing process of boundary definition within the ever-expanding lifespace occurs throughout adolescence, which frequently is played out at the contact boundary between the adolescent and her parents, particularly during earlier adolescence. This can result in running battles themed with responsibility, freedom, power and boundaries. When the therapist encounters an adolescent and parent, for whom conflict has become a fixed pattern within the parenting space, I very often find that difficulties have arisen not simply because the adolescent has become moody, hormonal, has fallen in with a 'bad' crowd, etc. but because the parent has not quite understood that his mode of parenting is failing to support his teenager developmentally. He is still trying to parent in a manner that worked with his son as a younger child and feels powerless to influence him now. Shame is sure to be present in the encounter; and it is not uncommon to hear a parent describe how he finds it very hard to like his son and issue (another) ultimatum – either behave or be gone. Parents surprisingly have little awareness of how hurtful and isolating the impact can be on their adolescent children.

No parent or caregiver can be receptive 100% of the time. Life happens, and it is beyond our capacity as human beings to maintain perfect relational connections. Sometimes the most well-meaning and supportive parents cannot 'be there' for their adolescent children. A parent can become distracted and preoccupied with his own life situation, and the adolescent experiences diminished receptivity within the parenting space during these episodes. A parent, for example, might be hurting; or becomes distracted by the excitement of a new relationship; he may be intensively focusing on a work project to the detriment of family life, or the adolescent's parents are in the process of separating. As these experiences become less figural for the parent, the parenting space becomes increasingly receptive once more. However, in many cases, non-receptivity characterises the parent-adolescent relational space. The adolescent who has inhabited a non-receptive parenting space characteristically does not feel known to his parent and is often agenda-driven, where the adolescent's life is closely directed and managed by the parent who has a desire for his son or daughter to be a "success" e.g. the adolescent having a pre-determined, non-negotiable academic path and career. The agenda can emerge in a compensatory manner in respect of the parent's own life experience and the adolescent does not have much of a voice in determining the direction of her life. The parent fails to notice or fully take into account the wishes and sense of emerging self of the adolescent. When I meet adolescents whose lives are agenda-driven, I hold the image of a topiary tree while we work: a dedicated and thoughtful gardener has created a structure around which the plant will grow and take shape, and so each is perfectly sculpted. Adolescents are not topiary trees. In other experiences, absence or some experience of separation has created a lack of receptivity within the parenting space. Perhaps there is irregular, insufficient or no contact between an adolescent and his parent. This can be the case when, for example, the parent-adolescent relationship has faded after parental separation. An adolescent who experiences a habitual lack of receptivity within the parenting space often describes feelings of insignificance and invisibility. This creates sufficient support to challenge his deep belief that he does not matter is the challenge.

Hostile parenting

This is the experience of a parenting adult's behaviour and way of relating which is actively shaming and destructive for the adolescent's emerging self-experience. In fact, it can be positively dangerous for the adolescent's sense of self to emerge at all within the parenting space. The parent-adolescent relationship is organised around the parent's abusive/addictive behaviours and the adolescent adjusts accordingly. He learns to be hyper-attentive to parental needs and the parent's feeling world, and to relinquish his own – this is in direct contrast to receptive parenting. In these cases, perhaps the parent is verbally, physically and/or sexually abusive; the parent is addicted to some substance or behaviour; or the parent is living with significant mental health issues which impact the parenting space. A *directly hostile* parenting space is one in which the parenting adult is actively and directly harming the adolescent, for example, through verbal, physical or sexual assault. *Indirect hostility* is created, not because of a direct insult, but where the adolescent is living with the fallout of a parent's addiction; abusive treatment of a partner; or symptoms of serious mental health diagnosis which severely impacts that parent's capacity to function, as an adult in general and as a parent in particular. An adolescent's recent description comes to mind of bringing her boyfriend home to meet the family. Her mother is a loving and caring woman, who, when she is agreeable to taking medication for her schizophrenic presentation, functions well in the world. She had ceased her medication for the moment, and just as my client and her boyfriend arrived home, her mother came running out of the house screaming and gesturing aggressively to the sky. A helicopter had flown overhead – a rare occurrence now, though a regular and unsafe feature of this woman's traumatic childhood, growing up at the height of the Troubles in Northern Ireland. Her daughter's chagrin was pervasive, as the experience echoed the familiarity of this feature within the parenting space.

In the instance of hostility, whether direct, indirect, or frequently both, it is the parenting adult who is creating and maintaining the distress and danger in the adolescent's experience. Whilst non-receptivity within the parenting space can create feelings of hopelessness at times, hostile parenting creates despair. The burning existential question for these adolescents is not, "*Who am I?*" but rather, "*What's wrong with me?*" Despair is a mixture of powerlessness, hopelessness and rage. This despair is internalised and is translated into a deep and core belief, namely, "*There **must** be something wrong with me*". Psychological chaos ensues.

The yearning and residual shame which many adolescents experience as they come to terms with the trauma of being parented in a hostile relational space can be immense. A deep sense of loss emerges which has to do with the absence of a meaningful parental presence in the adolescent's life. I am reminded of a 17-year-old client's description of standing by the graveside on the day of her father's funeral. She felt sad; though not about the man who had passed away – she was relieved he was gone from the world, which would now be a safer place for her. My young client felt sad because she became poignantly aware that she was burying her one chance to have a father. She described feelings of intense disappointment and emptiness as she stood by the grave: "I wanted and needed a dad, but not *that* dad".

Parenting space assessment is fundamental as it is primarily within these spaces that children experience, or fail to experience a sense of wellbeing and empowerment, the level of which is dependent upon the extent to which their yearnings for physiological, psychological and relational integrity are honoured. As adolescence gets underway, the young person is already deeply imprinted by the quality of receptivity within each parenting space. This synthesis of relational themes and experiences significantly determines his unique phenomenology, creative adjustment responses and wider lifespace expectation, especially with regard to contact with other people.

Other relational spaces

Assessment of relational dynamics which may be influencing the adolescent's self-experience also includes an interest with regard to the quality of connection between the young person and the wider cast of characters who populate his lifespace, both past and present. These include significant family members, the wider adult world and of course the peer landscape. The therapist is curious to discover how the adolescent and his siblings relate; if he is particularly close to grandparents and other relatives; if he is popular amongst peers, struggles to connect unless online with adolescents who share similar gaming or animation interests, or if he is essentially isolated. She also wishes to learn about how he relates to teachers and adults in authority; if other professionals are involved; and if she is seen as merely another interfering person in the long list of people who have become involved in his young life.

Wombspace as lifespace

Somewhat surprisingly, I have discovered that the adolescent's earliest experience may be exerting considerable influence on his present-day experience, and so I have learned to pay attention to this aspect of his life narrative also. Having worked for many years with younger children, whose parents implicitly understood that this experience directly impacted their children's functioning, and who readily and spontaneously volunteered details regarding their children's wombspace and birth experience, I became curious about how this context of pre- and perinatal process might continue to shape the individual through adolescence. This aspect of assessment is almost always revealing to me and fascinating for the adolescent.

My clinical hunch regarding the relevance, for the adolescent, of life before and during birth has been validated and informed by recent research, particularly within the disciplines of transpersonal psychology (Bennet and Grof, 1993), neuroscience (Krueger and Garvan, 2014) and biology (Lagercrantz and Changeux, 2009). Conception, gestation and birth are relationally embedded phenomena, and it makes sense to me that a relational field Gestalt understanding of development would include each person's unique wombspace and birth experience as notably formative.

Extending field theory

We are born into a field which exists long before our conception. These field conditions are relevant, and so, the therapist's interest extends to two years prior to conception, as she assesses the wombspace and wider lifespace conditions with regard to parental relational dynamics, other children, miscarriages, significant experiences and trauma. Typically, human beings inhabit a wombspace for 38 weeks, which is a considerable length of time. The wombspace may be a receptive, non-receptive or hostile environment for the developing foetus who, it has been established, is a sentient, responsive and relationally curious being. (Salihagic-Kadic et al., 2005) How parents feel about the pregnancy, the mother's temperament and the physiological aspects of the pregnancy for both mother and child, are all revealing of how the wombspace may have been experienced by the developing infant. Consider the scenario of a supported woman, in a loving relationship, who has yearned for a child and is delighted to experience a healthy and stress-free pregnancy, compared with a woman whose pregnancy is the result of a sexual assault by an abusive partner who continues his tirade of physical, emotional and sexual abuse throughout her pregnancy, who feels overwhelmed by having an unwanted child, and who sometimes drinks to escape her situation. Wombspace quality will be very different for each of these developing foetuses. Given the emergent body of knowledge from scientific studies of unborn and newborn children (Zimmerman and Connors, 2010), it is conceivable that events and experiences in utero not only imprint the infant, but that the imprint might endure throughout childhood and into adolescence.

Birth itself, when we think of it, must be a monumentally arduous journey creating physiologically, psychologically and interpersonally an entire lifespace paradigm shift. The change in the infant's life, following departure from the dark, cramped and muffled amniotic wombspace, could not be more pronounced. He now finds himself in an expansive sensory world of direct contact with the other as he encounters breath, touch, voice and gaze. Experiences during the initial moments, hours and days following entry into this new landscape for the delicate and vulnerable child are significant, with the potential for a loving, peaceful bonding process to intensify or for the trauma of invasive medical procedure, neglect or maltreatment to terrify him. Prior to, during and following birth, the developing infant experiences his lifespace as largely benevolent or as a threatening and dangerous environment.

It is possible that we accumulate experiential data and are meaning-makers right from our earliest moments of life, so that wombspace and birth experience shapes how we creatively adjust to subsequent lifespace conditions. Thus, including this major event from wombspace through perinatal experience in assessment can shed light on the adolescent's present lifespace experience. More often than not, the description mirrors the young person's contemporary struggle, revealing something of his phenomenology. For example, a wombspace saturated with maternal anxiety will likely infuse the child's emotional field who will be prone to anxious experiencing. Similarly, an adolescent whose creative adjustment seems an exaggerated response to everyday stress, and who habitually feels overwhelmed and in threat of annihilation, frequently will have experienced an essentially torturous birth. Even the smallest challenge seems crushing to him.

Structuring the assessment

Relational dialogue

A question-and-answer format, whilst satisfying the therapist's curiosity with regard to biographical and presenting symptom information, tends to implicitly set the therapist apart as some sort of expert. Adolescents, and often parenting adults, may take umbrage or feel disempowered at this power differential dynamic and already there is shame in the encounter. It is preferable to co-create a dialogue which fosters authentic relational contact, opening the possibility of support and adding a richer dimension to the meeting. The therapist aims to grasp a rich appreciation of this adolescent's lifespace, which includes interpersonal, intrapsychic, interprofessional and wider lifespace aspects of his experience. She also pays attention, with heightened curiosity, to the way in which contact is made within the lifespace, of which she has now, at least momentarily, become a part.

After a warm welcome, she immediately states her intention to extricate herself from any potential power struggle with the adolescent by articulating that she does not assume his attendance at today's meeting to be willing and that his active participation is not required. Attempting to foster his curiosity and communicate to him that he will be neither exposed nor shamed, she invites him to make his own appraisal of her and informs him that the principal decision-maker with regard to engaging in any ongoing therapeutic process will be himself. Adolescents often appear visibly more empowered and relaxed following this interaction alone. At various times throughout their meeting she will invite the adolescent into dialogue in a manner which conveys minimal risk of exposure, reminding him that he does not have to engage at all. They often do.

Regularly, parenting adults enter her office feeling uncomfortable, suspicious and prepared for an onslaught of 'bad parent' shame. So, openly conceding that it is a daunting prospect to present one's parenting to any professional, together with an invitation to parenting adults to also make their own assessment of the therapist, is both empowering and de-shaming. The assumption and acknowledgement of hesitancy and scepticism, on the part of both adolescent and parents, contributes markedly to the co-creation of a genuinely consensual and collaborative encounter. She supports each one to remain curious, mindful that they are all assessing.

The therapist intentionally spends as little time as possible in communication with parents prior to the initial meeting, despite their usual eagerness to furnish her with as much detail as possible about the situation. In hearing how the presenting issue is defined, she is most interested to witness how people respond to each other's description of experience. She invites the parent who made initial contact to begin by saying a little about what has brought them here today, always mindful of the potential for shame, particularly for the adolescent. And so, as the story unfolds, the therapist steps in and begins to shape the pace, direction, tone and interactive style of the meeting. Her questions and statements reveal an interest in coming to know the adolescent's experience in the world, who often is either unwilling to say much in front of parents or has no language for his experience. Even the most subtle nuance in her relating is an indicator to them all of the posture she will hold as this adolescent's potential therapist. The supportive relational tone through which she uncovers various aspects of the adolescent's experience matters considerably.

In paying attention to contact boundaries, the therapist notes the adolescent's capacity to hold his own in parental contact, how he makes contact with the therapist and his capacity for self-reflection, as she attempts to situate him developmentally. For example, she might meet a 17-year-old adolescent who is bright and articulate, whose dialogue reveals an impressive level of insight, and who connects readily with parents and with the therapist. Contact is fluent and supported. Conversely, the next 17-year-old client she encounters demands life on his terms, inhabiting an utterly impulse-driven lifespace and seems intent on blaming the adult world for his struggles. Contact is tentative; the risk of power struggle and of shame is high. This adolescent expresses his sentiments more like a huffy, belligerent 12-year-old than someone on the cusp of emerging adulthood.

Through careful observation of their intersubjective relatedness i.e. of what is said and what remains unspoken, language used, feeling responses, yearning, eye contact, breathing rhythms, tension, physical posture and their embodied experience in this relational configuration, the therapist begins to assess the various contact boundaries and considers how she may need to situate herself in response to these. Her unswerving focus is the emergent developmental status of the adolescent-parent relational space and her commitment to conveying her attempt to understand the adolescent's phenomenology.

Many adolescents enter a therapist's office determined not to say a word and find themselves warming up as they experience receptivity, realising that she might genuinely be interested in their experience. It is important that the therapist keeps the adolescent in mind at all times, filtering and translating information through his phenomenological lens and actively empathising with him, all the time careful to avoid entering into power struggles. Active empathy, tentatively offered, communicates to the adolescent that, whilst the therapist may not always be accurate, she is at least *interested* in grasping his experience. This in itself is a considerable statement of support and is almost always appreciated by the adolescent. Each time she tentatively and respectfully offers a hunch about how the adolescent may have experienced a particular lifespace situation, contact with him becomes subtly richer and less remote. If she is sufficiently attuned and her attempt to be actively empathic hits the nail on the head, this encourages even the most reticent adolescent into richer contact. The therapist pays careful attention to the fragments of contact between the adolescent and herself, noting any increase in verbal and nonverbal cues, such as eye contact, direct dialogue between them and other moments of reaching. The first witnessing of spontaneity from the adolescent informs her that trust is emerging – a fledgling trust in her to appreciate and support his yearnings for integrity.

All the time the therapist is also fostering connection with, validating and perhaps offering challenge to parenting adults. Her intention is to support their attunement to the adolescent's experience, whilst assessing their capacity to be receptive, careful here also to avoid shame. Her aim is to evaluate the potential for support available to the adolescent within each parenting space and to create a non-shaming context in which to situate his 'problem', reframing the presenting issue through a relational lens. It is important that she remains attuned to how she is experiencing the others and herself in the encounter, paying attention to immediate contact dynamics within the therapeutic space. Her embodied experience is especially revealing as she attempts to de-code and communicate a supportive appreciation of each person's moment-to-moment response, including her own.

Confidentiality

This is a complex area as the issue of confidentiality collides with development. Contact boundary development involves heightened experimental curiosity, coupled with inadequate developmental maturity, naturally leading in many cases, to problematic and dangerous situations. The therapist's dilemma is one of balancing the adolescent's need for privacy and ownership of experience against her ethical and legal responsibilities with regard to the young person's safety and wellbeing. *(See* Chapter 13 *for in-depth discussion on case management issues.)* It is important to raise the question of confidentiality during the assessment process to establish how much to disclose to parents and other professionals, aware that confidentiality is essential to the adolescent's trust in the therapist and therapeutic process. To establish clarity with regard to one's role with parenting adults, it is important that they distinguish between therapist as a provider of information, furnishing them with detail about the adolescent's exploits or as someone who is supporting overall development. The therapist invites the adolescent and his parents to consider the issue in an inclusive dialogue, framing confidentiality in terms of *black and white* issues and *grey* issues.

Following disclosure, black and white issues pose no dilemma as informing parents and potentially other agencies is non-negotiable. Examples include disclosure of sexual abuse, cases of suicidal or homicidal gestures, serious chemical dependence or the presence of a significant eating disorder. Grey issues offer a somewhat more obscure dilemma. It is helpful to acknowledge expectations which are likely held by both adolescent and parenting adults so as not to adopt the role of co-conspirator with the adolescent or information gateway with parents. Stating that adolescents typically reveal information to the therapist which might be concerning to parents, say perhaps cannabis use or experimental sexual activity with peers, she describes how an impasse will soon emerge if she reveals this information to parents: The adolescent is likely to understandably feel betrayed and withdraw from the process, probably resolved never to talk to an adult again. The parenting adults are likely to feel grateful to have this information. However, information alone is redundant in these situations. They may restrict his movements, discipline and lecture him – and adolescents being adolescents, he will find ever more creative ways to circumvent their influence and continue with his risk taking.

The therapist offers an alternative to them all in trusting her to hold these grey issues with the premise that she is interested in supporting the adolescent to become a more credible and responsible choice-maker. This has the effect of dissipating any anticipation of collusive alliance on the side of either adolescent or parent. It also creates additional safety for the adolescent who, otherwise, perceives the therapist as untrustworthy, withholding important aspects of his experience from therapeutic dialogue, thus compromising the work. This dialogue does not resolve grey issues; rather it draws conscious awareness to them, establishing confidentiality as an ongoing process to be negotiated, mirroring the shifting privacy boundary within the parent-adolescent relationship. It also importantly creates scope for the therapist to decipher how best to intervene when these issues emerge in the work. After all, artful intervention with grey issue material has the potential for developmental transformation. It is imprudent to proceed if reticence regarding the question of confidentiality is expressed at this point, otherwise power struggles are inevitable. In these instances, slowing down and supporting dialogue as confidentiality parameters are negotiated may very well reach to the heart of the developmental dilemma. This dialogue *is* the therapy, as contact boundaries are evolving within the encounter.

Initial session closure

As the initial meeting comes to an end, the therapist reviews the principal themes of dialogue, acknowledging and appreciating people's openness to exploring family process with her. She enquires about each person's feelings with regard to their meeting and the possibility of continuing their dialogue, reminding the adolescent of his opt-out clause and his balance of power with regard to decision-making. In truth, she knows already, having remained attuned to the adolescent's quality of contact during the meeting, whether he is readily willing to meet again. If the therapist senses uncertainty or ambivalence, or if her hunch is that an expression of openness to returning would be seen by him as a submission to the adult world, then rather than pressing him for commitment, she makes one of two interventions: she posits the dilemma that she has not gathered sufficient data with which to make an informed decision regarding engagement in an ongoing process of therapy and so suggests that they meet one more time so he has a greater sense of her and of what will be involved (i.e. she buys time). Or she invites him to go off and reflect on today's conversation; to consider the possibility of coming back and to get in touch if he feels like it. Through this intervention the therapist acknowledges that the more defended an adolescent, the more crucial it is for him to concretely experience empowerment in their contact episodes, and she is aware that requesting a direct response may compromise his integrity. It is unusual that, following this type of interaction, a guarded adolescent does not return at some point in the future.

Commonly by the end of the initial meeting, the therapist is satisfied that the assessment process has been thorough and has drawn to a natural conclusion, providing she feels that she has an adequate grasp of contact boundary dynamics within parenting spaces; that the adolescent is amenable to becoming her client and his parents are willing collaborators; that there is not an unexplored interprofessional domain in which to situate herself; and that she has adequate clarity with regard to direct, indirect and overt developmental issues. In situations where any or all of these strands are incomplete or lacking, she considers that the assessment process will be ongoing until all these potential power struggles have been defined and explored.

The therapist makes a call, based on the assessment's progress and on the adolescent's developmental location, with regard to the following session's configuration, assuming a subsequent appointment has been agreed upon. She may decide that it is most appropriate for them all to meet together again; that the adolescent and one parent should be in attendance; that she needs to meet other parenting adults (in the case, for example, where two acrimoniously separated parents will not tolerate sitting together in the same room); or that an individual meeting with the adolescent might be most useful next time. The therapist generally does not look for any future commitment beyond one or two subsequent sessions, which makes the process feel more tolerable for the adolescent.

References

Ainsworth, M. D. S. and Bowlby, J. (1991). An ethological approach to personality development. *American Psychologist*, 46, pp. 331–341.

Allen, J. P. and Land, D. (1999). Attachment in adolescence. In J. Cassidy and P. R. Shaver, eds., *Handbook of Attachment: Theory,Research, and Clinical Applications*. New York: Guilford Press, pp. 319–335.

Bennett, H. and Grof, S. (1993). *The Holotropic Mind: The Three Levels of Human Consciousness and How They Shape Our Lives*. New York: HarperCollins.

Krueger, C. and Garvan, C. (2014). Emergence and retention of learning in early fetal development. *Infant Behavior and Development*, 37(2), pp. 162–173.

Lagercrantz, H. and Changeux, J. (2009). The emergence of human consciousness: From fetal to neonatal life. *Pediatric Research*, 65(3), pp. 255–260.

Salihagic-Kadic, A., Kurjak, A., Medić, M., Andonotopo, W. and Azumendi, G. (2005). New data about embryonic and fetal neurodevelopment and behavior obtained by 3D and 4D sonography. *Journal of Perinatal Medicine*, 33(6).

Zimmerman, A. and Connors, S. (2010). *Maternal Influences on Fetal Neurodevelopment*. New York: Springer.

Chapter 3

Ongoing parental involvement

The adolescent's environment is predominantly, though not exclusively, a world influenced and shaped by parental connections. Healthy evolution of the parent-adolescent relational space during adolescence necessitates a transformation of the contact boundaries. Frequently the therapist encounters parents whose love for and worry about their child is comparative, though who often feel powerless to influence or help their son or daughter. Many parents experience the adolescent years as a loss, rather than an evolution of the parent-child relationship, as they stand helplessly by whilst their beloved and struggling adolescent rebuffs any parental attempts towards affection or advice. Parents do not matter any less than they did during childhood; they merely assume a more influence-based, less outwardly active role in the adolescent's world. Supportive reassurance from parents is immensely validating for the adolescent, whose ongoing experience of being received by his environment becomes integrated into overall self-experience: They have faith in me; I can have faith in myself and my expanding world.

The therapist's intention is to harness parental care and concern for the adolescent in a developmentally appropriate manner by facilitating parents to become more attuned and receptive. She does this by directing the assessment dialogue beneath presenting symptom issues (and its associated shamefully exposing descriptions of volatile behaviour or vulnerability) to the integrity level – making explicit each person's yearnings for physiological, psychological and interpersonal integrity within the parenting space.

The adolescent is often genuinely surprised to discover that a parent still loves or even likes him and had no idea that parents could be so understanding. He is heartened to learn that parents miss him and want him to be happy. These revelations can be transformative, as the adolescent may be inclined to assume parents to be hostile, judgemental, ignorant, controlling and lacking any capacity to relate meaningfully. Reparative dialogue which uncovers relational yearning functions to dissipate the isolation which frequently characterises the parenting space. This intervention can make all the difference in the world.

During assessment, a rationale for ongoing contact with parents is almost always offered as the relevance of their involvement in the work is usually significant. Exceptions include situations where exclusively one-to-one work with an adolescent is deemed the most appropriate intervention, or perhaps because of direct hostility within parenting spaces. Parental involvement may translate as peripheral support and an occasional few episodes of dialogue. More frequently, however, participation of parenting adults in therapeutic work is crucial for developmental progression.

Frequently, the adolescent's presenting issues are entangled in family process. This can easily be detected with careful attention to themes of dialogue and choice of language employed by parents. If the words *attitude*, *respect* and *trust* are used to describe the adolescent's manner within the family, one can assume the presence of overt developmental issues. Parenting adults will describe not being able to *trust* their son; who are concerned about his *attitude* and *how he speaks to them*; and who worry at his spectacular *lack of motivation* for anything with the exception of gaming and partying. The adolescent's experience is always a perfect complement to this, as he expresses his grievance about *not being trusted*; being *treated like a child*; and that his parents are *trying to control his life*.

(*It may interest the reader to note that I view the developmental journey to adulthood as typically beginning around age 11 and ending in the late 20s. Legally, a 22-year-old is deemed to be an adult; developmentally, however, he is far from adulthood. To this end I regularly involve parents of older adolescents and emerging adults in the process as this is often both developmentally appropriate and therapeutically helpful. Turning eighteen is not the same as becoming an adult, yet many clinicians will deem these young people 'adult clients'. This, to my mind, is clinical absurdity. For the psychotherapist, developmental status, not chronological age, ought to be the determining factor in field intervention work with adolescent and emerging adult clients.*)

Luke

Sixteen-year-old Luke was showing no interest in studying for his approaching GCSE exams, much to his parents' concern. As the dialogue swiftly moved away from study to adolescent-parent contact dynamics, it became apparent that Luke and his parents had reached a developmental impasse. As accusations and criticisms were being cast, I opened these issues for exploration by inviting them all to describe a typical school morning. A scene was described involving the adolescent refusing to get out of bed and having to be called repeatedly by an increasingly frustrated mother who was aware that the cascade effect of her son's tardiness (due to his playing a game console until 12.30 a.m.) was that everyone would be late. Luke recounted how his mother would badger him for not having packed his bag the night before, for not doing homework, for not eating breakfast, for keeping everyone late, for being irresponsible and for rolling his eyes when she was speaking to him. I turned to the adolescent and sympathised at how stressful these mornings must be for him with all the nagging. He agreed – finally, someone understood! I then asked his mother how she experienced these morning episodes. It surprised the adolescent to learn that his mother was equally miserable. I shaped the dialogue so that she articulated how she detested the role of 'nag' which she had assumed by default, and Luke's mother described what kind of contact she longed for with her son in the mornings. She painted the picture of a relaxed, drama-free, contactful morning where they both got along. This parental dialogue extended to exploration of the wider *parent-as-nag* and corresponding *adolescent-as-blasé* relational pattern which had become established since early adolescence. The father described his experience of shuttling between aggressive confrontation and indifference as he struggled to get Luke to heed his sound advice about how to conduct himself. Again, making explicit his yearning for more satisfying contact with his son created a softening of relational ground within the parenting space for both the adolescent and his father as I supported deconstruction of the monster myth which had been reciprocally created.

At this point I offered my support to move the adolescent and his parents out of this fixed and counterproductive mode of relating, aware that the adolescent's collaborative interest in proceeding would be paramount if power struggles were to be avoided. I shaped and facilitated their mutual agreement of a quid pro quo experimental arrangement (Kegan, 2003) that, providing the adolescent packed his bag the night before, got himself out of bed and was ready to leave the house at an agreed time; his mother, in return, was forbidden to nag in the mornings. Luke was charmed by the prospect of a parent being held to account for her totally unreasonable behaviour and so committed to honouring his part in the experiment. His parents were pleased with this arrangement, if somewhat sceptical. Having agreed to try out an alternative morning schedule, I reminded each party that this was simply an experiment, supporting them to hold interest in how it unfolded rather than investment in its successful outcome. I encouraged the adolescent to remain choiceful, opting out of the experiment whenever he wished, and sympathising with his predicament that if he did so, his parents would likely feel compelled to resume the nagging. In a playfully collusive tone, I indicated to the adolescent that I had figured out how this all worked and how to get parents off his back, adding that I would be happy to reveal my thesis in a private dialogue with him sometime . . . if he was interested. I suggested that we all convene to review the situation in two or three weeks. *(I find a weekly rhythm to be too intense for adolescents who scarcely have time to experiment with or to integrate any insight between sessions. My hunch is that this insistence on weekly sessions accounts for the notoriously high incidence of sporadic attendance and premature disengagement of any client group. No-shows are an unusual occurrence if the therapist is committed to following the work's natural momentum.)*

This intervention introduced the possibility of empowerment within the parenting space for both adolescent and parent, creating hope that the fixed pattern of fraught relatedness, which so unnecessarily defined their contact, might be transcended. Rather than the merit of the experiment hinging on how effectively the adolescent had managed to complete his morning tasks on time (in truth, I have little expectation of immediate success), I was attempting to support the adolescent to develop an inkling of insight that taking ownership of his experience would advance his capacity for leverage within parental relationships. Establishing this experiment, irrespective of its success or failure, was a figural step in supporting the filial contact boundary towards a more mutually satisfying and developmentally evolved status for both Luke and his parents.

Parenting strategy work

I suggested a separate appointment with Luke's parents, careful to assure the adolescent that the focus of our dialogue would strictly be supporting them to develop a less antagonistic parenting style towards him, and that I was not interested in indulging any diatribe against their son: it would be an opportunity for them to reflect on *their* behaviour, not on his. This created the assuredness of preservation of his integrity and a burgeoning notion that he had recruited the therapist as his advocate. He had.

I used this time with Luke's parents to explain to them that in all likelihood, their son was not, as they feared, exhibiting traits of some personality disorder, due to his spectacularly erratic and self-obsessed presentation. As they explored their expectations with regard to Luke's behaviour and their ensuing exasperation when he failed to exhibit a similar mindset to them with regard to housework, study and sobriety, they began to appreciate the unproductiveness of their approach. These very reasonable parents could not understand why their adolescent son was so infuriatingly unreasonable: life would be so much easier if only he would heed their advice and promptly follow all parental directives. I informed them that, as a psychotherapist, I do not diagnose . . . but if I were to proffer my analysis in this instance, it would be that this is an acute case of *rearing-a-16-year-old syndrome*, as an attempt to inject humanity into the situation and remind them of my non-judgemental posture. I offered them an explanation that throughout adolescence contact boundaries *develop* rather than instantaneously transform into the bilateral and differentiated contact we expect from mature adult relating. His father and mother began to appreciate that they themselves were shaping and facilitating the contentious dynamic with Luke. These parents realised that their expectations, as they stood, were a little unrealistic and were both grateful for and open to suggestion.

I coached them to obligate their adolescent to honour curfews and behavioural limitations and to complete tasks in return for increased freedom and other benefits, which would render the parents more influential and empowered. I also aided them in compiling two lists: the first of their expectations with regard to their son's behaviour and the second of things which were important to him (it is almost always possible to find things that matter to an adolescent: time with peers, social events, screen time, attire, smartphones, game consoles, etc.), supporting them to establish a simple contract with Luke whereby he stacked the dishwasher each evening after dinner in return for attendance at a local disco on Friday night; and a more complex contract involving parental contribution to his saving for a first car as payoff for containment of his verbal and physical aggression towards family members. Luke's parents could now, with some continued input on my part, begin to shift the balance of lifespace power to the adolescent, as was developmentally appropriate. This leant itself to the establishment of increased receptivity, trust and warmth within the parenting space.

I find that the universal difficulty with implementing parental strategies is not the adolescent's unwillingness to participate, but lack of parental consistency. In other instances where parental involvement will support the therapeutic and developmental process, I choose, where appropriate and as much as possible, to include the adolescent in this dialogue. Ongoing work in adolescent psychotherapy typically involves spontaneous inclusion of parenting adults in any given session. This is why I have designed my practice with two adjoining soundproofed offices and request a parent's attendance for the duration of the session to facilitate this process. At the end of each session, I may solicit the presence of one specific or several parenting adults for the following session, depending on how the work is progressing.

Parenting spaces and trauma

A sizeable percentage of adolescents who are referred for psychotherapy have experienced trauma (Briggs et al., 2013). The therapist examines the presence of trauma from the adolescent's phenomenological perspective, specifically focusing on the implications of parental influence on the adolescent as he attempts to lay claim to his life. Understanding the quality of parental connection in these instances is crucial as this will inform and underpin any therapeutic intervention. Following a traumatic event, it is not unusual for a disconnect to be experienced between the adolescent and his parents, as he becomes unreachable and frozen in his manner of relating. Remorphing the trauma-infused parenting space from non-receptive to receptive is a major aspect of the healing process, transforming the adolescent's lifespace experience. In other instances, it is the parents who are the traumatisers.

I am interested in the phenomenological experience of trauma for adolescents, and the consequent impact of this trauma on development. Ongoing dialogue with many adolescents over the years has led me to identify two qualitatively different experiences of trauma which I have named *Trauma-Within* and *Trauma-Without*. Trauma-without is an experience of trauma which is created from outside the family field, e.g., a family member's death through illness, a road traffic accident, rape by an outsider. These testing and often overwhelming experiences thwart the adolescent's developmental path; there is rupture and distress in the adolescent's experience of contact boundary. Trauma-without is often experienced as life-changing, with adolescents frequently expressing a sense that "life will never be the same again".

Trauma-within is the experience of trauma which emerges from the ground of family experience (e.g. parental addiction, abuse in all its forms of children/adolescents by caregivers). Hostile parenting is traumatising for the developing adolescent. It creates a degree of dispiritedness, shame and isolation which I do not meet in adolescents who have been through even the most brutal distress having occurred outside the family.

Trauma-without

Gearóid was 13 years old and the middle child in a family of three boys. Two years ago, his family were returning home from a day by the seaside when a drunk driver hit their vehicle. Within a short time, the emergency vehicles arrived at the scene and the family were brought to three different hospitals. His mother was taken in one ambulance, Gearóid in the next, his father and two brothers in the third. Gearóid's father and siblings escaped with minor injury. His mother received life-threatening injuries and was hospitalised for three months. Everyone, including Gearóid, thought for a while that she was going to die. Gearóid himself sustained considerable injury and was hospitalised for three weeks. He now faced several more years of surgical procedure and an intensive physical rehabilitation process. His parents brought him to see me as they felt they had 'lost their son'. Their description of Gearóid fitted perfectly with someone who was experiencing post-traumatic stress. This is what happened when we met.

Gearóid wasn't too sure about meeting me and like many adolescent males, was fairly monosyllabic in his dialogue. To step right in and get him talking about the accident would be to re-traumatise him – his terror was palpable behind the nonchalant veneer. So, following the contact assessment meeting, I undertook several one-to-one sessions with the adolescent with the emphasis on establishing rich therapeutic contact. After several sessions Gearóid told me that he had not been sleeping well and was having nightmares. We began to gently and tentatively court the unspeakable. I was supporting the other members of Gearóid's family also at this time as they struggled to come to terms with what had happened to the family. I met with his father who, as he spoke of the accident, described intense feelings of failure and worthlessness at not having been able to save his family. He was a firefighter and had attended similar scenes many times, but that night he could do nothing to protect his own family from the oncoming headlights on his side of the road. Tearfully shaking, he described how he now saw the lights every time he closed his eyes. Gearóid's dad brought him to my office each week, made himself a coffee and read the paper in the waiting room.

Gearóid had become withdrawn from his family for some time but liked this weekly ritual of a drive with his dad to my office and back. Sometimes I invited his dad to stay for a part of the session, and sometimes it was just Gearóid and me. As the weeks progressed, we talked about what life was like 'before' and what it had been like for him since the accident. He told me that he knew he needed to talk about the actual event, but he didn't know how or when. We talked about what it would be like to talk about it. His symptoms began to decrease, and he felt a little better. One day, as he was describing the anxiety he felt on car journeys, I could see that something powerful was happening for him. "You're back there now, aren't you?" I said gently. He told me that he could see the car crash and hear all the sounds. He put his head in his hands and was doing his utmost not to cry. I had a choice about how best to support this teenager in this moment. The answer was obvious to me – I didn't directly support him at all. I stepped out of the way and let his father do the supporting. My hunch was that it would be healing for them both. So I told him I would like to invite his dad in. He nodded that was okay, and so I called his dad and told him to sit by Gearóid, that his son needed his support. Silently he pulled a chair over to Gearóid, put both arms around him and pulled his son's head into his chest. As soon as he did this, Gearóid started to sob loudly. Before long, Dad's tears were falling on Gearóid's hair. When the tears subsided, they begin to talk about the night of the crash. The following week I met with Gearóid and both his parents. There was more tears and hugging, and important acknowledgement, initially from his dad and then from the adolescent, of how difficult this whole nightmare had been for Gearóid: his injuries and ongoing treatment, travelling alone in an ambulance to a strange hospital many miles from his home, not knowing what was happening, lengthy separation from his mother, whom he was sure he would never see again, his rage at the drunk driver who caused so much devastation to his family, the anxiety and isolation he has experienced since the accident. These few sessions proved transformative and life-giving to Gearóid.

I am not so sure that this adolescent would have experienced this depth of healing had his parents not been involved in the work. Indeed, the trauma had impacted the parenting space, and it was just as important for Gearóid's development to address this as it was to process his traumatic memories. The traumatic experience had rendered the parenting space non-receptive and frozen; and so to fully support this adolescent's development, Gearóid needed his parents' support and they needed to be able to support their son. This clinical example is fairly typical of how I support an adolescent who has experienced trauma-without – i.e. when the traumatic experience is something which has happened *to* the family as opposed to something which has happened *in* the family. The work was to support Gearóid to come to terms with something 'bad' that had happened. It is a very different experience to support someone who believes 'he is bad' because of what has happened in his life.

Trauma-within

Mick, aged 14, was doing poorly in school and had an 'anger management' problem. The school had tried everything; expulsion was on the cards if he did not improve his attitude. Therapy was suggested to his father as something which might help Mick to deal with his anger and to develop a more responsible attitude towards his education and to those in authority. His father thought this would be a good idea too – the boy was difficult to handle at home and he thought Mick might have ADHD 'or something'. Mick was disrespectful to everyone and constantly fighting with his older brother. With this adolescent, the referral route was predictable – an 'acting-out' symptom was identified. The tight feeling in my body as I spoke with Mick's father on the phone informed me that this father would be wanting therapy on his terms. The implicit message was, "This can't continue. Nobody knows what to do with him. You are the expert; you fix him." I felt that familiar pressure to 'deliver the goods'. This is what happened when we met.

I arranged an initial meeting with Mick and his parents. Only Mick and his father arrived. Mick avoided eye contact as he and his father came in and sat down. Why would he want to make eye contact? His father and I were going to sit and talk about how bad he was for the next hour. With raised eyebrows I would listen to the litany of offences. I would tell him that it was not acceptable for him to act in this aggressive way – it was doing him no favours and he was throwing his life away. He should know better. I would teach him strategies like counting backwards from ten to zero or to walk away to dissolve his anger in situations. I was another 'do-gooder' adult who was trying to change him. I would not take him seriously. He was armed and ready to defend himself from the shame which was coming his way. Mick wanted to get the hell out of there as quickly as possible, and who could blame him?

He and his father arrived at my office with an implicit assumption that there was something wrong with him. To be of any meaningful support to Mick I was going to have to quickly blast this unspoken assumption. That was not difficult, as I did not share it. If he was angry, he had reason to be angry. He may not have been containing and directing his anger appropriately, but there was nothing wrong with him. This was my baseline, and as soon as Mick picked this up, there would be a possibility of real connection between the two of us. I was not interested in his anger, or in any 'acting-out' symptom which brought this adolescent through my door. I was interested in getting to know Mick and seeing what happened when he and his father sat down to talk. I was interested that his mother had not come. I held a posture of curiosity and warmth. My only agenda was not to shame either of these people sitting here with me.

I began by announcing that therapy would be firmly on Mick's terms: I never work with teenagers who do not want to be here, and I won't ever make someone come if they don't want to. We were going to have a conversation and Mick would be 'sussing me out' (he smiled, and we had eye contact), so at the end of the conversation I wanted Mick to decide if he'd like to come back next time or not. Did that sound okay to him? "Aye." (His voice was in the room now too.) He didn't even have to speak – I'd like to hear from his dad, and if Mick wanted to respond or say anything, that would be fine. I wondered if that was okay? (He nodded his head in agreement whilst making eye contact with me.) I continued by adding that I had had a brief phone conversation with his dad, and it sounded like things are pretty tough for Mick. I told him that I had never met an unreasonable adolescent: young people who are angry have good reason to be angry, but it sounded like his anger is getting him into trouble.

I said that I would like to hear from his dad what he thought life was like for Mick. I had indicated that I did not intend to shame Mick. He was not sure what to make of me, though was more open to what might take place now. As his father spoke, it was important to nip the shaming tirade in the bud every time it started. It did not take long to get beyond the 'bad behaviour' track. Soon this irate and frustrated father was describing what life had been like in the family and the conversation shifted into a deeper mode. His son was no longer the focus of his dialogue – this created necessary breathing space for Mick. His wife left when Mick was 8 years old. She was alcoholic and towards the end became violent and verbally abusive with Mick and his older brother when she was drunk. Mick did not flinch. His father worked a lot and wasn't around as often as he would like. It was obvious to me why Mick might be angry, and I guessed that this adolescent was also feeling incredibly hurt, such was the extent of his integrity compromise. Translating hurt into anger seems to work as an excellent self-preservation mechanism for adolescents.

The mother-son parenting space was characterised by both direct and indirect hostility. I wanted to find out the level of involvement she had now in Mick's life, if any. At this stage I was not clear whether she would be involved in the work or not. Either way, the hostility had left a legacy which would need to be attended to. With all the focus on Mick's creative adjustment behaviour, the paternal parenting space had become non-receptive. I imagined Mick had experienced non-receptivity within the father-son parenting space for a while. Perhaps it had been characteristic throughout their relationship. Blame is unhelpful and unproductive in these situations, and it can have no place in the work. I remained curious and warm.

The art now was to create ground for deeper receptivity to emerge within the father-son parenting space. This would be a core, ongoing aspect of the work and a key support in the development of richer lifespace integrity for Mick. Offering support to the parent, so that he could find greater balance, created deeper capacity for him to support his son. First I supported Mick's father by expressing my sadness at what had happened and asking what the experience had been like for him. He talked about being left with two sons aged 13 and 8, whilst having a business to run; of how difficult and stressful it had been; of how angry and betrayed he felt that his wife left to go live with another man without even telling him; he hated her, they all hated her. He became upset and apologised for his tears. I stayed with his father for another while, and then I turned to Mick and remarked that this had really been very difficult for his father who had to carry a lot. I asked him what he thought it had been like for his dad. Mick wasn't being asked to account for his unacceptable, aggressive behaviour or say anything about himself. There was no obvious shaming agenda here; it was safe for him to respond. He thought it had been hard for his father. I asked him how he thought his dad had coped. Mick responded by saying that he felt his dad was a good dad and had made a good job of being a single parent. There was room for humour in this piece, and for the first time there was an experience of three-way contact. I guessed it had been a while since they smiled at one another.

His father's experience had been acknowledged a little by all of us. Now I shifted the focus of the dialogue: I wanted us to look through Mick's lens.

I could have asked Mick directly, though I suspected that the response might be a shrug of the shoulders and a comment from him such as "*Shit happens*". A valuable opportunity would have been lost. Adolescents often do not have language for their experience. When trauma-within is present, the adolescent's experience is commonly dismissed because it is too painful a reality – both for him and for other family members. I so frequently encounter adolescents who are not merely unwilling to talk about difficult experiences; it is apparent that they have some deep-seated, trauma-induced dumbness or aphasia with regards to their distress. The quality of their silence is less to do with resistance or ineloquence, and more a statement about being unconscious about being unable to speak.

Having a parent attempt to acknowledge the adolescent's experience is a helpful start in supporting an adolescent to give voice to and come to terms with his experience. It also gives him an experience of being seen and received by his environment. Aware that this part was very necessary for Mick, I asked his father what he thought this whole experience had been like for Mick – the years of living with an alcoholic mother, of having her walk out one day when he was 8, his journey since then. There was a sadness and softness in his voice as he spoke. His son cried himself to sleep for a long time after his mother left. He used to stand outside Mick's bedroom door and listen. He didn't know what to do or say, so he thought it was best to leave him. It used to break his heart. Mick's father cried a little and apologised for his tears again. (Mick was visibly moved, and I later discovered that he never knew until this moment of his father's presence outside his bedroom door all those years ago.) She hadn't even sent him a birthday card since she left; she made no effort to see him even though she lived in the next town. He, himself, had been very busy and had not always been there. Mick spent a lot of time on his own and had probably been very lonely; it had been really hard on Mick. His father had tried his best, but wee boys need their mothers. Mick and his father were now struggling to hold back the tears.

I indicated to Mick my hunch that his father had guessed well. He nodded in agreement. His father turned directly to him and said, "I'm sorry, son". There were some tears on both sides now, and for the first time in his life, Mick's experience had been acknowledged. And this acknowledgement had come with an expression of care and love. *Somebody **gives** a shit*. I imagined that came as a surprise to him. Later in the session I asked his father to describe his son: Mick was a great lad, very smart and capable. He could do whatever he wanted if he put his mind to it. He was determined and stubborn, a bit like his father. He was kind and direct – you knew where you stood with him. "You sound like you are very proud of your son" I said. "Och God I am surely" was the response. I turned to Mick. "He sounds to me like a dad who really loves his son". Mick nodded, and I saw a faint smile. "Of course I love him. He's my wee man," added his father. I asked him curiously if he knew that his dad felt all these things about him. He didn't. It was good to hear them. Later, as we brought the session to a close, I invited them both back again – maybe we would do a half hour with them both and a half hour with just Mick and I next time we met. Both Mick and his father agreed. We were off to a good start: focus on the 'acting-out' symptom had been re-directed to the context of Mick's experience. The potential for shame was immense otherwise. I continued to involve his father and later his older brother in the work.

During one-to-one sessions we worked to establish meaningful and safe relational contact. As Mick began to feel more comfortable with me he recounted a recurring dream: His mother was walking in the middle of a road carrying him in her arms. He was a small baby. She wanted to smoke and so removed one hand, putting it in her pocket to get her pack of cigarettes. Her lighter was in her other pocket, so she took her remaining hand away to fetch it. Mick dropped suddenly to the ground. He woke up trembling and crying just before he hit the ground. His heart was pounding. This dream had captured his experience vividly. It offered us a powerful metaphor to work with as he began to articulate his phenomenological experience. He remembered in meticulous detail the day his mother left – she made him help pack and carry her belongings to the car. He tearfully begged her not to go. It didn't matter about all the bad stuff, he just wanted her to stay. He cried that much after she drove off that he vomited. He was there by himself until his father came home: it seemed like forever. The fact that he was voicing his dream and his memories to someone was healing in itself, but it was not enough. Depth healing was required. Physiologically we store trauma (Van der Kolk, 2015): the day his mother left had been buried alive in Mick's muscles, bones and cells. We paid attention to what was happening in his body: he felt like he wanted to be sick, his legs felt like jelly, his heart was pounding, his chest was sore, he had a pain in his solar plexus like someone was sticking a knife into it. I knew because he told me and because I could feel his sensations in my body also. The tears come and they keep coming. With trauma, embodiment work is necessary as it supports restoration of physiological integrity (Levine, 1997).

Over the coming sessions Mick articulated more and more of his experience. Weaved through the dialogue another important aspect of the healing was occurring. We worked now at a cognitive level – reframing his experience without the shame. He had internalised the hostility, and so we had to put an end to the myth he had created of *The Defective Self*. We pieced together what he knew: His mother's father was a violent alcoholic. He was killed in the Troubles when she was 13 (Interestingly, she left when her eldest child was also 13). She was the eldest girl in a family of seven and had to leave school after his death to help take care of her siblings, most of them boys. When drunk she would regularly express the sentiment that men and boys ruin women's lives. She evidently and understandably experienced a strong sense of injustice for not having had the opportunity to get a decent education or good job. Subsequently, she held her husband and sons accountable for her unhappiness, for her drinking and for holding her back in life. Without blame or demonising, we looked objectively at his family situation and saw that maybe his mother's drinking and destructive behaviour was not because Mick was a bad child (which at 8 years old he was convinced of) but was an expression of the pain she was experiencing. This did not exonerate his mother or make it okay that she caused so much distress to Mick. Rather, it provided the adolescent with a wider perspective from which to contextualise and make mean-ing of his experience of them both within the parenting space. He had tried his best to be a good boy and make her happy, but it never worked – if only he could have been better! He understood now that it was not about him and finally could begin to separate out her behaviour from his self-experience.

Mick began to understand why he was so angry all the time. The destructive behaviour was a creative attempt to heal, although it did have its obvious limita-tions. So he reframed his experience of the legacy of inhabiting a hostile parenting space: "My mother was screwed up because she had a hard time and didn't have much support. She wasn't happy, and she drank to anaesthetise her pain. I get why she did it, but what she did wasn't okay. It wasn't her fault, but it wasn't okay. Her drinking and beating me and leaving wasn't okay; and it was about her, not about me". The cloak of shame was discarded, and the self was no longer experienced as defective. Mick's self-perception moved from "*There must be something wrong with me*". to "*Maybe I'm okay after all*". For the adolescent, this was a liberating place at which to arrive. He arrived at this place without the hostile parent being involved in the work. Healing was not about the parent changing their behaviour (if this happens it is wonderful, though it is rarely a realistic outcome), it was about acknowledgement of the adolescent's experience and a stepping back to see his or her experience from a less individualistic, more contextualised, self-in-and-of-the-lifespace perspective. The parenting space hostility which Mick had absorbed was dispelled. However, as this happened, his self-destructive urge did not automatically dissolve. And so, as Mick began to take himself seriously in the world, reparative work included attending to the despair which continued to infuse his lifespace. The adolescent now made deeper meaning of his experience in the world, grieving for what might have been. It was important to acknowledge precisely what had been lost: having had a parent who was not capable of meeting her child's needs; how terrible life had been because of the hostility; the differ-ence a receptive parenting space would have made in his life; the cost of having internalised the hostility throughout his childhood, etc. This process engendered self-compassion and created new ground for the adolescent to envision a mean-ingful future and to begin to find a place of belonging in the world. In time, the adolescent no longer defined himself by the quality of parenting space he experi-enced and had begun to stand in ownership of his life.

Creating deeper receptivity where there is a quality of non-receptive parenting is always very possible and an important focus of work with adolescents. Work-ing with a hostile parenting space is different. It is not simply a matter of creating greater receptivity. Reframing the space by developing a balanced perspective of the parent-adolescent relational connection is necessary to heal the adoles-cent's deep self-shame which permeates the space. Some women and men cause unspeakable hurt to their children, and often the damage to the parenting space is irreparable. The damage to the adolescent's self-experience is not. Mostly the adolescent's despair will not or cannot be healed within this space. There are other spaces. Inadequate parenting does not necessarily result in failure to thrive – other life-giving aspects of his environment can make all the difference in the world: an encouraging teacher or sports coach, a grandmother, a best friend, a guitar, a therapist. Very often, adolescents whose experience of being parented was less than supportive, arrive at adulthood as happy, confident, self-assured men and women – and they make wonderful parents themselves. They have found support elsewhere, and their healthy self-process is not due to the parenting they received, but in spite of it. Thankfully humans are wonderfully resilient and resourceful. And so the therapist must always hold a tremendous posture of hope when she meets her adolescent clients.

References

Briggs, E., Fairbank, J., Greeson, J., Layne, C., Steinberg, A., Amaya-Jackson, L., Ostrowski, S., Gerrity, E., Elmore, D., Belcher, H. and Pynoos, R. (2013). Links between child and adolescent trauma exposure and service use histories in a national clinic-referred sample. *Psychological Trauma: Theory, Research, Practice, and Policy*, 5(2), pp. 101–109.
Kegan, R. (2003). *In Over Our Heads*. Cambridge, MA: Harvard University Press.
Levine, P. (1997). *Waking the Tiger*. Berkeley, CA: North Atlantic Books.
Van der Kolk, B. (2015). *The Body Keeps the Score*. New York: Penguin Books.

The author wishes to thank The British Gestalt Journal for their kind permission to reprint an excerpt from a previously published paper within this chapter: Starrs, B. (2014). Contact and despair: a Gestalt approach to adolescent trauma. *British Gestalt Journal*, 23(2), 28–37.

Chapter 4

One-to-one engagement with the adolescent

Contact assessment involving the adolescent together with parenting adults, as the point of departure in therapy, is an important support to contact between therapist and adolescent during their initial one-to-one meeting, as much will have been communicated within their field of relatedness prior to this first encounter without the presence of parenting adults. In addition to information gathered in reference to the adolescent's lifespace context and configuration, the assessment process will have generated extensive data regarding contact boundary development, thus affording the therapist a reasonable appreciation of the adolescent's contact style and openness to their encounter.

A prudent prerequisite to the commencement of one-to-one work with the adolescent is the presence of even the faintest spark of openness to connecting with the therapist. During contact assessment the therapist remains attuned to any joining contact between the two, as evidenced in the adolescent's delicately nuanced expression of interested participation. His quality of responsiveness to the therapist may range from interest, readiness to dialogue and convivial warmth to patronising indifference, hostile silence and contempt. It is both premature and ill-advised to engage in one-to-one work with an adolescent who demonstrates no interest in connecting and whose contact remains rigidly contentious within the therapeutic space. The adolescent's demeanour may be translated as a statement of his faith in the therapist to support his yearnings for integrity. In instances where the basis of one-to-one contact is suspicion and mistrust, power struggling and mutual dissatisfaction are guaranteed. Respectfully stating that she does not think the adolescent is interested in engaging in further sessions locates any dilemma with the adolescent and his parents, which is wholly more beneficial than the therapist attempting to convince the adolescent why he needs to attend and how she can help him. This scenario promotes passivity rather than mutuality for the adolescent who sees the therapist as offering him a service, establishing an unhelpful power struggle from the outset. However, it is unusual for a young person not to respond favourably to the support afforded him in non-requestive contact during the initial assessment, and almost all adolescents choose to engage. The prospect of being understood, taken seriously and not being shamed by an adult, who seems genuinely interested and safe, holds an alluring appeal for most.

The objectives of psychotherapy with adolescent clients are to increase the integrity of and extend his lifespace; to get him interested in himself; and to support him to have a life worth living. By the end of the first one-to-one session, it is expected that some degree of progress will have been made with even the most traumatised adolescent. There are instances where the work is complete at this point and further sessions are unnecessary. However, for the most part, ongoing work is anticipated – contingent on the adolescent's willingness, of course. Psychotherapeutic intervention with adolescents need not be protracted, and in many cases the work is complete within six to eight sessions. The assumption that healing trauma, certainly in adolescence, ought to be a lengthy process, is unhelpful. The adolescent client has neither endured the decades of embedded shame nor the rigid feeling, thought and behaviour creative adjustments that his adult counterparts may have. It is a much simpler task to restore integrity in the young person and to support access to hope and vision for a life worth living.

Configuration styles

The therapist will have identified the adolescent's particular configuration style during the contact assessment. This insight supports her to discover the meaning of the adolescent's creative adjustments. An appreciation of each adolescent's configuration style also assists the therapist in determining how to modulate her own style of relatedness, the dialogue's focus and her interventions to support the co-creation of optimal therapeutic space integrity.

The adolescent develops a lifespace configuration style which shapes and is shaped by his wider lifespace experience. Whilst each adolescent's style is subtly unique, there are three principal modes of configuration through which his experience and perspective is constructed. I refer to these as *impulsive, inhibitive* and *directional*. Typically the young person recycles constantly between all stages throughout adolescence as he develops increased directionality within his lifespace. Directional proclivity implies a choiceful, considered adolescent who has a growing sense of ownership of his life and experience. There is self-assurance and composure in his contact style; he takes himself seriously – but not too seriously; is flexible, relationally attuned, insightful and balanced. His yearnings for integrity have been met to the extent that, for the most part, he is inclined towards physiological, psychological and interpersonal integrity as he moves purposefully and with vision through his lifespace: he is moving in the right direction.

We can expect that the adolescent will move through impulsive and inhibitive stages before reaching a more directional style of contact. For many adolescents, however, the impetus towards integrity is thwarted with the result that one particular configuration style becomes a fixed mode through which he organises his experience. His lifespace is characterised with either chaos or restriction and whilst developmental wisdom is always present in his creative adjustments, his integrity is likely being compromised. A considerable number of adolescents referred for psychotherapy have become caught in either an impulsive or inhibitive configuration style.

The impulsively configured adolescent is disposed to respond spontaneously within his lifespace. His emotional response tends to dictate his action response so that he does whatever he *feels* like doing. Provided the adolescent is interested in something or someone, he shows himself to be intensely focused and motivated. However, his propensity to indulge impulses renders him prone to boredom, inattention and restlessness unless captivated by an activity. Many younger adolescents (Siegel, 2013), particularly boys (Mortola, 2015), typically demonstrate this inclination towards impulsive configuration – for example, the junior exam student who chooses his game console over a study programme and who demonstrates no interest whatsoever in his future, much to his parents' chagrin. Over time we can expect to witness growing interest in more aspects of his lifespace as his future begins to matter to him. Greater ownership of experience results in a heightened capacity for impulse containment as the adolescent becomes more directionally minded.

For some adolescents there is a propensity towards inflexible impulsive configuration when, for example, an adolescent may have experienced a childhood and family life characterised by chaos and disruption to the degree that the impulse-driven environment has become the adolescent's internal working model (Howe, 2005). Similarly, the adolescent may have creatively adjusted to an experience of trauma through impulse indulgence, artfully avoiding overwhelming feelings of loss and vulnerability. Typically, his creative adjustment conceals an underlying sense of shame. He fails to take himself seriously, unless he is supporting his impulsive inclination. The adolescent's feeling world tends to be pronounced and more amplified than his less impulsive counterparts. Characteristically, containment of the expression of his feeling is problematic. Many, for example, are identified as having 'anger management issues' or receive a diagnosis of ADHD (Van der Kolk, 2015). For some, the feeling of being alive only truly happens when adrenalin is coursing through their veins. Life is a party shaped by high risk and potential addiction, and the adolescent's thoughts about the future generally do not stretch beyond the weekend.

The inhibitively configured adolescent, on the other hand, has no difficulty overriding his impulses. He is externally referenced, doing what he feels he *should* do, which is not necessarily a statement of personal integrity. He has a strong sense of duty and typically is described as a very *sensible* young man. However, he lacks spontaneity and frequently expends a great deal of energy overthinking situations, often experiencing himself as a bystander and not fully immersed in his world. This adolescent has a propensity to anxiety, which is the expected outgrowth of developing within an inhibitively configured lifespace.

The adolescent for whom inhibitive configuration has become a fixed pattern has developed a capacity to almost entirely dissociate from his impulses. He becomes preoccupied with certain goals which have more to do with environmental acceptability than with honouring his integrity, hence the directionless quality which so often characterises his efforts. His aspiration to be the top student or athlete, or to lose weight, is driven by inadequacy and collides with his tendency towards perfectionism. He learns to deny his tired and hungry body, remaining rigidly driven towards his underlying goal of becoming an acceptable human being. Where the directional adolescent *tries his best*, the inhibitively configured adolescent *has to be the best*. Outstanding grades, sporting achievements and weight loss, in the end, bring little satisfaction as he loses any sense of balance and perspective. He moves within a restricted lifespace, infused with rigidity, as his life becomes a punishing regime; his relentless drive lacks a directional quality and he experiences little enjoyment in life. The adolescent is typically miserable and lonely, living with tremendous psychological pressure, and his creative adjustments are an attempt to decompress.

For both the impulsively and inhibitively configured adolescent, the struggle has to do with *containment*. For example, Cathal, whose lifespace contact is shaped through reaction to impulse, has no interest in school, save for seeing his friends and disrupting classes; binge drinks each weekend and has been experimenting with drugs; spends many hours each day playing his games console and accessing pornography; and is prone to explosive outbursts when challenged by his parents, who feel they have lost their capacity to influence him. He has developed neither the capacity nor the inclination to contain his impulses. The therapeutic focus with Cathal is promoting his interest in taking himself more seriously and supporting him to develop the art of thoughtfully and choicefully relating to his impulses. Conversely, Kevin's academic progress is important to him and he works hard at his studies; he is a talented footballer and takes his commitment to this sport very seriously – spending additional time in the gym to complement his rigorous training programme, whilst managing his diet carefully to assist his sporting performance. Whilst Kevin may appear directional and successful, he approaches these activities with intensity and imbalance. He finds it difficult to accept less than an A grade in school: anything lower amounts to personal failure. He thinks obsessively about his sporting performance and fitness. If he feels his academic work is sub-standard or answers a question incorrectly in class, he bangs his head off his bedroom wall; if he plays badly in a match, he slaps and punches himself. In time, Kevin loses his place on the football team due to ongoing ankle and back issues, which could have been avoided if he had given his body sufficient time to heal from the original injuries; and thoughtful attention to his diet evolves into rigorous calorie counting and eventually to the development of an anorectic profile. Kevin's dilemma is not knowing when his efforts are *enough* as he sees his accomplishments as self-statements which belie an abiding sense that he, himself is *not enough*. The therapeutic challenge is to support him to feel like an adequate and acceptable human being, and not to singularly define himself by 'external' identity markers.

One of the therapist's primary objectives is to facilitate the adolescent's movement towards increasingly directional lifespace configuration, irrespective of presenting symptom issues. It is always useful to present a generic description of each configuration style to the adolescent, offering a hunch as to how he might be organising his experience within his world. The art is to stimulate the adolescent's curiosity about himself so that he begins to recognise his self-neglect and lack of integrity in such a way that it bothers him. This intervention is effective in developing both the necessary insight required to appreciate the redundancy of his rigid configuring and the concern to mobilise towards a more directional way of being. Insight, however, takes time to manifest into a transformed lifespace experience: the adolescent does not suddenly arrive at a place of directionality; he grows into it.

Initiating contact

The process of how physical configuration of the therapeutic space is negotiated and creative activity is initiated is revealing in itself. The assessment process will have afforded the therapist an idea of whether the adolescent is more inclined to frozenness or spontaneity, which informs her of the young person's capacity to make choices. A receptive and assured adolescent typically enjoys exploring the physical space, figuring out where to sit and what to do. In my office, there are three possible areas where we might locate: at a large table, by the sandspace or on beanbags. I offer the more supported adolescents a choice about location. Once that has been established, there is further choice with regard to an activity. For example, the adolescent who sits at the art table now has to decide on which media to work with – page or mask? markers or paint? watercolours or acrylics? I then note how he begins: whether he himself decides what to paint and how to go about it, or if he needs support to reach for the brush, choose a colour, dip the brush and make a first mark on the page.

Invitation to select either location or activity becomes an exercise fraught with anxiety for the more reticent adolescent, as contact is now already strained through expectation. Similarly, an adolescent client may choose not to engage in any creative enterprise, lest he be perceived as uncool and childish. In these situations, it is helpful to offer a rationale, more directive than invitational in tone, that exclusively dialoguing is simply boring and that fiddling with something makes the time more relaxing and interesting, placing some materials within reach. Throughout these exchanges, safety is created by ensuring that expectation, exposure and shame are excluded from any interaction. The therapist is closely attuned to her breath and body, remaining open and relaxed to cultivate a receptive therapeutic space. The manner in which these micro-episodes are co-created indicates more clearly the level of inertia or momentum present in the therapeutic space. Indeed, these initial moments of encounter also reveal a great deal about the adolescent's level of momentum and capacity for spontaneity within his wider lifespace experience.

Once both are physically anchored in the space, the therapist initiates a deeper level of dialogic process. Conscious shaping of contact and direction of dialogue during the initial one-to-one session is important to establish the culture and tone of the therapeutic space. It is helpful, from the outset, to remind the adolescent that this meeting, in addition to creating space to come to know each other more, is also useful by way of his evaluation with regard to any ongoing engagement. This explicit invitation to the adolescent to continue assessing the therapist artfully sidesteps power struggles, offers greater possibility of mutuality in the encounter and informs him that ongoing commitment is not an expectation. In these opening few moments the adolescent may not yet have spoken a word and feels under no obligation to do so as the therapist's contact is not requestive.

The contact assessment will have generated a rich supply of material to draw on, and so the therapist begins the dialogue by reflecting on the assessment process, offering hunches about the adolescent's experience in relation to his participation in assessment meetings and makes appreciative and tentative statements with regard to his general lifespace phenomenology. This stimulates the adolescent's memory and felt sense of their prior contact, bringing to mind an experience of previously established trust, and of continuity. Active empathy generates active participation and so the therapist also communicates how she has been impacted by the adolescent and his experience. It is at this point that, having taken care to create receptivity within the therapeutic space, she invites the adolescent into a back-and-forth conversation. Beneath the words, the therapist is consistently attuned to both their worlds of experience, particularly to the presence or absence of spontaneity in the adolescent's contact, which shows through in his capacity to hold his own in the dialogue. She remains attentive to the complexity of the nuances of their relating, including their embodied experience, their myriad micro-episodes of contact, the potential impact of her words and presence, as well as the adolescent's developmental location and configuration style. As she perceives the adolescent adopting a more remote posture within the therapeutic space or as an intervention to prevent intensity and shame, the therapist initiates sideways contact (see below), by switching focus to the activity or exploring other less exposing aspects of the adolescent's lifespace as a meaningful digression. This interplay between direct and sideways contact maintains balance and mutuality within the therapeutic space. Gradually, the adolescent's faith in the therapist as a genuinely interested dialogue partner grows. Therapeutic receptivity supports him to tolerate richer and increasingly direct contact, as his curiosity to explore his experiential world intensifies. Metaphorically speaking, the adolescent begins to feel the therapist's supportive hand at his back.

Sideways contact

It has been widely observed by those who study interactional habits within the animal kingdom that direct eye contact from human to animal is often perceived as predatory behaviour. The person is viewed as a threat which creates a flight, fight or freeze response in the animal. (Leopold and Rhodes, 2010) Adolescents, particularly traumatised ones, respond similarly to intensity of contact within the therapeutic space and so it is advisable to initiate *sideways contact* which will organically morph into more direct contact as trusting relational ground is cultivated; young clients may feel barraged and exposed otherwise.

Sideways contact diffuses any intensity in interpersonal relating, and many adolescents benefit from this less-intense quality of interaction in the beginning stages of therapy. With the exception of those adolescents who present as readily contactful and articulate, it is advisable to encourage engagement in some activity. Expansion of the therapeutic space to involve an activity, for example, doodling, moulding play dough or painting; or diversion of intense developmental dialogue to more light-hearted conversation, are effective for deflection should the adolescent require breathing space or when natural lulls emerge in the dialogue. In instances where greater reduction of intensity is required, the therapist may also engage in some simple activity herself, such as doodling or moulding play dough. The use of creative devices at this early point is principally to support the establishment of meaningful contact and to minimise intensity. The therapist who relies solely on verbal discourse with a tentative, self-conscious adolescent whose capacity for reflection is limited, or similarly, who elevates creative expression over interpersonal contact as the central focus, may risk restriction of contact for the adolescent. Sideways contact in the form of creative process is a support to richer lifespace and therapeutic contact for the adolescent, which does not give the therapist licence to move beyond the realm of psychotherapy. Angel or crystal therapy, using various card packs, energy healing, shamanism and other practices are *not* psychotherapy and numerous adolescents have recounted grim stories to me of previous therapists engaging them in 'weird stuff' which inevitably compromised the integrity of the therapeutic space. These additions risk bringing the profession into disrepute.

Sandspace: a three-dimensional integrity narrative

The clinician works to establish a therapeutic space whose conditions support optimal integrity for the adolescent. Creative expression through posture, dialogue and activity is a support to contact, leading to important developmental shifts in intersubjective relating and personal understanding. Even the most shamed adolescent will benefit from reparative interventions which activate his capacity to make meaning of his lifespace experience through the lens of his unmet yearnings for integrity. Creating an integrity narrative helps the adolescent understand and appreciate his lifespace experience, as his creative adjustments, however misguided and destructive they might appear, are reframed as expressions of the pain of unfulfilled yearnings.

The therapist is attempting to facilitate illumination and integration of the full complexity of the adolescent's lifespace in a manner which respectfully acknowledges his phenomenology, extracts shame from his self-experience and opens for him the potential of creating a more hopeful, choiceful and directional lifespace. Relying on verbal reframing of the adolescent's lifespace context may have limited impact for some young people, including the adolescent in the earlier stages of development; the adolescent whose lifespace configuration has become a fixed gestalt of impulsivity or inhibition; and the traumatised adolescent. For the client who is identified in any one, or indeed all, of these groups, words alone may not always reach the heart of his experience or sustain new awareness between sessions.

The adolescent benefits from interventions which include both dialogic appraisal and visual representation of his lifespace, as the imprint of visual cues has a greater tendency to remain with the adolescent and support fuller integration of new insights. Inviting him to artistically depict some aspect of his experience assists the adolescent in developing a richer appreciation of his lifespace. However, he may not always willingly respond to this invitation, and whilst artwork is certainly effective for some, there is a more powerful intervention through which the adolescent's lifespace and contact boundaries are made not only visible, but also tangible and three-dimensional. This method which essentially animates aspects of the lifespace by creating symbolic representations in sand, incorporating both dialogic and visual features, I call s*andspace.*

The more spontaneous adolescent needs little encouragement to begin defining his lifespace in the sand and reflecting on the artefacts he has chosen. However, many adolescents will not readily choose to work in this manner and so the process may be introduced as sideways contact initially. Rather than inviting the adolescent to the sandspace, it works best if the therapist 'brings the sandspace to the adolescent'. Preparation of the physical space of the therapy office is important: the positioning of the sandbox in the room must lend itself to a relational encounter. As the dialogue focuses on a developmentally significant issue, the therapist offers a rationale for introducing this manner of intervening by telling the adolescent that a visual representation of the issue will help *her* understand it more deeply. By doing so, the therapist takes initial ownership of the sandspace process, though her interest, of course, has an invitational twist.

Sandspace is useful for transcending verbal limitations, particularly for the younger or traumatised adolescent who may not have language for his experience. Introduction of figures and artefacts acts as an extension of and support to dialogic relating, as well as amplifying and adding richness to the issues being reflected on. The quality of sideways contact afforded through sandspace also staves the possibility of therapeutic space intensity. The therapist's tentative three-dimensional fashioning of aspects of the adolescent's lifespace is almost always captivating for the young person whose engagement moves in the direction of becoming increasingly interactive and spontaneous. Often this movement happens instantly. If the adolescent's curiosity heightens, the therapist invites the adolescent to participate in this sculpting process, metaphorically inviting him to take authorship of his lifespace. All the while, the therapist is supporting him to see through a non-shaming lens of possibility, which at times involves both of them reaching into, re-shaping and reframing the lifespace image which is emerging through the sandspace.

The therapist and adolescent gradually begin to co-create a dynamic sandspace which sheds light on the adolescent's phenomenology, as aspects of his lifespace are sculpted in the sand. Amplification of figures becomes an interactive process as dialogue emerges between various aspects of his lifespace. The process 'externalises' dilemmas and interpersonal conflicts in such a manner that the adolescent, metaphorically speaking, inhabits his lifespace and at the same time, stands outside it, looking in – and does so with support. The adolescent is supported to adopt a reflective posture, and in the process, reorganises his lifespace narrative with compassionate appreciation of how he has creatively adjusted to distress and insufficient support. Ultimately, this leads to greater ownership of his experience as he, in time, outgrows his previously compromising lifespace configuration and adopts a more directional posture. The co-construction of dimensions of the lifespace creates capacity for richer sensory development as the adolescent begins to *see* his issues and dilemmas with greater clarity. The visual impact of this lifespace perspective-taking remains viscerally, long after the session has ended, percolating within the client.

One important dimension of therapeutic work is to nurture and stimulate the adolescent's newly emerging developmental capacity to make meaning (Kegan, 2003). Trauma, distress and lack of support within his lifespace are all too often translated into shame-based self-statements, and so, interventions which support the adolescent in making contact with and meaning of aspects of his lifespace experience from a wider perspective are essential. Sandspace creations always have a specific developmental focus, and the experience of 'stepping back' and visually reflecting on one's lifespace is both compelling and healing. This intervention presents the adolescent with an opportunity to make meaning of his childhood experience, parenting spaces and expanding lifespace in such a manner that supports the establishment of rich integrity, voice and momentum within his lifespace.

As the adolescent and therapist three-dimensionally reframe the lifespace, expression of the therapist's accurate attunement creates a palpable sense of relief and validation for the adolescent whose phenomenological experience has been powerfully witnessed. The therapist's conscious attunement to the impact of the sandspace on the young person throughout the process is paramount. Otherwise she risks overwhelming the adolescent who may become flooded with painful and unbearable feelings and memories. Inclusion of some visual representation of support and hope is a guiding principal for each sandspace, even if the adolescent has, as yet, little sense of ever having a life worth living.

The therapist's faithful commitment to understanding, appreciating and validating the adolescent's phenomenology is a transformative experience for both (Orange, 2011). Not only does the process support the adolescent to grasp a more contextual appreciation of his first-person experience, it also supports empathic resonance in a manner which dialogue alone does not quite seem to access. Allowing oneself to be profoundly moved by another's suffering, whilst personally demanding, gifts the therapeutic space with deeper dimensions of validation and integrity (Levinas and Nemo, 2011). It is also, of course, important for the therapist to reach out during this reframing process by communicating the personal impact of bearing witness to the adolescent's experience on her. In this way, reframing the adolescent's experience through sandspace creates richer therapeutic contact, as the adolescent quite literally has a sense that the therapist *sees what it's like*. For the adolescent, amplification of his phenomenological experience and reframing of his lifespace context in a de-shaming, supportive and compassionate manner is accomplished more extensively and profoundly through the visual sculpting of his lifespace in this dynamic, three-dimensional manner than through reliance on an exclusively verbal intervention. Typically, following such attuned interventions, integrations and shifts in contact are pronounced.

Aoibheann

Aoibheann agreed to speak to someone after it was discovered that she had been self-harming. Following the contact assessment, which was attended by the adolescent and both parents, I met with Aoibheann for several one-to-one sessions. During the first of these, she chose to paint a picture which depicted her falling (Figure 4.1).

As the adolescent painted, I shaped our dialogue by reframing aspects of the contact assessment and tentatively sculpted the family dynamics as I imagined she might experience them. Aoibheann's appreciation of the endeavour to respectfully understand and reflect her phenomenology supported the emergence of her voice. The adolescent's curiosity was sparked and she began to open about the impact of parental conflict: she did not know why her parents were still together and figured they were nearing the point of separation, adding that she was worn out by their constant arguing. For the second one-to-one session, Aoibheann chose to sit by the sandbox and as the dialogue unfolded, I invited her to create a sandspace that would reflect how family life felt to her. She placed a large number of animals in the sandspace to represent parental conflict, finally arranging a nest containing two eaglets in an elevated position using a wooden mallet. Aoibheann described how she and her younger brother, represented by the eaglets, had adapted through withdrawal (Figure 4.2).

I suggested to Aoibheann that the self-harming made sense in the context of this stressful situation, explaining the very human need to find some manner of creatively adjusting to the intensity of living in a family field characterised by ongoing parental conflict and the threat of parental separation; concern about her little brother; and her own pressure to succeed academically and socially. The adolescent responded to this contextual reframing of the self-harming by talking more profoundly about how she experienced her lifespace. To support the understanding and validation of this experience, I invited Aoibheann, during the following session, to depict what it felt like to be her. She placed an agonised figure next to a knife and pool of blood, the visual power of which aroused sadness in the adolescent for the struggle she was experiencing (Figure 4.3).

Figure 4.1 Aoibheann falling

Figure 4.2 Escaping parental conflict

Figure 4.3 Aoibheann's agony

Parallel dialogue

Frequently, particular situations and struggles within the adolescent's present-day lifespace mirror aspects of his pre- and perinatal experience (Bennett and Grof, 1993). The therapist, when attempting to express her empathic attunement about certain features of the adolescent's life, at times may focus her empathic dialogue on the young person's phenomenology of birth. Having gathered information with regard to the adolescent's pre- and perinatal experience, she tries to imagine what his experience of wombspace, birth and earliest days in the world may have been, offering this empathic resonance to him as if she were referring to his present-day situation. Actively empathising at two simultaneous levels powerfully supports the paradoxical approach to change (Beisser, 1970). This is particularly effective when despair or an impasse has emerged for the adolescent.

Meeting Aoibheann in her despondency has the potential to create momentum within her lifespace, and I began to actively empathise with her struggle to be born, the resonance of which may somehow continue to be experienced years after the event. I had discovered during contact assessment that Aoibheann had experienced a protracted labour, enduring the intensity of crushing contractions for two and a half days before adequate cervical dilation and movement into the birth canal. I chose my language carefully, speaking to both her present day and birth struggles: "It sounds like this is an intensely dark and tight space you're in just now, and that

Figure 4.4 "Me feeling human again."

it feels somehow that you are stuck here with no end in sight. I imagine you feel the pressure closing in on you at times in a way that overwhelms you. My hunch is that, much of the time, you feel that you can't take any more, except that it keeps coming and it seems to get more and more intense. It must be lonely and scary in there by yourself with hardly room to move. This is just terrible, it's too much for you and I'm going to stay here with you in this dark and compressed space until we see a light at the end of the tunnel". The adolescent almost always responds to this depth of attunement and feels met in the struggle as the therapist becomes a psychological midwife, so to speak, supporting the adolescent to birth into a new way of being in the world. Aoibheann's self-harming behaviour ceased following this session.

Further one-to-one sessions focused on creating faith in herself and a clear vision for her expanding lifespace, in spite of the stress of ongoing parental animosity. Aoibheann's voice and spontaneity emerged as she grew interested in herself again. The adolescent's sandspace representations depicted increasing hope and directionality, with one such sandspace portraying supportive lifespace influences on one side and more challenging ones on the other. In the middle she made a channel with a boat containing the agonised figure and one which she named 'me feeling human again', being stewarded towards an eagle, which represented the potential of who she was becoming (Figure 4.4).

Secrets

There are times, both during contact assessment and in one-to-one work with an adolescent, where the therapist finds herself tolerating confusion and uncertainty. A dual reality emerges within the work which consists of a superficial level of clarity, yet the therapist holds a strong sense that information is being withheld. Many adolescents, however, do not reveal their secrets. The therapist's agenda is not to challenge the adolescent's reticence or to draw out secrets. Instead, registering to herself the sense of tightness and lack of clarity supports the therapist to remain grounded and contactful.

I am reminded of a 17-year-old client, Caroline, who had come to therapy because she was depressed and anxious. During the contact assessment, her parents seemed very supportive and receptive. They were at a loss to know why their daughter felt so terrible and she herself could think of no particular reason why, suddenly over the last six months, she had begun to feel so overwhelmed in the world. Caroline had abruptly withdrawn from her college course, had returned home to live with her parents and found a job in a local store. We worked together for several months, exploring various aspects of her lifespace as the adolescent experienced some relief from her symptoms. There was a distinct lack of fluency in our contact, which is characteristic when working in the presence of secrets. Some two years later, I received an unexpected message from the adolescent, seeking an appointment as soon as possible. Some weeks previously, Caroline, who had recently been promoted in the job which she loved, had suddenly announced to her parents that she had handed in her notice. Following a heated exchange between the adolescent and her parents, Caroline burst into tears and revealed that her dramatic departure from college a few years earlier was the result of having woken up as she was being raped by a fellow student who had entered her room in the middle of the night. As Caroline spoke, it emerged that her new work promotion involved travelling around the country, staying overnight in hotel accommodation. As she lay awake in a hotel room, listening to the sound of male voices passing by her door, she became petrified that someone would break in and sexually assault her again. The adolescent could not bear the terror and insomnia, and subsequently resigned from her job.

The quality of contact within the therapeutic space upon Caroline's return had been vividly transformed as there was no longer a secretive aspect to our relating; instead, clarity and fluency were the characteristics of our contact. Working within the presence of secrets is common and occurs when the adolescent determines that to disclose some particular aspect of her experience will create exposure and unsafety. In Caroline's case, she made the decision not to reveal the sexual assault during her first episode of therapy because telling me meant that she would have to face into what had happened, which terrified her. The initial round of therapy created some relief, which, she informed me later, was helped along by alcohol and cocaine, until the pain of keeping her secret surpassed the fear of disclosure.

Common therapeutic responses

Translation of therapeutic responses into actively empathic responses supports the paradoxical approach to change (Beisser, 1970) and in doing so, creates deeper empathy and movement. The therapist's embodied feeling, thought and behaviour responses within the therapeutic space are important illuminators, creating access to more information regarding the adolescent's lifespace experience. A spirit of curiosity and openness, and a conscious awareness of these responses within the co-created field of contact introduces an added dimension of therapeutic richness (Jacobs, 2017) and lifespace momentum for the adolescent. For example, the therapist may find herself reacting initially with intolerance towards an adolescent who feels depressed and unmotivated, judging him for choosing to stay in the doldrums and feeling indignation that he has not implemented the useful strategies she has given him. As is tempting with adolescent clients, the therapist repeatedly finds herself trying to change how he thinks and feels, growing frustrated that he is 'not helping himself' (and making her look bad). Realising that she has been succumbing to pressure to fix the client, the therapist attends to the remoteness and isolation which has emerged within the therapeutic contact and re-establishes I-Thou contact with the adolescent (Buber, 1970). In this instance, as the therapist becomes mindful of her feelings towards the adolescent and the pressure she is exerting within the therapeutic space, she actively translates her awareness as a statement of how unacceptable this adolescent may experience himself and be experienced in the world, and of how he likely feels pressured by those around him and possibly even by himself, to be different. The therapeutic encounter for the adolescent now has a much greater probability of creating meaningful depth and relief.

Therapeutic responses are diverse and unlimited. However, there are several which become particularly familiar for the adolescent therapist. The two principal therapeutic responses which emerge for therapists in the work with adolescents are *urgency* and *despair*. The less-experienced therapist repeatedly finds herself operating out of these responses. Therapeutic space integrity is maintained by understanding urgency and despair responses as information about the adolescent's feeling world and translating these into active empathic responses. With urgency, the therapist commonly engages in power struggling with the adolescent, parenting adults or other professionals. She is gripped by a sense of having to *do something* which is characterised with imbalance and exaggerated effort. Whilst situations regularly arise which call on the therapist to mobilise, very little is accomplished satisfactorily when urgency is shaping these interventions. When this occurs, the therapist is inclined to overreach and even panic; she may end up feeling and looking foolish. This is usually accompanied by the adolescent's distinct lack of concern. Similarly, with despair, the therapist may develop a collapse response, feeling powerless to influence such a dire situation. She finds herself helplessly sighing and lost for words. Ironically, her most empowering and helpful intervention for the adolescent is to become aware of and step out of the despair. For example, in response to a despair co-transference, the therapist may say something like, "I imagine you feel helpless about this situation and you don't hold much hope about anything good happening. It sounds like you're almost despairing; as if you've given up and all you can do is sigh when you think about it". Invoking the paradoxical approach to change by acknowledgement of urgency and despair reinstates balance and integrity within the therapeutic space, ensuring the therapist's grounded attunement and receptivity. Whilst they are helpful illuminators, little progress is made when urgency and despair are present in the therapeutic encounter as they breed remoteness in contact.

A common therapeutic response in the presence of trauma, is desensitisation, where the therapist's capacity to respond is dampened (Wilson and Lindy, 1994). The parallel process reflects a desensitised field, where potentially all, including the adolescent, parenting adults and other professionals, remain peculiarly unaffected by troubling situations. I am reminded of a recent supervisee who felt her client was progressing well and the work was nearing termination stage. As we explored the dynamics, the description of her 12-year-old client's experience certainly was cause for concern. However, my supervisee had been unaware of how desensitised and frozen she herself had become in the work. This young girl lived alone with her father, who still bathed her and in whose bed she slept each night; she described feeling frightened and unsafe with him; she self-harmed, ate only one apple each day and appeared underweight. The therapist is often so blindsided in the presence of a desensitised field that even the simplest awareness does not occur to her, including, in this case, initiation of child protection measures.

The adolescent who inhabits a traumatised lifespace becomes artful at numbing the awareness of distressing feelings and unsafe situations. This numbing quality can extend into the therapeutic space, and to attend to this, the therapist must stay in rich contact with all she perceives.

Counselling vs. psychotherapy with adolescents

Psychotherapeutic work with adolescents involves assessment of the wider dynamics at play within the young person's expanding lifespace in addition to addressing presenting symptom issues. Meeting key parenting figures, where available and appropriate, to witness contact process between the adolescent and significant adults in his life, and intervening to harness their support, if possible, for the young person's development is a key and ongoing therapeutic task. One-to-one work supports the unpacking of the adolescent's phenomenological experience and the expansion of his meaning-making capacity, as he moves in the direction of becoming more empowered and choiceful within all aspects of his lifespace. Psychotherapy with adolescents supports the adolescent's overall developmental pathway.

Many helping professionals attend to direct issues which have been identified in the adolescent's life, focusing on modifying thoughts, behaviours and feelings. Cognitive and behavioural methods are employed to help the young person cope (Fuggle, Dunsmuir and Curry, 2013); or perhaps an art or play therapist will employ some creative process to support the adolescent either verbally or non-verbally in a non-directive therapeutic encounter (Riley, 2010). I refer to all of this work as *counselling*. The work characteristically takes place individually between the counsellor and adolescent, save for an assessment meeting when information is gathered from parents about the adolescent's context and behaviour. The adolescent may begin to express his experience, often feeling relief at being understood and met with support. Symptoms may improve or vanish. However, this one-to-one work can create difficulty as the adolescent may be neither willing nor able to present facts and concerns to the counsellor in a reasonably objective manner: a 13-year-old's face-saving version of events may vary considerably from that of the adults in his world, though often the counsellor's hands are tied in these situations. The philosophy that it is not the therapist's business to believe or disbelieve, but to empathise, may work for adult clients. The therapeutic space may become compromised when she adopts this posture with teenage clients. The adolescent is also prone to finding ways of engaging on his terms. For example, he may refuse to dialogue about some important aspects of his experience. It is not uncommon to hear of situations where the adolescent and counsellor spend session after session discussing music tastes and sporting interests whilst the reason for referral, that he has been expelled from school, having been caught supplying cannabis to other students, is not ever addressed. It is both important and necessary to find non-shaming topics for dialogue with adolescent clients at times; however, these conversations are developed to establish relational ground, so that deeper work can take place. They are a means to an end, not the principal focus of the work. The counsellor may inadvertently support the emergence of a collusive, avoidant counselling process which meanders superficially. The counselling relationship might offer sanctuary to the adolescent, though does not always attend to the developmental context of the young person's experience. At other times, the counsellor may embark upon a programme of change, attempting to influence the adolescent's world of feeling, thought and behaviour. However, if this happens prematurely, the clinician often experiences a non-collaborative quality in the contact. In these instances, the counsellor may well be *talking at* rather than *dialoguing with* the adolescent, who adopts a passive role and becomes set for failure, as he has not fully invested in this 'collaboration'. The work lacks a quality of mutually active participation and therapy is 'being done to' the adolescent.

Psychotherapy with adolescent clients cannot be reduced to a set of techniques. The emphasis is on the relationship and supporting the development and expansion of the adolescent's lifespace. Each adolescent's developmental journey and lifespace dynamics are truly unique, and so it is folly to reduce therapeutic intervention to a one-size-fits-all technique-driven exercise. The most powerful dimension to the work is contact: the capacity to sit into and appreciate the adolescent's phenomenology. The adolescent's greatest yearning, (and the deeper the trauma, the stronger the yearning) is for his phenomenology to be empathically and compassionately witnessed and for that appreciation to be communicated to him. He needs to know that he is seen and that he matters, despite how unbearable the thought of this seems to him. We know this, yet the pressure to undertake time-limited work with measurable outcomes, focusing on modifying thoughts and behaviour in the short term, is ever-increasing (McWilliams, 2011). Fully meeting the adolescent, supporting his meaning-making, de-shaming and reframing his experience are what heals.

References

Beisser, A. (1970). *The Paradoxical Theory of Change*. Palo Alto, CA: Science and Behaviour Books.

Bennett, H. and Grof, S. (1993). *The Holotropic Mind: The Three Levels of Human Consciousness and How They Shape Our Lives*. New York: HarperCollins.

Buber, M. (1970). *I and Thou* (W. A. Kaufmann, Trans.). New York: Scribner. (Original work published 1923).

Fuggle, P., Dunsmuir, S. and Curry, V. (2013). *CBT with Children, Young People & Families*. London: SAGE.

Howe, D. (2005). *Child Abuse and Neglect*. Basingstoke: Palgrave Macmillan.

Jacobs, L. (2017). Hopes, fears, and enduring relational themes. *The British Gestalt Journal. V* 26(1), pp. 16–20.

Kegan, R. (2003). *In Over Our Heads*. Cambridge, MA: Harvard University Press.

Leopold, D. and Rhodes, G. (2010). A comparative view of face perception. *Journal of Comparative Psychology*, 124(3), pp. 233–251.

Levinas, E. and Nemo, P. (2011). *Ethics and Infinity*. Pittsburgh: Duquesne University Press.

McWilliams, N. (2011). *Psychoanalytic Diagnosis*. New York: Guilford Press.

Mortola, P. (2015). *Bam! Boys Advocacy and Mentoring*. New York: Routledge.

Orange, D. (2011). *The Suffering Stranger*. New York: Routledge/Taylor & Francis Group.

Riley, S. (2010). *Contemporary Art Therapy with Adolescents*. London: Jessica Kingsley Publishers.

Siegel, D. (2013). *Brainstorm*. New York: Jeremy P. Tarcher/Penguin Books.

Van der Kolk, B. (2015). *The Body Keeps the Score*. New York: Penguin Books.

Wilson, J. and Lindy, J. (1994). *Countertransference in the Treatment of PTSD*. New York: Guilford Press.

Chapter 5

Separation and complex family configuration

Most parenting adults are aware that the experiences of separation and complex family configuration are likely to present challenges for the adolescent. Subsequently, many seek psychotherapeutic intervention for their children as they identify the need for additional support for their adolescent sons and daughters as they integrate the relational redesign of their lifespace.

More typically, however, the presenting issue may be understood as somewhat or wholly unrelated to family process; however, these lifespace dynamics are likely to be shaping the adolescent's present-day experience, regardless of the passage of time since the events themselves unfolded. Parental separation may have occurred much earlier in childhood or prior to the adolescent's birth; parents may not ever have been in a relationship; a biological parent's identity may not be known to the adolescent; the presence of new partners and step-siblings may have long since been established in the adolescent's lifespace. Commonly, neither parenting adults nor therapist may fully appreciate the potential legacy and influence of separation and complex family configuration for the young person, failing to understand the adolescent's creative adjustments and shame dynamics as potentially stemming directly from these family integrity issues, however unconnected they might appear (Kalter, 2006). The adolescent himself experiences no conscious connection between his current experience in the world and familial relatedness; these things don't bother him, and he doesn't even think about them. Consequently, it may seem curious to everyone that traces of dissonance begin to manifest through adolescence. However, each of us knows adolescents who, as children, experienced hardship and seemed to adjust well, only to 'go off the rails' during adolescence. The adolescent may not necessarily be troubled by separation and parental relationship dynamics; however in adolescence, the young person is developmentally propelled to perceive his lifespace experience through a new, more sophisticated phenomenological lens (McConville, 1995). Unresolved childhood dilemmas are inclined to re-emerge as the developmental impulse of adolescence takes hold. And so, bearing in mind the young person's growing capacity to appreciate context, his developmental thrust to make meaning of his lifespace experience and a more vivid and vigorously configured feeling world, the emergence of a more visceral response begins to make sense.

Parenting space integrity

From countless conversations over the years with adolescents who have experienced parental separation and have found themselves growing up within a complex family configuration, I have concluded that these youngsters, in general, have a remarkable capacity to adapt to evolving and potentially challenging family situations *provided key parenting adults remain receptive and attuned.* Their angst has more to do with being overlooked than with the remodelling of family life. Adolescence provokes a response to the experience of non-receptivity and hostility within parenting spaces, especially where separation and family reconfiguration feature.

Separation dynamics differ somewhat to the experience of complex family configuration, with both creating its own set of challenges for the young person; however, children frequently experience both lifespace reorganisations simultaneously. For example, one parent may leave the parental relationship and family home having met someone else, and immediately the world of family relatedness is complexified, even more so if the parent's new partner also has children from a previous relationship. The challenge of adjusting to the perplexity of so many threads of experience may overwhelm even the most robust child who cannot possibly integrate all that is changing within his lifespace, particularly if parental hostility and struggle emerge in response to these dynamics. An adolescent whose parents separated in these circumstances when he was 5 years old is likely to shrug his shoulders when I express my curiosity about his experience of family. Typically, as we unpack and explore his childhood phenomenology, he uncovers shame, insecurity and confusion which have been suppressed. I have come to appreciate that his familiarity with the situation does not equate to his acceptance and full integration of it; so when I hear the words, "I don't really care", I may translate this as, "I care very much and I'm hurting a great deal".

Separation

It is not possible for parenting adults to separate from one another without some experience of separation being felt within the parent-child relational field (Pryor and Rodgers, 2002). Physical relocation is common, which often equates to less availability within the parenting space. Unless the dislocating parent is reassuringly attuned and receptive, the child typically feels that this parent is separating from *him* also, which, in many cases (Kalter, 2006), is all too true. This personalising of the separation process creates a threat to the child's sense of security, which, if coupled with parental hostility, creates a precarious lifespace scenario. When children are troubled, most seek out parenting adults for comfort and support. During the separation process, ironically, it is parents who are creating the difficulty and who are usually in a state of stress themselves, potentially becoming non-receptive or hostile as the separation process unfolds. This may add an additional layer of confusion and isolation for the struggling child.

Separation situations are not always painful and range from benign to greatly disturbing for the young person. Some bring more relief than vexation, particularly if the parent who leaves is characteristically non-receptive or hostile; the hurt is more to do with the quality of parent-child relationship than with the actual separation process. For example, Erin, aged 5, inhabited a non-receptive parenting space with her father, who was expressly disinterested and an immature young man by all accounts. Similarly, Anna, aged 6, had witnessed and experienced her abusive and terrifying father's hostility since her wombspace and felt safer with him gone. Neither expressed remorse nor a wish to have much contact with their father throughout their childhood.

However, both adolescents held deep yearnings for parenting space integrity and felt the absence of a receptive paternal parenting space in their lives: I don't miss having *that* father though I miss having *a* father. The shame of living within a non-receptive or hostile parent is felt more poignantly as adolescence gets underway and it is likely that paternal parenting space shame was shaping their creative adjustments to some extent. During the teenage years, Erin presented with a growing dependency on alcohol and cannabis; Anna was a high-achieving anorexic. In addition to specifically appropriate interventions related to their presenting symptom issues, exploration and reframing of parenting spaces facilitated considerable healing.

Some children find themselves in living situations where they are informed that parents are going to separate in time – maybe at the end of the academic year, when a house is sold, or when financial conditions make it possible. Living with this sense of *imminent separation* is unsettling for adolescents who may witness parents relating more harmoniously as they experience the relief of having decided to separate. Parents may negotiate family life with minimal or no communication, and one parent, for example, may move out of the parental bedroom and begin to share a child's bed or sleep elsewhere. In other instances, parents may have arrived at a mutual or forced acceptance that their relationship is over and one or both may quietly be exploring other relationships. The adolescent typically finds it difficult to share a home with parents who live distinctly separate lives. The experience of living together in this quasi-separation situation creates a dual reality which is confusing for children; family integrity is greatly compromised as the adolescent lives with the knowledge of what will inevitably happen. The experience of living with imminent separation also occurs when a parental affair is unearthed, where the adolescent must tolerate a family life infused with betrayal and uncertainty which may or may not herald the end of his parents' relationship. This may also happen when parents constantly argue and fight, where it is clear to their children that they are unhappy in the relationship, particularly when threats of separation are overtly expressed. Living with imminent separation experience is akin to driving a car, knowing that one will crash, though not being sure at exactly which point along the road this will happen or what damage will be caused. I cannot imagine how unnerving that would be.

Other adolescents experience separation more as a gift to the family than a crisis, provided the separation is on their terms, with minimal disruption. I am reminded of a 13-year-old client who presented with anxiety and whose parents had separated two years previously. Louise described how they would endlessly quarrel and how she resented her father. When he moved into another house nearby, family life was positively transformed. The parents were instantly happier; home was more peaceful; her relationship with both parents improved considerably and the parents quickly developed an amicable relationship. Separation created considerable relief and lifespace enhancement for everyone, yet Louise feared that her parents would divorce or meet new people, "*because it would become real then*". She had come to terms with the initial stage of separation and dreaded further disconnection and loss within her family experience. Her anxiety emerged when she discovered that her father was dating. For Louise, her father moving out was not so much experienced as parental separation than family lifespace expansion which resulted in greater family cohesion. She was distraught that family integrity had now been challenged.

Complex family configurations

Evolving interpersonal relations in the form of new family configuration is routinely an extension of separation for the adolescent, who now finds himself inhabiting additional parenting spaces, irrespective of how he feels about new partners. The adolescent himself may be receptive, non-receptive or hostile within these new relational spaces, which often sparks controversy with parenting adults (Papernow, 2013). Whilst parents are wholly entitled to move on and seek fulfilment in their lives, parental dating, if lacking receptivity and attunement to the adolescent's sensibilities, brings with it added insult. The child may watch his father or mother become infatuated with someone, expressing excitement, obsessively checking messages and spending time with the new partner, which the young person may translate as a statement of parental disinterest in *him*. Children often feel overlooked when new partners are introduced. The adolescent may also have adopted the role of surrogate partner with a parent who depended somewhat on his support. A new adult relationship now renders his parenting space role redundant; he is displaced and feels lost. His reaction is more to do with his loss of relational status than accepting the parent's new partner. In fact, many report liking new partners despite their best efforts at contempt. Parents may also move in and out of several relationships throughout their son or daughter's childhood, creating ongoing relational interruption.

New adult connections create the likelihood that other children will enter the evolving family landscape, either as existing children of parents' partners or new births within these relationships. This may generate vulnerability for the adolescent whose status and position may be transformed and whose relationship with parents risks becoming more remote (Papernow, 2009). This insecurity may manifest in non-receptivity or hostility towards others within the newly configured sibling group.

Engaging parents

When parental separation and complex family configuration are features of the adolescent's lifespace context, contact assessment includes appraisal of the impact of these changes in family structure. The therapist explores the three principal dimensions of experience related to these issues:

1   Parental capacity to sufficiently contain both inappropriate behaviour and information from their children. All too often the adolescent becomes a receptacle for interparental hostility which, according to their phenomenological description, is decidedly the most distressing aspect of these situations.

2   The extent to which the adolescent has adopted a supporting role within the parenting space. Familiar postures for the adolescent in these situations include parental go-between, confidante, advisor, counsellor, pseudo-parent and home-maker. As the struggling parent looks to their child for support, the cost of this premature immersion in adult-world dynamics is a heightened sense of responsibility and conflicted loyalties which renders the young person hyper-attuned within parenting spaces, to the detriment of his own lifespace expansion.

3   The depth of parental attunement to the adolescent's needs, feelings and developmental location throughout the separation and reconfiguration process. Some parenting adults are prone to demonstrating a spectacular lack of sensitivity to the adolescent's experience as they become preoccupied with other people, situations and powerful emotions.

Fortunately, many separated couples negotiate parenting and co-parenting dynamics gracefully, with containment and great attunement. The willingness of both parents to attend contact assessment meetings together is a major statement of hope that they hold, or at least are open to developing some capacity to contain interparental conflict and to negotiate adult-world dynamics appropriately, to be as supportive as possible to the adolescent. It is always concerning when one parent completely refuses to engage when the other is present; however, safety issues may necessitate this, as in the case of an abusive ex-partner. It also may be ill-advised for the therapist to engage the hostile parent in these situations.

If it emerges during the initial assessment meeting that one of the parenting adults present is a step-parent and not the adolescent's biological parent, it is wise to sensitively ask this person to leave the meeting, with a possibility of re-engaging at a later time. There is less risk in offending a parenting adult than the therapeutic space becoming compromised from the outset due to the adolescent being forced to endure a contact assessment meeting in which the step-parent's participation is strongly resented, particularly when the therapist engages this step-parent by inviting him to make statements about the adolescent's experience and behaviour. The therapist's reluctance to automatically assume amicable relational dynamics between the pair indicates to the adolescent that she is mindful of and interested in his phenomenology. He is always grateful for this considerate intervention, irrespective of his feelings towards parental partners.

During contact assessment, as the issue of separation is named, it is important that dialogic exploration is focused through the adolescent's lens. Parents, at this point, may feel the threat of exposure and so it is advisable to remind them that the therapist is not about to ambush the assessment and replace it with an impromptu couples therapy session, nor is it her wish to procure a detailed description of the reasons for relationship breakdown as this is none of her business (except as it relates directly to the adolescent's experience). The therapist assures parents that her interest in their relational dynamics extends only to how this might be affecting their child. Even if these lifespace changes occurred years ago, it is likely that a young child's meaning-making and experience of parental separation continues to shape his creative adjustments in adolescence, and so it is important to attend to the parents' description of the relational dynamics which have shaped his lifespace. Useful points to discuss include each parent's memory of how their child experienced the separation and family reconfiguration process and the evolution of parenting space relatedness since time in the wombspace.

It is regularly the case that parenting strategy work will be a necessary intervention to support containment of animosity and adult-world dynamics; and so, as the dialogue unfolds, the therapist evaluates the appropriateness and usefulness of having both parents present during subsequent sessions, assessing how capable they are of being reasonable with one another. Future meeting configurations may include all three together, the adolescent alone or with one parent and parents either individually or together. Therapeutic intervention may involve challenging parents who rely on their children for practical and psychological support to seek this support elsewhere within the adult world. The therapist's intention is to create deeper receptivity and attunement within parenting spaces as the impact of tolerating interparental hostility and holding inappropriate family responsibility on the adolescent becomes apparent. She does this by appealing to the parents' love, care and concern for their child, as she extends their awareness of how detrimental and potentially traumatising their insensitivity has been. These aspects of the work can prove challenging as many separated parents characteristically descend into dualistic thinking about one another and about situations which involve them both, overlooking their children as they are blind-sided by shame. Unfortunately, it is not always possible to reach beneath a parent's rigidity and lack of insight. Ongoing involvement of one or both adults may be a redundant exercise in this case, as themes of loyalty and collusion feature in a redundantly recycling manner where parental animosity is a fixed gestalt, potentially compromising the therapeutic space for the adolescent. It is also wise to remain cautious with regards to hidden parental agendas of recruiting the therapist as an ally against the opposition or drafting her into legal battles. The work, in these situations, is to minimise contact with parenting adults and to reframe for the adolescent a harsh and uncompromising parenting space more as a reflection of parental rigidity than as a statement of care about the child, in the hope of dislodging some of the internalised shame which may have accumulated over the years.

Addressing the adolescent's phenomenology

Whether or not the adolescent appreciates that these lifespace dynamics may still have influence in his life, no matter how removed and irrelevant they seem from his present-day experience, it is important to explore his phenomenology with regards to family relatedness. This exploration is always both revealing and meaningful as the young person begins to appreciate the context of his experience. Separation and new family configuration are relationally complex, often creating a sense of confusion within the lifespace. Over a relatively short time period, dramatic changes may have been experienced within the family space in general and within parenting spaces in particular. There are many features which present potential challenge, including adjusting to a radically transformed lifespace, witnessing parental struggle and interparental hostility, and negotiating contact boundaries with parents and other existing or new family members. Lack of acknowledgement of any of these aspects of experience creates an additional layer of shame as the child's experience is discounted; he learns to 'just get on with it'. Frequently the adolescent has endured many years of confusion, conflict and parental dislocation without much or any validation of his phenomenology. In fact, in most instances, it is within the therapeutic space that the adolescent first gives voice to his experience, either because of prior unwillingness on his part or lack of attunement within the adult world, or both. Therapeutic work creates space to integrate and make meaning of these lifespace transitions, whether long-established or contemporaneous.

During one-to-one work the therapist expresses curiosity and confusion as the presence of complexity within family dynamics becomes apparent. Bearing in mind that the adolescent responds to visual representations of his lifespace as a support to his meaning-making process, the therapist suggests that seeing the adolescent's family configuration depicted in the sandspace might create some clarity *for her* in their dialogue. This three-dimensional sculpting of family process supports the adolescent to articulate the integration of this web of family relatedness within his overall lifespace experience. Through his portrayal and description of the evolution of each person's presence within his lifespace, the impact of all this relational reconfiguration becomes increasingly apparent to him. Weaved through this more context-appreciative lifespace narrative are the accounts of his experience of parenting spaces prior to, during and since separation; his understanding of the reasons for separation; his experience of parental dating and adapting to a more populated family space; and his experience of negotiating the duality of being co-parented in disparate fashions, living between two houses and having two sibling sets. The therapist's interest in and validation of his phenomenology supports the adolescent to make greater meaning of his lifespace experience as creative adjustments are reframed through the lens of yearnings for physiological, psychological and interpersonal integrity.

The shame of being overlooked

Fifteen-year-old Emer was impulsively configured: difficult to control and prone to aggressive outbursts at home, drinking with her friends and living life on her terms. Her disinterest in school work and antagonistic attitude towards teaching staff and other students had created a situation where she was facing expulsion. Her parents and school principal were perturbed that Emer was not in the least bit concerned about her situation or her future, and when referral to me was suggested, the adolescent reluctantly attended the contact assessment meeting.

I quickly assessed that both parents lacked much attunement to Emer's experience, understanding her belligerent attitude as 'teenage hormones' and making statements such as, "Emer's problem is that she has no manners and cares about nobody but herself". From the parental perspective, it certainly looked this way. However, I guessed that the adolescent's attitude and behaviour was motivated by threat to her integrity. My intention was to support parental awareness of this. The parents' hopeful anticipation and Emer's dread-filled pre-empting of a dialogue focused on her creative adjustments were promptly waylaid as I shaped our conversation towards underlying yearnings for integrity. As parental separation was named, I suggested that it was important for us to take some time to explore this aspect of experience, assuring the family that shameful exposure was not my agenda. I invited Emer to listen as I supported her parents to reflect on their separation in terms of parenting space receptivity.

My initial wondering was related to the passage of time since they had all sat together in a room. Oftentimes this is revealing in itself as years may have passed, or perhaps today is the first time that the adolescent has ever had this experience in conscious living memory. Tensions are diminished through acknowledgement that this meeting configuration in itself is unfamiliar and potentially uncomfortable, as this revelation often creates an important and rare moment of joining for all three present. In Emer's case, it had been two years since she sat with both parents together. Emer's mother declared that she discovered her husband's affair and they separated immediately. He moved in with his new partner, leaving his wife, Emer and her 10-year-old brother in the family home. It is important that the therapist models containment, intervening with robust composure during decidedly tense moments. She must ensure the contact assessment meeting does not morph into a parental battle ground. Otherwise she will lose the adolescent for sure. And so I stepped in, inviting them to reflect on how this situation might have been experienced by Emer. They seemed to think that she was 'fine' about it all as she did not say anything to the contrary, though in hindsight it might have been difficult for her. It was clear that both lacked much appreciation of Emer's distress or that current creative adjustments may have been an indirect expression of this. Adversarial parents may initially remain more rigidly configured than more mutually allied parents, and so Emer's mother remained fixed on her daughter's presenting issues, whilst her father objected to revisiting this old ground and was expressly dismissive of any connection between events two years ago and his daughter's exasperating attitude and behaviour. Disengaging from power struggles by offering an observation that, whatever the cause, their daughter seemed very unhappy and was not taking herself seriously in the world, adding that it may be worth looking beneath her behaviour to her experience in the world – specifically to her experience within parenting spaces as these are significant relational spaces – supported the shift from confrontation with the therapist to deepened receptivity for the adolescent. By offering this rationale, the therapist, more often than not, achieves the desired outcome: metaphorically speaking, the parents are supported to redirect their gaze away from each other and the therapist, and towards their daughter. And so, as the adults began to trust that they were being engaged as parents, rather than ex-partners, exploration of parenting spaces prior to, during and since separation softened the ground somewhat. Whilst this was a hopeful development, ongoing parental involvement and parenting strategy work to create more appropriate containment and attunement would also be necessary, for sure.

As the dialogue became more moderated, I invited Emer to respond to what she was hearing. She described feeling constantly criticised by her mother and less aggravated by her father, though she did not see him that much. In a few words, the adolescent had communicated a great deal of her experience and I tentatively translated her statements. I offered a hunch that she had arrived at the reasonable conclusion that her mother no longer loved her and that her father cared more about his new partner than he did about her – and that she desperately missed her parents. She nodded her head and began to sob; her parents were also visibly moved. She had said enough for now, and so I invited her parents to respond to my expansion of her statements, supporting their articulation of the impact of seeing their daughter's distress. Bearing direct witness to a child's expression of her experience has more influence on a parent's capacity to attune than anything a therapist might say; and for many warring parents, this moment is the first experience of genuine co-parenting for some considerable time. The voicing of Emer's experience also had the desired effect of diverting the parents' attention away from a focus on finding solutions to manage her behaviour towards reflection on their relationships with their daughter.

During one-to-one work with Emer, we reflected on the initial meeting and began to explore her phenomenology in more depth. She acknowledged that her creative adjustments were to do with how unhappy she felt, concluding that, as parents were prone to do, hers had confused the expression of pain with adolescent pugnacity. As the adolescent had experienced the benefit and healing of the contact assessment, there was receptivity and fluency in our contact; Emer's initial resistance had dissipated as her faith that shame would have no part in our relating had grown.

As Emer described her lifespace experience, I invited her to depict the main features of this in the sandspace (Figure 5.1). She selected a number of figures and arranged them in a line across the centre of the sandbox, keen to articulate the significance of each. Below is a description of Emer's experience which was unearthed as we dialogued about each figure in succession, beginning left to right.

Figure 5.1 Emer's lifespace representation

The adolescent described her father's girlfriend as a dragon, resenting her because the relationship began as an affair whilst Emer's parents were still married. She saw the dragon as a 'homewrecker' and as singularly responsible for her family breakdown. Emer had taken offence that this woman was always with her father and disliked this woman's two children, whom she referred to as *brats*.

Emer's parents were depicted as children, because they acted like children. She remembered how she discovered the separation. She was sitting alone at the kitchen table doing homework one winter's evening when her father came into the house and sat down opposite her. He told her that he had met someone else and was leaving her mother, adding that he would see her each weekend. The conversation was brief, one-sided and framed in terms of the parental relationship, with no space given to Emer's experience. After a very short time he stood up, unwittingly turned off the light and left the house. He was gone and Emer remained alone in the dark kitchen, bewildered and tearful. As Emer's replayed those initial moments of discovery she said, "*It's like World War One in the trenches. A bomb has just gone off and everyone is dead. I think I saw it coming but I didn't want to believe it*". She had never attempted homework since that night as it reminded her of the conversation with her dad.

It had been agreed that each parent would tell one child and very soon afterwards, her mother and younger brother came home. Both were distraught. And whilst she encouraged the children's relationship with their father and endeavoured to conceal her contempt for her ex-husband and his new partner, Emer's mother's bitterness and contempt remained. The adolescent reflected on how her mother had changed since the separation, describing a stressed and shamed woman whose contact style has become non-receptive. She reflected on the experience of feeling disliked and unloved by her mother and how she was beginning to rethink that assumption following the contact assessment and her mother's softening since the meeting.

Next she spoke about her younger brother who had found the separation process very difficult and often cried for his father. Emer resented how cherished and spoiled he was by both parents; how he told tales and how they believed everything he said; how she got blamed for everything; how he looked for attention from both parents; how he was always there when she was with her father; and how generally annoying it was to have a younger brother. A picture began to emerge that Emer's father was somewhat inaccessible to her and I became curious as to how much time she spent alone with her father. It transpired that Emer could not remember ever being alone with her father in the two years since her parents had separated. Their meeting ground was always his new home which he shared with his partner and her two young children, and contact always involved both Emer and her brother. We explored her feelings around this and she became tearful as changes in the paternal parenting space were acknowledged and validated. She missed her father terribly.

The fifth figure she situated in the sand represented her mother's brother, who had moved into the family home one week after her parents separated. He needed somewhere to live, and financially it was a sensible move for her mother. However, when her uncle came to live with Emer's family, he adopted a parenting role, setting household chores and curfews; and reprimanding her for speaking rudely to her mother, fighting with her brother and not doing her homework. She continued to find this additional disruption to family life very difficult to accept and disliked her uncle immensely.

Emer placed Jane next, with whom she had been best friends since nursery school. They shared a love of horses, spending Saturdays together at the local riding school and sharing a dream of opening their own equestrian centre one day. They both had also experienced parental separation and confided in one another about their situations. Emer and Jane lived near a forest and had a favourite tree into which they had carved their names. One evening, the previous year, Jane was found hanging from the tree. Emer's sorrow was palpable as she voiced her experience of losing a great friend through such tragedy. It emerged that she had received little support since Jane's death and had not spoken before today about the experience. I offered a hunch that Jane's death had brought with it even more isolation regarding her family situation, as Emer had nobody to talk to since then.

The desk represented school, which she detested and which had become a hostile landscape for her. Emer described feeling agitated as she walked through the school gates each morning, noticing herself become clenched and aggressive. Apart from one or two teachers and a small group of friends, she experienced the school community as insufferable and found it impossible not to be reactive to these 'idiots'. School was boring, academic work was pointless and the worst part was how she would inevitably get the blame for *everything*, when clearly she was the innocent party. I empathised with her predicament of having to endure so much injustice, knowing that we would revisit this scenario when she felt more supported and had arrived at a more balanced lifespace perspective, when she would then be open to taking greater ownership of her experience.

Emer chose a foal to represent herself, principally because she loved these creatures. As we unpacked the analogy of herself and the foal, she identified feeling young, delicate and vulnerable. I noted that the foal was not standing, to which she responded that it was because her feet still felt unsteady under her. Emer's statement created space for us to explore a little of her sense of lifespace insecurity. We began to appreciate that she had been devastated by the accumulation of experience over these past two years, and I told her that I imagined the little foal was nursing a broken heart, which prompted both tears and compassionate appreciation for herself.

The other horses symbolised her affinity with these animals, how they understood her better than anyone, and the sanctuary which was afforded her when she was with them. I listened with interest as she came to life telling me her hopes for the future to become a horse trainer, therapeutic riding instructor or mounted police officer. I was also mindful that we had just happened upon a directional aspect of Emer's experience which would be important to amplify during subsequent sessions, pitching her combative posture in the world as a threat to the realisation of her dreams. Adolescents develop more impressively when they engage in power struggles between their impulsivity and directionality rather than staging them interpersonally, and this worked a treat in Emer's case.

Incorporation of sandspace in our initial one-to-one encounter revealed a depth of experience which created relief and offered Emer a level of clarity about her lifespace phenomenology which had been previously obscured. Lifespace appraisal, involving acknowledgement and validation of her experience, was a crucial step towards a more directional proclivity. Appreciating the adolescent's creative adjustments, in this case Emer's obstreperous behaviour, as a statement of yearning for integrity, enables the therapist to reach the adolescent at the heart of her experience and heal shame. Awareness of the adolescent's phenomenology also supports intervention with parenting adults as the therapist works to promote containment and attunement in cases where separation and complex family configuration are aspects of the adolescent's lifespace experience.

References

Kalter, N. (2006). *Growing Up with Divorce*. New York: Free Press.

McConville, M. (1995). *Adolescence: Psychotherapy and the Emergent Self*. San Francisco: Jossey-Bass Inc.

Papernow, P. (2009). *Becoming a Stepfamily: Patterns of Development in Remarried Families*. New York: Routledge.

Papernow, P. (2013). *Surviving and Thriving in Stepfamily Relationships*. New York: Routledge.

Pryor, J. and Rodgers, B. (2002). *Children in Changing Families*. Malden, MA: Blackwell Publishers.

Chapter 6

Complex parenting spaces
Adoption, fostering and loss

Unique challenges are presented for the adolescent who experiences displacement, estrangement or death within biological parenting spaces and who, as a result, inhabits additional temporary or permanent parenting spaces, or lives without any replacement parent figure in his life. In instances where biological parents' care for the child is either forcibly or voluntarily withdrawn, it is generally necessary to identify other more appropriate parenting spaces within which the young person may be placed. The child, no matter how young, is impacted by this cycle of rupture and connection, which may occur once or episodically throughout his childhood (Bowlby, 1988). As adolescence gets underway, meaning-making and integration of his complex parenting space experience becomes developmentally compelling; however, without sufficient support his creative adjustments configure to establish more elaborate defence from awareness and discomfort associated with this lifespace complexity.

Adoption

Multiple levels of trauma are possible in the early life experience of the adopted child, including prenatal and birth trauma, relational rupture with biological parents, and temporary care situations prior to adoption, in addition to the overwhelm of entering a new family landscape. The legacy of enduring such turbulent lifespace conditions, within which the adolescent may have been exposed to substantial integrity threat, is likely to be immense. An anticipated consequence of this traumatic imprinting is impaired regulation of physiological, psychological and interpersonal process, resulting in disorganised contact boundaries which may be ongoing throughout the lifespan. Creative adjustments typically include impulsive configuration or rigid compliance and invisibility which are a statement of historical and ongoing interpersonal insecurity. Anxiety is also typically present.

The inclination in psychiatry towards a schismatic view of the child's presentation and contact style being understood as observable symptoms of specific disorders and somehow disconnected to his lifespace context, has resulted in adopted adolescents, widely and oftentimes erroneously, receiving diagnoses which reflect their traumatically disorganised contact boundaries without due attention or support being afforded to the impact of pervasive parenting space interruption on the child's development (Van der Kolk, 2015). Diagnostic labels relating to attentional and hyperactive pathologies, mental health issues, dyspraxic physiology, autistic tendencies and fetal alcohol syndrome are standard (American Psychiatric Association, 2013); comorbidity is common, and medication is frequently prescribed (Ingersoll, 1997).

It has been my experience working with adopted children and adolescents that the therapeutic space is infused with yearning for recognition and validation. However, I repeatedly meet adopted adolescents who have had previous experiences of therapy throughout childhood and adolescence and who have neither had their adoption acknowledged by the therapist nor been invited to explore this aspect of their lifespace experience. The traumatised child is rendered dumb, and due to the level of physiological, psychological and interpersonal dysregulation present within the traumatised adolescent's lifespace, it is likely that he will not have language for his experience. His bewilderment and isolation risk becoming more deeply entrenched and his voice more muted if the therapist misses her cues to liberate him from the frozenness of the traumatic imprint. Appreciating the phenomenology of adoption and its associated creative adjustments supports the therapist to cultivate a contextually sensitive therapeutic space.

Curiosity

The adolescent may be referred for therapy at his own request, identifying the need for support as he seeks greater clarity with regards to his lifespace narrative. More typically, direct or overt developmental issues are highlighted as problematic features of family life, whereby the adolescent's impulsive or inhibitive configuration and self-defeating behaviour creates cause for concern. When adoption is named as a feature of the adolescent's lifespace, the therapist is primarily interested in the degree of openness or defensiveness present within the system regarding the experience of adoption. The adolescent may be reluctant to probe the circumstances and relational dynamics surrounding his adoption as this may feel potentially overwhelming for him, possibly due to developmental limitations in his capacity for reflection and insight. However, in many instances, his reticence has more to do with fear of offending adoptive parents than honouring his own personal yearnings for integrity. In these situations, parents may explicitly or implicitly inhibit the adolescent's curiosity, which is viewed as a threat to family integrity. Ambivalence is often present, and whilst many parents appreciate the adolescent's wish to discover more about his identity, at the same time, they may feel deeply apprehensive that reconnection with a birth family may translate into alienation within their own. They also fear that their child may be pained by what and whom he discovers. Some adoptive parenting spaces are so rigidly configured that the wish to explore adoption or seek out birth parents is experienced as an insult in which they personalise his curiosity as a shameful statement about his feelings towards them as parents.

Eliminating threat from and establishing support for his curiosity is paramount, whether or not the adolescent chooses at this point to actively explore the experience of his adoption. Support for curiosity is validating for the adolescent and minimises the shame potential inherent in the exploration of previously unexamined aspects of his lifespace narrative; otherwise his searching may be steeped in the guilt of trespassing into forbidden territory (Verrier, 2009). If, during the contact assessment, the therapist senses that her invitation to dialogue feels like an infringement of family boundaries, she can be confident that discouragement of curiosity is a field condition. When the adolescent's desire to search appears inhibited, the therapist intervenes to soften the ground within a rigidly configured family field to ensure optimal parenting space receptivity as the adolescent explores both the meaning of his adoption and possibly also actively seeks out information and birth family members. Creating field conditions which foster the adolescent's curiosity empowers him to make meaning of the experience as he attempts to integrate the phenomenology of being adopted into his overall lifespace identity – whether he chooses to pursue this endeavour now, at some point in his future, or not ever.

Disappointment

As his capacity for meaning-making develops, there is, throughout adolescence, an expansion of awareness that his adoptive status may be the nexus from which much of his lifespace experience stems. The adolescent's relationship to the temporality of his adoption, not simply as an event which happened in early childhood, but as a core and ubiquitous lifespace dynamic, can be unsettling for the young person who frequently experiences himself as dislocated and isolated within his family space and wider lifespace situation. He often describes his phenomenological experience as living in a *dual reality*, identifying, on one hand, with his established status as an adoptive family member, whilst the obscurity and bewilderment of his early life experience remains strangely removed from, yet is forever shaping his lifespace experience.

Romantic or painful experiences and fantasies are shared with the therapist, which have to do with a sense of belonging and connection within both family spaces. Threads of anguish and existential isolation may emerge as he considers why and how his birth parents could have abandoned him, and as he contemplates what life might have been like had he remained with his birth parents, or been born as the biological child of his adoptive parents. The shame of this hidden reality is compounded if the adoptive family field cannot tolerate the duality of his experience, implicitly understanding that he must suppress that which is unacceptable. This double bind must be attended to for integrity to be restored.

A major theme which infuses the adopted adolescent's lifespace is *disappointment*. As he describes his experience, it is often apparent that he holds and may also perceive a strong sense of disappointment around his existence within the family field. If this is the case, he inevitably experiences relief in the unpacking of this shame. The adolescent may feel chagrined at having been placed for adoption or at being a disappointment to adoptive parents that he is not their own offspring, or because he considers that parenting him has been burdensome. I frequently hear the adopted adolescent describe himself as the fall-back option, or 'Plan B', viewing his presence in the family as mitigator of parental pain at not being able to conceive their own child.

In many instances, the adolescent engages in therapy without prior knowledge about his parents' decision to adopt and he typically finds the dialogue fascinating, if somewhat intense at times. Adoptive parents demonstrate varying degrees of appreciation of the impact of early life trauma on their child, as they themselves adapt to the demands of complex parenting – a role which has commonly emerged from the parents' own traumatic experience of loss as a result of fertility issues. With regard to the parenting of their child, often the adolescent's perception regarding his adoptive parents is accurate as parenting adults feel disheartened and disconnected. Some describe the overwhelm of parenting such a complexly configured adolescent and express regret over the discrepancy between their expectations and the reality of raising an adopted child. This is a statement of parental overwhelm rather than a statement about his existence and needs to be explicitly and sensitively reframed as such for the adolescent. More commonly, however, the experience of parental disappointment is vastly outweighed by devoted love for their child whom they could not love any more if he was their biological offspring and who see his presence as an immeasurable gift in their lives. Here, the insecure adolescent's propensity towards viewing his lifespace through a pessimistic lens is challenged as the therapist supports parents to convey to their child that love and disappointment are not mutually exclusive: the adoption was borne out of loss *and* they love their son *and* they find the challenge of adoptive parenting a difficult one at times *and* they would not change him for the world. Disappointment does not spell rejection. In situations where conception issues played no part, it is always encouraging for him to discover that the parents' decision emanated exclusively from an empowered yearning to adopt a child, as opposed to emerging from loss and disappointment on their part.

It is important to create space for the acknowledgement of disappointment for everyone as this dislodges internalised shame and pressure and reaches a new depth of relational clarity and connection. This reparative intervention extends beyond parenting spaces, which is important, as commonly, this expectation to disappoint is also pervasive within the adolescent's wider intersubjective experience as he struggles with acceptability. Growing acceptance of the dual nature of his lifespace reality, with the co-existence of paradoxical or divergent experience pertaining to both his personal identity and family space, assists the adolescent's integration process as he reaches a consciously held existential posture of *'I belong and I don't belong'* with regard to both families.

Paula

In the summer after first year of university, 19-year-old Paula made the decision to engage in therapy as she felt overwhelmed by certain lifespace dynamics. She had been in therapy previously as a child and younger teenager, though her adoption had never been discussed. Paula was prone to anxiety, and her lack of faith in herself had become more exposed since stepping out of the familiarity of her childhood environment. She was also concerned at her excessive dependency on a college boyfriend.

I met initially with Paula and her parents, both of whom were largely receptive to their daughter and to her relationship with her adoptive status. At 16, on Mother's Day, Paula expressed a yearning to discover more about the circumstances surrounding her adoption and was actively supported by her parents to do so. Paula's exploration involved frank dialogue with her adoptive parents, accessing social work records and meeting members of her birth family. She discovered that she was removed from her biological mother at birth as the result of multi-agency concern regarding this young woman's capacity to care for her child due to her continued involvement in a violent relationship with the child's father, a diagnosis of borderline personality disorder and alcohol dependency. Paula was placed in foster care until her adoption at fourteen months old. Devastated at the realisation that they were unable to conceive, her parents chose to adopt, and Paula was the nominated child. They also adopted a second child, Peter, who was now 15 years old.

The adolescent's birth mother was open to reconnecting; her biological father had died over a decade ago from alcohol-related issues. Paula visited her mother every couple of months and they communicated relatively often by text message until her mother's death by suicide just as Paula was beginning college. Her search also revealed that she had three older siblings, one of whom had been killed some years previously in a road traffic accident. All of her biological siblings had been placed in foster care, and she now had somewhat unsatisfactory, sporadic contact with the two surviving siblings, with whom she experienced a confusing and paradoxical relationship of connection and alienation.

Paula and her parents recounted the intensity of childhood separation anxiety and fear of abandonment which characterised both parenting spaces. As a child she could not bear to be separated from her parents, yet found it difficult to trust them. Her parents felt that she was driven by insecurity, constantly clinging and pushing, endlessly testing their love and receptivity, and fearing the inevitability of rejection. They expressed sadness that their love for her was not adequate to heal her early lifespace trauma. They described feeling pained and haunted by thoughts of what she might have experienced prior to being adopted, including the strong likelihood of wombspace violence in addition to the toxicity of maternal alcohol abuse. Paula was grateful for the deeper level of dialogue with her parents and for their support and acknowledgement. It helped to hear how steadfast their love for and parental commitment to her was, even if she had not always trusted it.

During one-to-one dialogue, Paula described her bewilderment growing up with the knowledge that she was adopted, not sure precisely what this meant, but understanding that somehow it was a secretive aspect to her identity. She spoke of a deeply held childhood conviction that her defective personality was responsible for the rejection by her birth mother and so she understood that there was something inherently wrong with her – a belief which still dominated her self-experience. Paula related her experience of feeling different and disconnected throughout her childhood. This isolation gave rise to fantasy about her birth family identity. At sixteen, she decided that she could not tolerate another Mother's Day without finding out about this birth mother and so her curiosity culminated in an urgent need to discover her origins in the world.

On the day of their reunion, Paula's yearning was replaced with detachment and ambivalence, which had long since become a familiar experience for her when pressured. When the meeting was over, she felt strangely disoriented yet more grounded than ever before within her lifespace, both repelled by and yearning for her birth mother, whom she referred to always as Jane. Within the therapeutic space, she articulated her experience of contact with Jane and processed complex feelings about the life and death of her deceased biological parents and older brother. The adolescent also spoke of her experience of how reconnecting with and discovering details of her birth family had impacted relationships within her adoptive family. I supported deeper acknowledgement and voicing of her experience by inviting her to make representations in the sandspace of her birth and adoptive family configurations, which she entitled *"Welcome To Headfuckville"* and which facilitated the articulation of a more visceral experience of inhabiting the dual reality of an adoptive lifespace. Paula's meaning-making of her identity within adoptive and birth family systems and within her wider lifespace experience was facilitated through support for her curiosity, acknowledgement of family-field trauma and disappointment, and active validation of her dual reality. The shame and isolation of her experience dissipated as she was met in her bewilderment, complex duality and loss. This resulted in relief and clarity for Paula and the promotion of more empowered, choiceful and directional contact boundaries within her world.

Ava

Fourteen-year-old Ava's adoptive parents brought her to therapy as she had disclosed to them that she was transgendered. As I supported the adolescent to explore her emerging gender identity, therapeutic dialogue included supporting the meaning-making and integration of all aspects of her lifespace experience. Ava had been adopted from Thailand at 18 months old, having spent the time prior to this living in an orphanage. Her parents had always been open and supportive about their daughter's adoptive status. However, Ava had no inclination to discuss this aspect of her identity. During initial one-to-one sessions the adolescent communicated her rigidity and lack of curiosity by shrugging off her adoptive context as significant in any way: "I'm adopted, so what?" Ava was disinterested in exploring and integrating the experience of her transracial adoptive identity and its influence within her expanding lifespace.

As trust deepened within the therapeutic space and Ava became interested in exploring more aspects of her lifespace, she introduced the issue of her adoption gradually and with curiosity. The adolescent described a pronounced experience of difference within her family and peer relationships because of her physical appearance. She recalled, as a child, yearning for people to know that she was just the same as them, hating her dark skin and wishing she looked like her parents. One very painful aspect of her childhood was the doubt and disbelief expressed by other children as they discovered that the woman whom she loved so dearly could possibly be her mother. Ava talked about being 'made to feel Asian' by people, whose contact with her emphasised her otherness: the adolescent referred to feeling as if she may as well have had the words 'I'm adopted' tattooed across her forehead. An increase in self-consciousness during adolescence created reluctance to be seen in public with her adoptive family, which was exacerbated by some expressing surprise when she spoke with an Irish accent, as people assumed she wasn't Irish. Ava continued to struggle with her appearance, and the experience of body dysmorphia was deeply tied to her yearnings to belong.

As the adolescent explored the racial composition of her family, Ava also began to talk about her adoption. She recalled how during a family trip to Thailand when she was 8 years old, she endured a sense of estrangement and bewilderment, petrified that her parents might leave her there. Her fantasy was that they had decided that they no longer wanted her and were delivering her back to the orphanage, choosing a new baby to bring home with them as her replacement. When they returned home, Ava refused ever to think about or discuss her adoption with her parents again. Tentatively, the adolescent began to speak of what she knew of her experience in Thailand prior to adoption: she had been living in an orphanage, having been found in a cardboard box, without record of a name or birth date.

Integrating all the dimensions of her lifespace experience is an ongoing experience for Ava, who has been attending psychotherapy for the past four years. In that time, she has begun what is likely to be a lifelong journey for her of processing and integrating many aspects of her experience including the experience of abandonment in infancy, tolerating not having access to the details regarding her birth family and earliest days in the world, life in an orphanage for over a year prior to being adopted. In addition, Ava has begun to make meaning of the experience of growing up as a transracial adoptee, talking about dimensions such as the expectation she feels to explain her adoption to the many people who enquire where she is from or who ask directly if she was adopted, as well as episodes of racism she has had to endure.

As Ava has grown to appreciate the significance of her adoption history and has begun to integrate her identity as an adopted adolescent into her overall lifespace experience, her voice has emerged and she has become more embodied. The emphasis on the transgendered aspects of her identity has receded and Ava has begun to articulate growing ambiguity with regard to being transgendered. Ava is developing a capacity to appreciate the complexity of her identity. The adolescent's curiosity has begun to emerge in respect of her Thai culture and identity and Ava has expressed some interest in revisiting the country of her birth. Involving Ava's parents in the therapeutic process has been important in supporting them to become more attuned to their daughter's phenomenological experience of negotiating a lifespace in which she experiences a dual and complex reality. The theme of *'I belong and I don't belong'* has resonated deeply with her.

Foster care

The necessity to place a child in foster care typically, though not always, suggests parenting spaces characterised by abuse and neglect (Howe, 2005). Removal from a family home by social workers and relocation within an unfamiliar environment amplifies and adds to the original trauma of being maltreated by parents. The short-term, non-permanent nature of many foster care situations often translates into multiple placements which may include both family and residential care settings (Newton, Litrownik and Landsverk, 2000), with many children remaining in the system until the emerging adulthood years and being separated from siblings in the process. The impact of this catastrophic lifespace instability is unimaginable.

Contact within foster parenting spaces ranges from receptive through to hostile, and transitioning from parenting space to parenting space becomes an anticipated aspect of the adolescent's experience, sometimes involving abrupt and dislocating changes in elements of his lifespace such as neighbourhoods, schools and friendships. The adolescent is also faced with having to repeatedly adapt to changes in his physical living space and family culture. Powerlessness, shame and exposure in these types of circumstance create despair and further magnify the fostered adolescent's sense of futility at ever being received with integrity, increasing the likelihood of his involvement in compromising behaviours and relationships. The adolescent's creative adjustments are frequently troublesome and laced with high risk, belying a vulnerability he has learned to artfully conceal to survive.

One commonly resented condition of the fostered adolescent's experience is a life scrutinised by professionals who, whilst their intention may be to care for the young person, are sometimes experienced by him as controlling, shaming and dismissive. I once worked with a fostered adolescent who, together with her best friend, sneaked off to a concert and hooked up with boys. As their teenage escapade was discovered, she raged at how her friend's parents grounded the girl for three weeks whilst a case conference was convened in respect of the fostered adolescent's behaviour, the outcome of which meant that even more professionals became involved – one of whom was appointed to undertake anger management work with her due to her outburst at the meeting. Regrettably, the level of practical, psychological and interpersonal support available to the many adolescents who grow up in foster care situations is wholly and disturbingly inadequate and as a consequence of his heavily compromised and highly dysregulated lifespace, the probability of mental health issues (McCann et al., 1996), addiction (Vaughn et al., 2007), homelessness (Baker, 2018) and prison (Berman and Dar, 2013) greatly intensifies for the young person (Guishard-Pine, Coleman-Oluwabusola and McCall, 2017), as if he has not suffered enough. Perpetuation of the foster care cycle also occurs in some situations where parents, who themselves were fostered and who struggle to give their children the appropriate care and receptivity they themselves were deprived of, are deemed ill-suited to remain in the role of parenting adult having become neglectful and abusive themselves (Howe, 2005).

Shane

After he had cooled off, following an increasingly common episode of thrashing his bedroom and being verbally abusive to a foster carer, Shane approached her and expressed his concern that he was becoming an angry person and feared turning out like his father. He asked for help. I met this 16-year-old several weeks later, having spoken briefly with his foster carer and social worker. The adolescent's father was serving a prison sentence for killing his wife, Shane's mother, during a domestic violence incident when Shane was 6 years old. He and his two younger siblings had initially been placed with family members. However, this aunt and uncle had two children of their own and felt increasingly pressured raising five children, three of whom had been extremely traumatised. After four years, it was decided that Shane and his siblings would be relocated; however, no suitable single placement was identified for the three children, so Shane was separated from his sisters. He experienced two short-term foster care situations until being placed with a couple at twelve years of age, who were the ninth and tenth parenting adults he had encountered within the space of six years, and with whom Shane continued to reside. In time, I involved these present foster carers; however, the starting point of our work was one-to-one contact with Shane, out of respectful appreciation of the multiplicity and fragmentation of parenting space experience which he had endured. Reparative relational work with this couple who fostered him, whilst necessary, was not a priority in our work at this point.

The co-creation of a therapeutic space, sensitively modulating to the adolescent's yearning for and fear of support is integral, otherwise sporadic engagement and abrupt endings are common features in the work with the fostered adolescent, mirroring his fixed relational pattern in the world. For the adolescent who has experienced so much trauma and lifespace dysregulation, his life often feels to him like a shameful, scrambled mess. He has little sense of perspective and so, the process of supporting an adolescent, such as Shane, to create a lucid and comprehensible narrative involves clear delineation of his lifespace experience into temporal chapters. Actively empathising with his phenomenological experience of enduring these bewildering lifespace circumstances, as well as expressing the impact of him and his story on me, creates a sense of being seen and of mattering. Craving for this care and acknowledgement is balanced with the threat and vulnerability which comes from trusting.

We began by exploring the myriad contact boundaries associated with his experience of foster care and our initial contact involved broad representation and reframing of his childhood and early adolescent years to lay the foundation for the emergence of a de-shamed, coherent lifespace narrative. Shane recalled each separate foster situation, including how it began and ended, and came to understand his creative adjustments to life in the system. He described his experience of social workers and other professionals who had become involved in his life over the past decade, many of whom he detested. Focus on his life in foster care also involved dialogue about his experience of contact with his siblings and his father, as he articulated the sadness and longing of having a remote, though loving connection with his sisters. He also described ambivalent feelings towards his father, whom he feared and detested.

More in-depth meaning-making involved exploration of his formative years prior to his mother's violent death. He recalled a turbulent and unsafe childhood, sharing memories of his father being drunk and shouting, of hiding under his bed, of his mother lying on top of him to prevent his father beating him, of his father ordering him to fetch his birthday gifts from his bedroom to then place them in the fire as punishment for wetting his bed. He remembered his mother with tenderness and missed how she tucked him into bed every night, said night prayer with him, told him she loved him and kissed him tenderly on the forehead. This experience of feeling safe and loved had eluded him since. He had not cried himself to sleep in years, though still periodically slept curled-up in the hot press when he felt in need of her warmth.

As our dialogue unfolded and contact deepened, we edged closer to discussing the nature of his mother's death and subsequent splintered family reconfiguration. I indicated to Shane, from the outset of our work that I was not so much interested in his sensational story as interested in *him*, and so he trusted that my curiosity lay not in the detail of what had occurred, but in his experience of these devastating events. He had no conscious memory of the night his mother was murdered, except a vague recollection of emergency personnel and flashing lights. He spoke of his bewilderment of missing his parents and trying to understand that his mother was dead and his father was in prison, accused of her murder, whilst at the same time, adjusting to an abruptly and radically reconfigured lifespace, living in his aunt's home, away from the familiarity of his neighbourhood, school and friendships, and being visited now by social workers and other professionals. This phase of the work involved attending to the complexity of his grief in addition to the inconceivable shame and trauma of having had one parent killed by the other.

As Shane developed compassionate appreciation of his lifespace experience, he was supported towards a more directional configuration. We began to explore how he had creatively adjusted to the shame of his sensational family narrative by associating with peers whose parents were also hostile. He described how there was little risk of exposure and judgement with friends whose backgrounds were also dark and traumatic. We began to deconstruct the myth of the defective self which shaped his interpersonal world. As his shame diminished, the less inclined he became to aggressive outbursts and destructive friendships. With support,

Shane gradually integrated the complexity of his lifespace experience thus far and began to envision a future which was not singularly defined by his trauma.

Parental death

For an adolescent, the trauma of a parent's death can be complex and extensive. He may arrive at a therapist's office with an urgent need to talk about what happened and how it has impacted him. However, he is more likely to show up hesitantly, flooded and without language for his experience. It is vexing to recall the number of bereaved adolescents who have communicated to me their exposing and distressing experiences of having encountered an insensitive counsellor who insisted on the adolescent prematurely focusing on his grief through interrogation and agenda-driven interventions; or similarly, who adopts such a passive posture as to render the adolescent frozen, whilst she waits in vain for his readiness to articulate his experience. In both situations, it is obvious that neither counsellor appreciates the adolescent's need to be held with active empathy to allay his fear, so typically associated with losing a parent, that accessing his voiceless overwhelm may annihilate him.

There are so many aspects to his experience that launching into dialogue about a parent's death with a reticent adolescent is premature, without sufficient relational ground and contextual appreciation. The circumstances surrounding a loss of this nature are significant and have a bearing on the phenomenology of the adolescent's grief. Notable features include his age at the time of the parent's passing; the adolescent's prior relationship to his parent; the nature of the death which may have occurred suddenly as the result of an accident, suicide or natural causes, may have been expected following a lengthy illness, or may have been a violent death; and other lifespace conditions including the young person's contact style and support structures. Creating a receptive therapeutic space begins with attending to safety. The therapist's intention is conveyed in her posture of warmth and non-invasive interest and is amplified through her elucidation of the conditions of their encounter. She advises him from the outset that they will not discuss the death unless he is disposed to do so, which injects momentary relief and some semblance of trust that threat of exposure remains low for now.

Addressing temporality

Rather than simply discussing the specific details of a parent's death, acknowledgement and integration of many elements of this major lifespace event is necessary for the adolescent to fully experience and transcend his grief. Appreciation of the quality of contact and depth of receptivity which defined the parenting space establishes the extent of loss experienced through the parent's death. Losing a receptive parent is heart breaking, though this makes the adolescent's grief less likely to be tangled in shame. Grief is often a more complex and problematic process for the adolescent who experienced the parenting space as either non-receptive or hostile. He may creatively adjust by idealising their relationship or by avoiding any difficult feelings associated with his experience within the parenting space. His ambivalence towards the parent, both in life and in death, may arouse feelings of guilt and self-reproach. He may also experience relief at an abusive parent's passing. Sensitive validation and reframing of the deceased's impaired capacity to attune and support him discourages the adolescent's susceptibility to translating the parent's failings into a statement of self-contempt.

A second aspect of supporting the adolescent's temporal experience of his parent's death is acknowledgement of the present and potential future impact of the parenting adult's absence within the adolescent's lifespace. Loss within a receptive parenting space results in pervasive feelings of sadness and loneliness for the adolescent who, in his present life experience, poignantly senses the imprint of the parent's presence and misses that parent desperately. He is both comforted and pained by the presence of cherished memories; and when he thinks of the future, he laments the fact that this parent will never watch him play another football match, see him graduate or meet grandchildren. To begin with, his lifespace reconfiguration creates anguish and he commonly feels opposed to continuing in the world without his parent – which is not the same as wanting to die or making plans to end his life, but rather an expression of despair, which will hopefully recede in time and with support.

The adolescent who has experienced non-receptivity or hostility may also experience sadness as he feels his parent's absence throughout his present and future lifespace; though this is likely to be coupled with a conscious or concealed experience of sorrow, anger and regret that this parenting space transpired to be so disappointingly unsupportive. At times, the adolescent's deepest sadness is in relation to the fact that circumstances were such that he does not care as much as he would like to in the face of losing a parent and feels relief upon a parent's death. I recall Ellen, an adolescent who endured being psychologically tortured and deprived of receptivity throughout her young life. Following her mentally unstable mother's death by suicide, she found it difficult to be comforted by people who came to pay their respects at the wake. The adolescent spoke of her yearning for people to sympathise with her, though not because her mother had died. The real tragedy for Ellen was that she was more relieved than sad that her mother had passed away. There is a darker quality to this grief which tends to create despair and high levels of shame.

Recollecting the death

Once the quality of parenting space has been established and the adolescent has spoken of his experience of life with and without his parent, it is anticipated that sufficient ground will have been created in which to discuss details of the parent's death itself. This ground includes the emergence of mutual recognition of precisely what the adolescent's loss means to him, so that beneath his description, both adolescent and therapist appreciate and continue to actively acknowledge the enormity, for him, of what has happened.

Through the unfolding narrative, the adolescent is supported to connect with and describe his phenomenology of the death, as the therapist invites him to voice his experience. Ever mindful of the impact on her client, the therapist's sensitively attuned interest in the dialogue aids the adolescent to express details such as how he learned of and whether he was present at the moment of his parent's death; his experience of the wake, funeral and burial; his thoughts about what might have happened to his parent following death; and his fear that similar catastrophic events would happen to himself or other family members as well as the potential cascade of interpersonal shifts which may have occurred as a direct result of the death. It is crucial that the therapist remains deeply empathic during these tender and heartfelt moments, lest the adolescent experience further abandonment. Framing the death within the context of other contemporaneous lifespace challenges also encourages more compassionate self-regard for the adolescent, as in the case where he had also been experiencing anxiety, taking important exams or been the target of bullying behaviour at the time of his parent's death.

This comprehensive acknowledgement and witnessing of the legacy of losing a parent through death, which includes a realistic and de-shamed portrayal of their relationship, insightful appreciation of the adolescent's reconfigured lifespace and an account of his experience around the time of the parent's actual death, creates the possibility of transcending the heavy-heartedness and embracing his lifespace with renewed interest and hope, not defined by the loss.

Ronan

Ronan's father was killed in a farm accident almost a year prior to our initial meeting. The adolescent was 14 at the time and since then had been reluctant to return to school. I ensured that contact assessment focused only minimally on the death, to ensure the adolescent felt neither exposed nor overwhelmed. At the beginning of our first one-to-one meeting I suggested a ground rule that we would not talk about his father's death unless Ronan introduced it into the dialogue. This seemingly counterintuitive invitation to avoid focus on his grief was an intervention aimed at establishing the therapeutic space as non-invasive, undemanding and safe. The relief created by this intervention alone was significant, as he was not waiting for me to throw a grenade into our dialogue and force him to talk about his painful situation.

Ronan was somewhat unsure about therapy and ambivalently chose to paint a mask whilst we dialogued about the contact assessment and his passion for farming. He enjoyed our conversation and warmed up well in contact, though towards the end, indicated that he felt 'happy enough' and did not see the need to continue coming. Stepping out of the power struggle, I suggested that we make a pie chart of his feeling world, which he willingly agreed to. I indicated that he did not have to reveal the context of his feelings, but simply identify their extent. Ronan was surprised to see how little happiness there was in his life and voluntarily, and with gentle support, reconsidered his decision about terminating the work for the moment.

Throughout the following sessions, Ronan told me more about his impressive knowledge and love of farming. He was the eldest of three children and the only one who had been interested in helping his father on the family's farm. Weaved through our dialogue about sheep, machinery and livestock marts, the adolescent described the relationship he had with his father. Apart from when he was at school, Ronan spent as much time as possible with his father, going everywhere with him. His favourite place in the world was sitting in the passenger seat of his dad's jeep as they checked on the animals and travelled around on farming business. He remembered with particular fondness helping his father during the lambing season, which was always a special time on the farm. Ronan and his father had talked about how one day he would take over the farm, the thought of which delighted the adolescent. I remarked that Ronan appeared to have lost more than just a father, but also his best friend, co-worker and inspirational role model. This was an important intervention, as it revealed the therapist's appreciation of the depth and significance of the parenting space. As the adolescent began to reveal in more depth his experience of the parenting space, it became clear that they idolised one another and that Ronan's life had not been the same since his father had passed away. He gradually began to touch and articulate his loneliness.

We discussed his present-day life structure and how the imprint of his father's presence was everywhere for Ronan, who felt the desire and responsibility, in equal measure, to step into the role of 'man of the house' and had taken over the running of the farm with the help of his grandfather and some neighbours. He saw school as an unnecessary and redundant exercise, refusing to attend as it interfered with his farming activity. He no longer had time for friends as the sheep kept him busy. Without a hint of objection and despite his drive and passion, this 15-year-old's days were long and labour intensive. I sensed that the extent of Ronan's effort was closely related to a desire to preserve a connection to his father and to live his life as a statement of loyalty to his father, irrespective of the cost to himself. Waiting for a tender moment of joining, I shared my hunch that his dad would have been very proud of his son – an intervention which conveyed my understanding of his unspoken yearnings. The adolescent became tearful and later we agreed that, whilst painful, it would be important to talk about what happened, in his own time. Predictably, during the following session, he again voiced his doubts about committing to therapy as it took up valuable time, which I translated as a statement of anxiety and dread about encountering more of his pain. I put it to him that if he were to attend every Wednesday fortnight at 5.00 p.m., we would be finished just in time for the local sheep mart at which I would ensure his attendance. He was delighted and so we continued therapy with Ronan and a trailer load of sheep being driven to my office each fortnight.

As relational ground is cultivated, adolescents trust to reach into the support, revealing more of their lifespace phenomenology and engaging with increasing spontaneity. And so, Ronan mentioned that he wrote poetry and would like to show me some of his work. It transpired that his compositions all featured the relationship with his father and his father's death. He carried a small notebook and pencil in his pocket and wrote his poetry whilst standing in fields looking at the sheep and lambs. It was during these moments that he felt closest to his father and often cried to himself. One of his poems focused on the day his father died. He asked me to read it, and afterwards he began to talk about the day, describing the accident and how guilty he felt that he was at school when it happened. The adolescent remembered the feelings of bewilderment and urgent powerlessness he experienced on seeing his father lying cold and motionless in a coffin, the pervasive sadness he felt that his father was no longer in the world, and how he still found it unbelievable. He replayed his fantasy of the farm accident and wondered if his father experienced much pain or knew he was dying. These thoughts haunted him. Ronan also spoke of the anxiety and insecurity he experienced when his mother was away from home. He was terrified that something might also happen to her and that he would be totally abandoned and left to carry the entire responsibility of caring for his siblings, the family home and the farm, which he feared he would not be able to bear. This conversation was extended and his experience supported by including his mother in our sessions at this point. Focus on these aspects of his experience supported Ronan to confess that he was not especially enjoying his life, which led to him describing the relentless pressure and exhaustion he felt. I offered a hunch that if his father could overhear our conversations, he may not be impressed. The adolescent agreed, and this intervention provided him both with relief and a new lens through which to perceive his experience.

It is likely that Ronan will always feel sad about his father's death, though the intensity of his pain and despair was gradually replaced with hope and renewed interest in expanding his lifespace. This process unfolded as the adolescent was supported to fully appreciate and take ownership of the phenomenology of his father's death, including the extent of loss experienced with his father's passing, the meaning of this loss in his present and future life, and his experience of the death event itself. As the adolescent's grief dissipated and he let go of the need to live his life as a testimony to his late father's memory, Ronan's lifespace became more self-referenced and directional in focus. His passion was still to be a farmer and work his father's land, though he also reconnected with his ambition to attend agricultural college and admitted to missing his friends and not having a social life. After exploring the possibility of hiring regular help on the farm whilst he studied, Ronan made plans to return to school and re-engage with his peers as I reminded him that it was possible to both enjoy life and miss his father desperately, explaining that these feelings were not mutually exclusive. This gave him explicit permission to experience enjoyment which was not laced with guilt and, in time, he warmed back into life.

References

American Psychiatric Association. (2013). *Diagnostic and Statistical Manual of Mental Disorders* (5th ed.). Arlington, VA: American Psychiatric Association.

Baker, C. (2018). Coramvoice.org.uk. Available at: www.coramvoice.org.uk/sites/default/files/999-CV-Care-Leaver-Rapid-Review-lo%20%28004%29.pdf [Accessed 28 Mar. 2018].

Berman, G. and Dar, A. (2013). *Prison Population Statistics*. House of Commons Library. Available at: www.parliament.uk/briefing-papers/SN04334.pdf

Bowlby, J. (1988). *A Secure Base*. London: Routledge.

Guishard-Pine, J., Coleman-Oluwabusola, G. and McCall, S., eds. (2017). *Supporting the Mental Health of Children in Care*. London: Jessica Kingsley Publishers.

Howe, D. (2005). *Child Abuse and Neglect*. Basingstoke: Palgrave Macmillan.

Ingersoll, B. (1997). Psychiatric disorders among adopted children. *Adoption Quarterly*, 1(1), pp. 57–73.

McCann, J., James, A., Wilson, S. and Dunn, G. (1996). Prevalence of psychiatric disorders in young people in the care system. *BMJ*, 313(7071), pp. 1529–1530.

Newton, R., Litrownik, A. and Landsverk, J. (2000). Children and youth in foster care: Disentangling the relationship between problem behaviors and number of placements. *Child Abuse & Neglect*, 24(10), pp. 1363–1374.

Van der Kolk, B. (2015). *The Body Keeps the Score*. New York: Penguin Books.

Vaughn, M., Ollie, M., McMillen, J., Scott, L. and Munson, M. (2007). Substance use and abuse among older youth in foster care. *Addictive Behaviors*, 32(9), pp. 1929–1935.

Verrier, N. (2009). *The Primal Wound*. London: BAAF.

Chapter 7

Anxiety, depression, self-harm and suicide

These presenting issues are creative adjustments in response to the shame of compromised integrity. The creative adjustment emerges initially in the form of feeling which stimulates an expressive response: anxiety and depression are feeling responses to the loss of integrity. Self-harm and suicide attempts, in turn, form part of the adolescent's behavioural repertoire as his impulse to discharge the potency of intolerable feelings intensifies. For example, the adolescent may feel anxious and despairing as a result of the chaos of family life; these feelings may become more pervasive in time and extend throughout his lifespace so that angst and despondency shape much of his feeling world experience. Behavioural-level creative adjustments are designed to manage and relieve the intensity of these feelings. School refusal or self-injury may become part of his coping repertoire. Similarly, the adolescent may withdraw from many aspects of his lifespace through inertia or to avoid anxiety provoking situations. If the therapist's intention is to support the young person's wider developmental process rather than solely addressing and ameliorating symptoms, then supporting him to make meaning of these creative adjustments as valid responses to compromised integrity within his expanding lifespace is a valuable therapeutic intervention.

Anxiety: assessment and intervention

The origin of anxious presentation is an experience of threat to lifespace integrity. Something is at stake: his physical or sexual integrity, his place in college, his sense of belonging and mattering, even his life. The adolescent may have endured one isolated incident, or ongoing and multiple experiences which have jeopardised his sense of safety and wellbeing. These include, for example, birth trauma, invasive medical procedure, growing up in an abusive or neglectful environment, feeling overlooked or abandoned by a parent, being in an accident or taking an important exam. Whether the threat has been acute or chronic, its *imprint* may continue to shape the adolescent's experience and a sense of threat begins to pervade his lifespace, against which he understandably feels compelled to protect himself (Van der Kolk, 2015). This sense of threat, which is experienced in varying degrees of physiological, psychological and interpersonal unease, and which may continue to be experienced long after the original threat has receded, is often translated into the most innocuous of situations. This inevitably results in some degree of lifespace restriction, as the adolescent attempts to negotiate his world in such a way as to avoid amplification of the tension and dread which infuses his experience.

The intensity of having to tolerate anxious experiencing may lead to trans-marginal stress (Lake, 1981) for the adolescent who is tortured with obsessive thoughts and compulsive behaviours. Similarly he may grind to a halt, where the thought of even the faintest degree of expansion of the lifespace feels impossible for him, as evidenced by the growing number of adolescents who spend their days largely within the confines of their bedrooms (Saitō and Angles, 2013). Characteristically, the anxiety dynamic is increasingly experienced as controlling of family life. Interpersonal contact, family and social activities are adjusted according to the adolescent's endurance threshold. As the disconcerting nature of anxiety leaves the adolescent feeling agitated, out of control and overwhelmed, parents, in turn, feel powerless, frustrated and bewildered. Unconscious lifespace restriction also supports regression to a much safer time when parents are the lifespace managers, which is why anxious adolescents commonly present more like toddlers than teenagers.

Physiologically the adolescent has a lurching feeling in the pit of his stomach, feels nauseous, sleeps poorly and may experience panic attacks. Psychologically he feels restless, overthinks, has difficulty concentrating and tends to catastrophise. Interpersonally he withdraws, feeling pressured in relational encounters and safe with only a handful of people, if any. For example, I am reminded of Tim, a 22-year-old adolescent who had been randomly attacked by a group of teenage boys several years previously. During the assault he was kicked until he was unconscious, urinated on and dumped in a bin. He was singled out simply for being a goth with dreadlocked hair who dressed in alternative clothing. As a result, he became fearful of being outside and soon afterward, dropped out of college and stopped socialising. Tim felt that the experience completely changed his personality from an outgoing, positive person to a nervous and withdrawn individual. He was diagnosed with generalised anxiety disorder following the attack.

The therapist is presented with troubled individuals whose sense of urgency and expectation is palpable. Panic attacks, school refusal, catastrophic thinking, obsessive-compulsive disorder and all other forms of anxious presentation are symptoms (American Psychiatric Association, 2013). Of what, initially the therapist may have no hint or idea. The situation does not initially require the therapist to know what is happening and what to do about it. The art is *to tolerate not knowing*, and to do so in a composed, contactful, fluster-free manner. The assessment process is an exploration of the relational, developmental, existential and situational contexts of anxiety, together with the meaning which is made of this anxiety. The therapist becomes artful in side-stepping the symptom-level dialogue by offering a rationale for widening the lens. She invites the adolescent and his parents to indulge her curiosity momentarily, so that she can better understand these symptoms, therefore ensuring just the right technique match. Of course, this is not a digression from the work. She does not intend to return to a major focus on technique, which is not to say that technique does not have a place; it has a supporting role. Her challenge is precisely not to succumb to pressure to find a solution and work at the symptomatic level alone. However, the therapist commonly experiences herself as pressured, de-skilled and anxious, as a therapeutic response to the urgency. (If the therapist is instructing on breathing techniques, doing relaxations, setting tasks, giving concrete coping strategies, etc., during the first part of therapy, before she appreciates the lifespace dynamics which may be at play, then it is likely that she will have entered into a rescuing role: rescuing the adolescent, the adults and probably mostly herself.)

As a creative adjustment to the anxiety, the adolescent commonly holds rigid control of his life in an attempt to counteract an underlying feeling of being very out of control. The adolescent develops two familiar mantras: '*What if . . . ?*' and '*I just can't . . .*' Characteristically, this translates into varying degrees of lifespace restriction, for example, school attendance wanes as it becomes easier not to have to negotiate the school day with all its social and academic pressures and which necessitates being away from home. The therapist may, understandably, reach for a rational response to the irrational process. However, it is unlikely that the adolescent will feel met in these therapeutic moments. Rather, getting the adolescent back to full school attendance is not the therapist's primary goal. Becoming interested in and heightening awareness of the adolescent's phenomenological experience; getting the adolescent interested in himself; creating support to extend his lifespace – these are critical tasks in her enterprise.

Context enquiry during contact assessment is illuminating – both content and process of the dialogue shed light on contact boundary development and on the adolescent's lifespace configuration. The therapist becomes interested in how the adolescent makes meaning of the anxiety. Similarly, she tries to discover the level of insight and awareness present within parenting spaces. Parental responses to their anxious children range from ambivalence, frustration and over-protection through to compassionate understanding. Often there are other pockets of anxious experiencing in the field and quite often one or both parents are prone to it. The therapist's intention is that this exploration will become centre-stage in a truly collaborative and contactful dialogue. Re-engagement with school will be an expected outgrowth of attendance to wider lifespace dynamics.

It is important to understand the context of the anxiety when an adolescent is referred for therapy, as therapeutic intervention differs somewhat depending on the lifespace conditions. Situational anxiety, where the adolescent feels anxious as a natural response to an event, for example, taking important examinations, requires the therapist to support the adolescent to regain perspective in addition to offering immediate cognitive and behavioural strategies to counteract the anxiety (Tubridy, 2018). In other situations, the adolescent may have been diagnosed with a psychiatric or neurodevelopmental disorder such as schizophrenia or high-functioning autism, where anxiety is a recognised symptom of the condition

(American Psychiatric Association, 2013). In these cases, the therapist may support the adolescent to grow to understand and manage symptoms in a manner which results in minimal lifespace restriction. Yet still, anxiety arising as a symptom of post-traumatic stress or the shame of being overlooked (Van der Kolk, 2015) calls on the therapist to support the meaning-making process and attend to physiological, psychological and interpersonal integrity repair, which tends to neutralise the anxiety either wholly or in part.

John

A shaming experience such as intimidation by a peer or teacher may precipitate an adolescent's refusal to attend school. However, in many cases, a less-subtle developmental dynamic is influencing anxiety-induced withdrawal behaviour. Lifespace wisdom is commonly at play, despite all outward appearances of anxiety's unwelcome presence and discomfort for the adolescent. Anxious adolescents hold a passive relationship to their lifespace, with a powerfully implicit sense that *'my life is not my own'*. The therapist can expect the emergence of anxiety as par for the course in these situations. Ameliorating symptoms and encouraging adolescents to return to school may satisfy everyone – the adolescent, parents, the school community and indeed the therapist. However, appreciating the expression of developmental tension which may be concealed within anxious school refusal opens the possibility of creating developmental momentum. For the adolescent, some preoccupation with parental dynamics is typical. For example, the therapist frequently encounters anxious, school-refusing adolescents whose anxiety is a creative adjustment to the absence of rich parental contact. The adolescent may poignantly feel the insult of not mattering to a parent and translates this into a self-statement that '*I* don't matter'. This may be the case when a parent becomes dislocated following separation, is habitually caught up in work and other activities or seems to express obvious preference for other family members. Some adolescents experience pressure and expectation within these non-receptive parenting spaces. For example, parents may be agenda-driven particularly with regard to academic performance.

I am reminded of John, a 17-year-old adolescent who experienced regular panic attacks and felt unable to attend school. Whilst concerned about their son, his parents' primary consideration was to have this boy return to school as a matter of urgency. John's father, who was an accountant, had essentially chosen his son's exam subjects and directed John's college application process. John was a compliant boy, and there was an expectation that he would study accountancy and join his father's practice.

One challenging aspect of the work when anxiety is a presenting symptom issue is wider lifespace rigidity and lack of interest in exploring the *meaning* of the anxiety. Typically, in situations such as John's, the father's one-dimensionality and expectation may make him somewhat of an intimidating presence for the therapist who prefers to exclude him from the therapeutic process or does not push when he is 'too busy' to attend. Consequently, the therapist may have minimal contact with this non-receptive parent, which is unfortunate as his contribution may potentially be transformative for his son. The intense pressure, expectation and fear of disappointing parents, coupled with a dissatisfying lack of contact, which has characterised the adolescent's lifespace is transferable to the therapist, who now focuses intently on returning the adolescent to school and removing anxiety symptoms as a response to pressure. This is an unfortunate scenario as the therapist is simply adding to the intense pressure which characterises an anxious adolescent's experience.

So, for John, it was necessary to slow the process down, engage parents and support each of them to reflect on family culture. I remarked at how much emphasis was placed on John's academic and career path and offered a hunch that the adolescent may have felt that his parents related to him more as a student than as a person in his own right. A nod from the adolescent verified this hypothesis and he was supported to articulate his frustration, revealing that his father only ever spoke to him about academic matters and that he received validation only following exam success. I suggested to his father that John may not feel known to him. This intervention created access to interpersonal yearning which, when supported and drawn out, shifted parental focus away from school and career agendas as they began to attune more deeply to the adolescent's experience. John's father expressed sadness and acknowledged being agenda-driven. As we explored his own experience, the father revealed a propensity to anxiety which he managed through a linear focus on work. It also transpired that, during his own adolescence, he did not feel known to his father. Expression of his own boyhood yearnings for a more fulfilling paternal relationship created empathic resonance and supported this parent to become curious to know his son.

It later transpired, during one-to-one work, that John had no desire to become an accountant. The unconscious developmental wisdom inherent in his inability to attend school was obvious: if debilitating anxiety symptoms persisted, he would not be able to complete his exams, be accepted onto an accountancy study programme and eventually join his father's practice. This adolescent's anxiety symptoms, culminating in school refusal, were an expression of his compromised integrity within the lifespace. It would certainly have been a disservice to the adolescent to engage at the symptom level and put him back on his father's elected life path for him by getting John back to school, without sufficient exploration of the relational dynamics which were underlying and shaping the adolescent's wider lifespace experience. The successful outcome of therapy in a situation such as John's is not simply facilitating a return to school but supporting the adolescent to trust his experience and adopt a posture of choiceful ownership within his lifespace.

Caitriona

When the therapist encounters an adolescent who has endured an experience of *trauma without* whose symptoms have emerged as a direct response of the distress he endured, assessment is straightforward. However, it is also not uncommon to meet adolescents whose anxiety appears to be an exaggerated response and utterly disconnected to any aspect of his life situation. These are particularly disconcerting situations for the therapist whose competence and knowledge are challenged. One option is to consider psychiatric referral as this presentation may warrant diagnosis and medication. Whilst this is sometimes an appropriate call, nevertheless I have encountered numerous adolescents and emerging adults over the years whose presentation resembled a major mental health disorder and which was diagnosed and treated as such, only to 'mysteriously' disappear in time. Developmental crisis may mask as psychological disintegration. Pathologising the adolescent is certainly one way to avoid shame as a clinician. However, working phenomenologically to understand the meaning of anxiety symptoms may be more revealing, supportive and productive.

For several months, Caitriona, aged 13, had been experiencing panic attacks, had become phobic about food, could no longer tolerate touch, refused to attend school and rarely left her family home. The sudden onset of these symptoms had left everyone feeling bewildered and unnerved, particularly as Caitriona had been a high-functioning child in the world until now. Contact assessment involved the adolescent, both parents and a profusion of expectation. I was mindful that if we were to launch into an analysis of symptoms, this would inevitably create exposure and shame for the adolescent as well as generating urgency within the therapeutic field.

To create therapeutic conditions which would get to the heart of this adolescent's experience, the focus of dialogue was widened as I attended to cultivating safe relational ground. I learned that Caitriona was the eldest of three children and had recently transferred from primary to secondary school. Our conversation revealed that during a family summer holiday, whilst having dinner in a restaurant, she mistakenly ate something which contained eggs. (She is allergic to eggs, wheat, nuts, and dairy products.) Caitriona experienced a mild reaction, which included slight wheezing and flushing. The restaurant manager, as a precaution, called an ambulance and she was taken, with her father, to hospital to get checked out. She required no medical intervention, very soon returned to the resort and enjoyed the remainder of her family holiday. However, on her return home, anxiety symptoms erupted with sudden and paralysing force. Her parents could make no sense of this, and as parents are prone to do, spent countless hours reassuring her and providing rational explanations as to why she shouldn't behave and feel the way she did. Rationalisations are always understandable and always unhelpful in these situations.

I became curious about the food allergies and discovered that, for the first eighteen months of her life, Caitriona had suffered with eczema so severely that she was wet-bandaged and slept upright in a car seat at night. During this time, she was hospitalised regularly with breathing difficulties and other complications, often having been brought there by ambulance. She endured countless invasive medical procedures as an infant. Her parents spoke of fearing that she would die during some of these episodes, sometimes sitting by her hospital cot, praying she would make it through the night.

The parents were somewhat upset at recalling this experience. Tying the threads together, I offered a hunch that the recent excursion to hospital may have activated some previously well-hidden memories and feelings. Human beings, even the very youngest of our species, when overwhelmed, do not forget. They may hold no conscious cognitive memory whatsoever of a traumatic experience, nevertheless, they are imprinted. Anxiety may form part of a creative adjustment spectrum in response to this insecurity and overwhelm (Van der Kolk, 2015). Beneath this creative adjustment we unfailingly discover hurt and loss, inevitably concealing deep-seated yearning. When integrity is threatened or impaired, our innate capacity to relegate the distress to some dissociated ground of our experience is activated. Anxiety may or may not begin to manifest at this point. However, future lifespace conditions often configure to act as a catalyst for the unearthing of this overwhelm. The emergence of oppressive, often debilitating anxiety symptoms at this point is not uncommon (Wheeler, 2002).

Caitriona became tearful at this point and revealed that she felt frightened getting into the ambulance, terrified that she would be kept in hospital and that she could die there. She had no idea why. The family began to appreciate that recent events may have created a reverberation to early childhood trauma. From this point, the adolescent and her parents grew less preoccupied with symptom amelioration and instead became interested in the underlying distress which may have been shaping Caitriona's experience. And so we collaboratively explored and made meaning of the emergence of this traumatic childhood experience. Staying with this piece generated an added depth of support and connection within the therapeutic space.

Happening upon a medical history narrative which resonated was likely to be one aspect of a much wider developmental context for the anxiety. And so, I began also to look for developmental tension within the adolescent's lifespace, curious about the wider implications of Caitriona's status as an emerging adolescent for her and for her parents. As the story unfolded, I learned that as soon as the diagnosis of food allergies was made, the child's health improved dramatically. Both parents subsequently became meticulous at regulating Caitriona's lifespace with regard to food – play dates, birthday parties and school outings were all carefully managed. Their supervision had not ever faltered . . . that is, until the holiday restaurant experience. We began to explore the less obvious implications of this. The threads revealed themselves gradually: the timing of the family holiday was significant, as this heralded the transition to secondary school, which to Caitriona and her family meant the end of childhood: becoming less dependent on her parents and more invested in peer friendships, eventually heading for college and leaving home. Both she and her parents were aware that the responsibility for dietary management was beginning to transfer to Caitriona. We discovered that death anxiety was at the heart, not just of her experience as a sick infant, but was also presently pervasive and shaping her experience during this transitional episode in her developmental process. It would now be the responsibility of this

13-year-old to prevent potentially fatal anaphylaxis (she informed me that she knew of one young person in her neighbourhood who had recently died from the condition). She was terrified that she would die, and understandably, her expanding lifespace felt threatening and hostile to her without her parents' ongoing direct supervision. This manifested in her becoming phobic about food and even about being in contact with other people, for fear that they may have consumed food to which she was allergic. It became clear that this was a life-or-death situation for Caitriona. Her presenting symptoms were less perplexing now.

The second strand of this developmental aspect to our inquiry had to do with Caitriona's parents, who were fearful that she would not be as vigilant as they had been with regard to her condition. They knew that adolescents were prone to conduct themselves with reckless immaturity and neglect; and that could cost their daughter dearly. This dietary management aspect in the care for their daughter had been a major feature of their parenting spaces throughout childhood and was drawing to a natural conclusion as adolescence beckoned. In addition, they felt that they had been competent caregivers up until this point and were anxious about how to parent a child who was not entirely dependent upon them. As we unpacked this experience, they expressed a sense of impending redundancy and sorrow that Caitriona was no longer their 'baby'. Like so many, they understood adolescence as the loss, rather than evolution of the parent-child relationship and were expecting an inevitable disconnect through the teenage years, holding deep concern about what might happen behind that rigid adolescent boundary. Their daughter's anxiety had been holding these fears at bay.

The developmental wisdom of the anxiety became evident: there were lifespace gains to be had with managing the bewilderment of anxiety symptoms as opposed to facing the vulnerability of the adolescing process for this adolescent and her parents. As the work progressed, the rigidity within Caitriona's lifespace softened considerably. I intervened with several concrete cognitive and behavioural techniques, promoting anxiety-free movement, as the adolescent risked increasing contact with people and food, and learned to tolerate and steadily trust being in the world again. This technique emerged organically and was relationally framed. Technique, if not grounded in contact and strategy, may provide only momentary relief. Parenting strategy work was also an important component of this phase of therapy as Caitriona's parents learned the art of relating to and parenting their child as an emerging adolescent. Reparative work with this adolescent meant attending to developmental process and involved seeing beyond the creative adjustment of her anxious presentation to the hidden yearnings for physiological, psychological and interpersonal integrity. Acknowledgement and support for these yearnings neutralise an anxious lifespace.

Depression

The phenomenology of depression is such that the adolescent tends to feel pervasively sad, with a curtailed capacity to experience pleasure. The adolescent is often saturated with shame, which is largely self-directed, and holds a deep conviction about his unworthiness. Despair and disinterest characterise much of his behaviour (McWilliams, 2011). His diminished experience of self is carried in his breath as he tends to sigh a lot, breathing out more than he breathes in. Breathing, and life itself, require a great deal of effort at times. Often he cannot be bothered with either, experiencing sensory dulling, inhabiting a joyless, grey, inhospitable world. He experiences his lifespace as devoid of personal meaning and adopts a posture of withdrawal and restriction (Yalom, 1980).

Many adolescents enter therapy having been previously diagnosed (either by a doctor or following an online search) as being depressed. All too often this very common labelling of his creative adjustment disempowers the young person, who is supported to adopt a passive posture towards his feeling world and to see himself as having been afflicted with some ailment which is treatable by medication. Whether or not depression is explicitly named, exploration of lifespace dynamics during contact assessment may suggest a depressive presentation. At this point, it is useful to reframe any potential labelling of depression as a creative adjustment, which is not the same as denying the presence of depression. Rather it is a redefining of the adolescent's *relationship* to his feeling world which supports both him and his parents to appreciate the context of this depressive edge, and assessment involves an exploration of wider lifespace dynamics. Typically, though not always, there is less of an aura of mystery surrounding an adolescent's depressed presentation, compared with his anxious counterpart, as he is not so disconnected from the ground of his experience. Hence, there is often less urgency shaping the therapeutic encounter. Translating depression into a more contextually focused experience is usually met with recognition and openness, especially when it is offered following the description of painful and unsupported integrity experience. The depressed adolescent will almost certainly have experienced some form of traumatic loss or other integrity threat and many have grown-up with a depressed parent (Downey and Coyne, 1990).

As with any adolescent, irrespective of presenting symptom issue, intervention with a depressed adolescent involves supporting him to make meaning of his experience and of his creative adjustments to life situations. Lifespace imbalance is assumed and so, encouraging the adolescent to make changes in areas such as sleep, screen time and diet, is also a necessary step. Creating momentum within the lifespace will be impeded without some kind of vision for a meaningful future to counteract despair for the adolescent, who may be struggling to make sense of his life in the face of significant integrity compromise.

Aoife

Fifteen-year-old Aoife had become increasingly disheartened within her lifespace. Depressive symptoms had begun to amplify recently, resulting in decreased school attendance and withdrawal from friendships. The adolescent lived with her mother and younger sister. Her mother struggled with addiction, and her sister with an eating disorder. When she was 6 years old, Aoife's father died in a house fire from which the rest of the family escaped. Since childhood Aoife had experienced psychosomatic symptoms, specifically pains in her chest, stomach and head. Sleep had also been a difficulty for Aoife, who slept beside her mother and regularly experienced vivid nightmares, from which she would wake terrified and upset. The adolescent self-harmed and had taken several overdoses. When I met with Aoife and her mother during the assessment, despair was tangibly present in the contact. Mindful of the limited support available to the adolescent within an indirectly hostile parenting space, I decided that working principally in one-to-one work with Aoife would be more beneficial than involving her mother.

As Aoife made meaning of her lifespace experience, she began to appreciate how feeling, thought and behaviour-level creative adjustments were a response to difficult and unsupportive family lifespace dynamics. Aoife spoke about the house fire and how she missed her father, recalling how family life had become progressively more painful following his traumatic death. She spoke of her mother's growing dependency on cannabis and alcohol over the years, and of how she now felt that she mattered to nobody, as her mother's attention, when sober, was almost singularly focused on Aoife's anorexic younger sister.

Aoife began to understand that nothing much would change without her first finding balance, and so, her tentative interest in creating healthy structure in her day-to-day life gradually increased. The adolescent saw that she was sleep deprived and began to boundary her screen time. She started to attend school a little more regularly, spend time with friends and play football again. These shifts in themselves improved Aoife's mood somewhat. However, for her to feel that her life was worth living, it was crucial to create vision for a meaningful future that she could strive towards. Adolescents have a remarkable capacity to tolerate adversity once they appreciate that it is possible to author a lifespace not defined by the shame they have experienced. And so, I watched for the first spark of significant enthusiasm to emerge, which came as Aoife spoke about her love of animals and shared her hope to one day work as a veterinary nurse. The adolescent was visibly energised as we explored online descriptions of the role of a veterinary nurse and the pathway to gaining this qualification. To morph her vision into momentum, I made contact with the school principal, informed her of the situation and requested that she set up a visit to a local veterinary surgery. The principal did this and accompanied Aoife on the short trip, during which the vet invited Aoife to spend a week on work experience later in the school term. Following her time spent in the surgery, Aoife, who had been greatly encouraged by the vet, demonstrated renewed commitment to her studies to attain the grades necessary to be accepted into the practice as a trainee. Aoife continued to visit the surgery weekly and demonstrated a great capacity to soothe distressed animals, becoming known within the veterinary practice as their 'animal whisperer'. Her experience of belonging and connection supported greater optimism, creating momentum within her lifespace, and psychosomatic symptoms also ceased. Development and nurturance of vision and momentum for the adolescent ensured that, whilst still finding family life difficult, she would neither be consumed nor defined by her experience within parenting spaces.

Self-harm

Despite its obvious risk, there is a healing wisdom in this behaviour-level crea-tive adjustment as it acts as a ventilating system for transmarginal intensity of feeling, with the supplanting of psychic pain into physical pain (Gardner, 2001). For example, Ian had been sexually assaulted at 8 years old by a much older adolescent. He became so frustrated when gaming or rowing with his parents that he would hit himself, bang his head, cut his body and punch walls so hard that he sometimes broke bones. Following these self-harming incidents, Ian would curl up on his bed and sob, feeling very young and heartbroken. The momentary morphing of his anguish into the pain of physical wounds felt like validation for him, enabling him to receive comfort and affection from his parents who, with the exception of these moments, experienced their son as unreachable. After each epi-sode, he readopted his impassive and withdrawn posture, until the next incident. In time, processing of the sexual trauma neutralised his propensity to self-harm.

While some adolescents, like Ian, injure to feel the pain they have become so capable of numbing, others feel compelled to self-harm to create relief from the intolerable intensity of feelings (Gardner, 2001). I am reminded of Deirdre, who felt as if she was endlessly drowning in her emotions, unable to escape the pain of living in a family home with warring and neglectful parents. Her father drank heavily and was verbally abusive; her mother confided in Deirdre about the mari-tal relationship and shared a bed with her daughter. Momentary relief descended as Deirdre cut her body with razor blades. This adolescent's self-harming behav-iour was a creative adjustment to the stress of living in a toxic and inescapable situation.

Whilst it may feel counterintuitive for the therapist to suppress her inclination to furnish the adolescent with strategies for changing or stopping the self-harming behaviours (particularly as the work with adolescents is so commonly steeped in expectation to intervene with urgency at the symptom level) it may not always be always useful to embark upon a behaviour modification programme – at least initially. The self-harm has emerged as a creative adjustment response to the ado-lescent's compromised integrity and so therapeutic intervention focuses on sup-porting the adolescent's meaning-making with regard to integrity yearnings and to arrive at a place where he doesn't feel it necessary to engage in self-injury any longer. As Ian and Deirdre explored their lifespace dynamics and were supported to transcend the shame of their experience, self-harming behaviour ceased with the emergence of vision and momentum.

Some adolescents wear their scars as honour badges and actively encourage peers to follow suit. It is a mistake to explain away copy-cat behaviour as merely a succumbing to peer pressure. Whilst a yearning for acceptance within the peer landscape may be a major motivation, not every adolescent will mimic this self-harming behaviour. Each adolescent who self-harms, even in copy-cat mode, is giving expression to some lifespace imbalance which warrants exploration and support.

Suicide

As feeling-level creative adjustment extends beyond a general experience of melancholy and meaninglessness to transmarginal despair, the exit strategy of suicide may become a fantasy or viable option for the adolescent. In the same manner that many people like to sit close to a door so that they have access to an escape route, should their experience in a room become too intense, so the adolescent who is struggling within his lifespace may feel soothed by the thought of ending his life as a statement to himself that he has some choice and does not *have* to endure his present difficulty (Joiner, 2007). For some, this thought creates sufficient breathing space and tolerability so that he does not act on this feeling impulse.

At times, the fantasy and feelings of suicide move into the realm of behavioural creative adjustment and the young person's yearning to act on his impulse is initiated. His chagrin may emerge from shame which has been deeply etched into his lifespace experience and as his level of distress transcends the margins of how much he can bear, his feeling about taking his life is translated into a behaviour response as he reaches for a rope, a bottle of pills or his car keys. He can, just as easily, feel driven to behave suicidally in a momentary wave of despair, identifying suicide as a reasonable response to an unreasonable situation to which he sees no alternative (Shneidman, 1998). In both these instances, the transformation of his transmarginal despair into a behavioural impulse to end his life is often catalysed and intensified by the presence of alcohol and drugs in his system.

Once the adolescent commits to this behavioural-level creative adjustment, he may feel compelled and driven, such is the intensity of the suicide impulse at this stage. As the adolescent begins to see the wisdom and gift of his death both for him and for those close to him, a lifespace withdrawal process commences (Joiner, 2007). The adolescent who has mobilised to act suicidally is often difficult to reach within the therapeutic space as he is between worlds, so to speak. With the knowledge that his struggling will soon come to an end, he may experience peacefulness and clarity (Shneidman, 1998). However, his contact is disembodied and this quasi-serenity creates a disconcerting feeling for the therapist, much like the eerie silence which descends in the wake of an explosion. As the therapist assesses that an adolescent's creative adjustment response is at a suicide behaviour level, she initiates a case management response whereby she informs parenting adults and other appropriate professionals to mobilise as much support and supervision as possible for the anguished adolescent during this intense period (see Chapter 13 for discussion on case management).

The adolescent's creative adjustment to integrity compromise needs to be addressed in a composed and unflappable manner as the therapist attunes to the potential therapeutic responses of urgency and despair. Whilst these are certainly present within the situation, it is unhelpful if they shape and define therapeutic contact with the adolescent, as this will create even greater remoteness in their encounter. Exploring the phenomenology of the suicidal feelings or suicide attempt reveals much about the young person's relationship to his lifespace and opens the possibility of reframing the shame which has led him to consider such drastic measures. Wisdom and reason are always present in the adolescent's draw to suicide, despite how unwarranted and unreasonable this may appear to the adults in his life.

Suicide as a momentary wave of despair

Fionn, aged 16, was admitted to hospital following an attempt to hang himself, which was quickly discovered by a parent whose intervention saved his life. Fionn's parents brought him from hospital to my office in terror and desperation. As I spent time with this teenager and his parents, exploring his lifespace, I heard a description of Fionn's life as very supported. His parents were receptive; he had experienced no trauma, was centrally located within his peer landscape and was an intelligent and capable young person. Fionn attended a co-ed school with his best friends, some of whom were members of the local rock band in which he played lead guitar. His girlfriend also attended the school. Fionn's lifespace appeared to be a wholesome environment and the adolescent had presented as happy and very engaged in his life up until this incident, which was experienced, naturally, as a bewildering and catastrophic shock for his parents.

During this emergency appointment I spent some time alone with the adolescent, who revealed that some hours prior to his suicide attempt, had discovered that his best friend, who was also a band member, had been secretly dating his girlfriend behind Fionn's back. As we unpacked this experience, Fionn articulated how, in one moment, everything changed: how could he ever show his face in school again? He had lost his girlfriend, his best friend, his band, his status. He was a laughingstock, and everyone had probably known about what had been going on behind his back for weeks. Fionn described himself as "the village idiot" and felt that his whole life had been a lie. The life he knew was over, and he could not imagine finding a way to live again.

When I became curious as to the meaning of Fionn's suicide attempt, he revealed that his creative adjustment response to the shock and shame of this lifespace rupture was to teach his girlfriend and best friend a lesson by killing himself. His motivating thought was the image of these two stood by his graveside on the day of the funeral, looking down at his coffin in a six-foot-deep hole in the ground: they would be sorry *then*, and he would have the last laugh. A simple intervention supported him to expand his perspective and begin to reconsider the scenario. I said, "I get that they would have been sorry then . . . but after the funeral they would get to walk out of the graveyard and live the rest of their lives . . . and you would be still in that coffin six feet in the ground. That seems a heavy price for you to pay to make them feel regret". Fionn's response was, "Oh yeah, I never thought of that".

Fionn had lost his place of belonging within his peer landscape and felt he had nowhere to go. Had he ended up taking his life, it is reasonable to anticipate that his parents would have spent the rest of their lives haunted by how they had failed him as parents, holding themselves somehow accountable for his death. Yet, from Fionn's perspective, hanging himself was a reasonable response to a wholly unreasonable situation. Death by suicide, for Fionn, would have been a statement about loss of belonging within his peer landscape, not about parenting spaces. For Fionn, it did not matter that his parents loved him: that was not enough. As with many adolescents in similar predicaments, shame shapes the creative adjustment and the impulse to withdraw from the lifespace becomes captivating. I have met countless adolescents, like Fionn, for whom the experience of social suicide catapulted them into suicidal process, such is the urgent need to belong with peers during adolescence.

Suicide as a statement of transmarginal shame

For some adolescents who have been traumatised, particularly those whose development has been unsupported because of non-receptive and hostile parenting spaces, living with pronounced psychological torment may eventually become unbearable (Herman, 1992). Creative adjustments may momentarily distract from the undercurrents of despair and isolation which shape his lifespace. However, as the adolescent experiences transmarginal shame, he sees suicide as the emotional painkiller par excellence, and this becomes an increasingly valid and sensible option for him. His suicidal experience is a statement of transmarginal despair, and it is vital that, with sufficient relational ground, the therapist addresses this distress and reframes his lifespace in a de-shaming manner as early as possible in therapeutic contact.

I received a telephone call from a concerned father with regards to his son, who had grown increasingly subdued and isolated over recent weeks. His father was terrified that this young man was making plans to end his life imminently, having learned that Rory had given social media passwords to an ex-girlfriend requesting that she post notice of his death in the coming days. I arranged to meet with the adolescent and both parents. Only Rory, who was 21 years old, and his father attended.

I was struck by the intensity in this adolescent's body, breath and silence. Rory presented as a seemingly unreachable and very flat adolescent. His eyes were pained and distant. He appeared very uncomfortable in the contact, as if the pressure of either having to utter words or sit in silence might overwhelm him. Suicidal and deeply traumatised adolescents are often incapable of reaching out, so I stepped in from the beginning and framed the encounter with supportive dialogue. I remained keenly aware of my body: breathing, slowing down, open and attuned. This embodiment is contagious, and the adolescent also relaxed somewhat. I indicated during the session that I would like to meet with both parents and Rory told me sharply and definitively that under no circumstances would he agree to his mother becoming involved in the process in any way. I wondered about the painful context of this statement.

As Rory gradually engaged in the dialogue, I learned that he was studying as an undergraduate. An extremely intelligent and capable young man, he was unable to concentrate and had lost his focus and momentum recently. He had performed poorly in a recent exam and a two-year relationship had also ended. These experiences, which he was finding difficult to come to terms with, appeared to have precipitated a crisis which had resulted in him spiralling into depressive energy and had culminated in him making plans to end his life imminently. As the session drew to a close, I felt we had established a tentative thread of connection. I made contact with his doctor, recommending further support. The GP informed me that Rory had recently walked out of a psychiatric assessment because he felt it was a "joke" and refused to engage with psychiatric services or take medication. I suggested to Rory's father that he take time off work and supervise his son, which he agreed to do. We met frequently thereafter for several weeks until the intensity dissipated, before extending the interval between appointments.

During subsequent sessions, it emerged that Rory's parents separated when he was 11. He was the eldest of two children, and he and his younger sister left the family home with his mother and went to live in a city some distance away. He visited his father at weekends. Prior to this, Rory had grown up on a farm in a small, close-knit rural community, with good friends and a love of farming and rugby. Throughout childhood he had been deeply embedded in his family and community life, with a strong sense of belonging. On the cusp of adolescence, his familiar lifespace, rather than expanding, suddenly disintegrated. He experienced a deep disconnect – being taken away from his father and friends, away from the farm and his rugby team, attending a new school in a new and foreign world which he detested. He had never forgiven his mother for this and had cut her out of his life since the age of 16.

It was necessary for both Rory and his frantic father to be held in the therapeutic space as both were deeply distressed and in need of support. As with many fathers and sons I meet, their relationship was characterised by immense, though unexpressed love and a large measure of relational awkwardness. I extended our dialogue, and they both spoke of their relationship with one another, the separation and move away from home, the impact of these past few months on his father, whose tears were translated into a statement of care and love. As we explored the context of his developmental journey and I supported more direct receptivity within the father-son relationship, Rory began to warm up to life again.

Some weeks later Rory felt strongly suicidal once again. During this time, he felt somewhat resentful of therapeutic support as he experienced peaceful and positive feelings about ending his life. He attended – in spite of his urge to disengage. I challenged his reticence about his mother participating in the therapeutic process as I knew that meeting her would afford me a deeper appreciation of his experience. I offered him a rationale for this meeting, stating that I would like to experience her for myself and wanted to hear how she talked about her son, assuring him that the content of his dialogue with me would remain off-limits during the dialogue. Whilst Rory refused to be present during the encounter, he was willing to tolerate the meeting when I suggested that his father would also be present.

I experienced Rory's mother as somewhat intimidating and icy in her contact, to which my response was a feeling of shrinking and being muted. The adolescent was keen to meet with me after the session and I scheduled a session with himself and his father later that evening. Respectfully I shared my experience of his mother, expressing my disappointment for Rory that she seemed strangely unmoved by his anguish. I offered my hunch that his interest in hearing about the meeting was a statement of curiosity and hope that she may care. Rory softened, and I acknowledged his yearning to have a loving, affectionate mother, adding that I imagined he experienced his own mother as 'formidable' as he was growing up. This word, for Rory, captured and authenticated his experience, invoking tears and opening the dialogue more deeply.

Rory's father described how the pregnancy was unplanned and that his mother resented having a child, showing him little warmth and attending only to his basic care needs during infancy. The couple stayed together for the sake of this child and had a second baby, though struggled to find happiness in their relationship. Rory indicated how his mother never let him forget that he was a 'mistake' and described the profound shame he carried about his existence in the world. His mother was prone to aggression at times and Rory recounted several significant incidents, including how, when he was aged 10 years old, his mother forced him to sleep in the car for several nights. During his early adolescence, when they argued, she would not speak to him for months at a time and would refuse to cook for him or do his laundry. When he was 16 years of age, his mother told him he was no longer welcome in the home as their arguments were becoming more frequent. Rory moved in with his father. I reframed the hostile maternal parenting space and the ensuing transmarginal despair which was shaping his experience. This lancing of the boil, with active empathy and support from both myself and his father, reached the heart of Rory's experience and created relief.

Over time Rory made meaning of many aspects of his lifespace through a more contextually focused, de-shamed lens. The adolescent became open to exploring his inhibitive configuration style within his lifespace and made meaning of his creative adjustments to the hostility and shame of his unwelcome existence in the world. Compensatory experiences which contrasted sharply with the overwhelm included finding status as a gifted academic and sportsperson – aspects of his life which gave him a feeling of control and power. Reflecting on his recent relationship breakup, he came to appreciate that betrayal of his girlfriend throughout their two-year relationship together with the juxtaposing experience of his dependency and devastation in the face of her rejection of him was a mirror of the ambivalence he experienced within the maternal parenting space. This rejection induced transmarginal shame which Rory believed would dissolve by annihilating himself.

As a result of parenting space hostility and a sudden, unwelcome rupture of his lifespace experience as an emerging adolescent, Rory had little expectation of belonging and being met meaningfully in the world and so it had become a lonely and hostile place for him. As Rory made meaning of his experience, he warmed up to life again and despite a complex and painful childhood, has learned to appreciate himself as a valuable and unique human being, with much to give the world.

References

American Psychiatric Association. (2013). *Diagnostic and Statistical Manual of Mental Disorders* (5th ed.). Arlington, VA: American Psychiatric Association.

Downey, G. and Coyne, J. (1990). Children of depressed parents: An integrative review. *Psychological Bulletin*, 108(1), pp. 50–76.

Gardner, F. (2001). *Self-Harm: A Psychotherapeutic Approach*. Sussex: Brunner-Routledge.

Herman, J. (1992). *Trauma and Recovery*. New York: Basic Books.

Joiner, T. (2007). *Why People Die by Suicide*. Cambridge, MA: Harvard University Press.

Lake, Frank. (1981). *Tight Corners in Pastoral Counselling*. London: Darton, Longman and Todd.

McWilliams, N. (2011). *Psychoanalytic Diagnosis*. New York: Guilford Press.

Saitō, T. and Angles, J. (2013). *Hikikomori: Adolescence Without End*. Minneapolis: University of Minnesota Press.

Shneidman, E. (1998). *The Suicidal Mind*. New York: Oxford University Press.

Tubridy, Á. (2018). *When Panic Attacks* (3rd ed.). Dublin: Gill Books.

Van der Kolk, B. (2015). *The Body Keeps the Score*. New York: Penguin Books.

Wheeler, G. (2002). Compulsion and curiosity. In M. McConville and G. Wheeler, ed., *The Heart of Development: Gestalt Approaches to Working with Children, Adolescents and Their Worlds Volume 1: Childhood*. Cambridge, MA: Gestalt Press, pp. 165–181.

Yalom, I. D. (1980). *Existential Psychotherapy*. New York: Basic Books.

Chapter 8

Eating disorders

The adolescent's relationship to his body is conditioned by the relentlessly bombarded media dictate that the state of his physique determines his degree of acceptability in the world. Perpetuation of this dangerous myth has led to both genders feeling increasingly pressured to toe the line, with girls striving for a sylphlike frame and boys for the Adonis or metrosexual look (Muris et al., 2005). This body objectification is an aspect of a wider externalisation culture which shapes how the adolescent feels about his lifespace. He is guided to view himself as a decent human being only in so far as he looks and acts the part – understanding that image seemingly means everything in today's world. The directionally configured adolescent tends not to be so driven by the externalisation process, being interested in and defining himself by much more than simply the perceived beauty of his physical frame. However, the body can become an object of great insecurity and distress for the more impulsively or inhibitively configured young person. Many are tortured in this 'external casing' which must be starved, groomed and sculpted into shape in the search for acceptability and worth.

The wider environment's relationship to food in the first world has evolved dramatically in recent years with a high-calorie, low-nutrient diet of abundance being extensively promoted and supported. This culture of indulgence is matched by the mutually incompatible assertion that the path to satisfaction is discipline and restraint, with the promulgation of fad diet and fitness programmes. Simultaneous environmental endorsement of both impulsive and inhibitive body care in equal measure is confusing for anyone. Many adolescents, mirroring the wider world's conflicted mindset, develop imbalanced perspectives and practices with regard to body shape, food and exercise. It is normative for the adolescent to be dissatisfied and preoccupied to some degree with body image, and more so in today's world given his extensive exposure to the fantasy that a toned and slender body equates to happiness and acceptance. However, as preoccupation enters the realm of problematic eating behaviour and high levels of body shame, these creative adjustments point to a compromised integrity at the heart of his symptomatic presentation.

The adolescent's psychological wellbeing and process of self-nourishment through eating are inextricably linked, so that any significant lifespace disparity has the potential to impact the experience of food intake. The distress may be directly related to the experience of eating, such as the presence of a phobic fear of vomiting or swallowing in response to a choking or vomiting episode in childhood. However, it is more likely that a pattern of restrictive and/or compulsive eating becomes established due to emotional adversity not directly connected with food (Lask and Bryant-Waugh, 2013). In these cases, avoidance, restriction, refusal and compulsive eating are statements of integrity compromise and have little to do with weight and body shape preoccupation. I am reminded of one adolescent whose parents had recently separated and who refused to eat during weekends spent at her father's new home, both as a statement of contempt at having discovered that his affair had precipitated the separation, an in the hope that, having aroused sufficient adult concern for her wellbeing, she would no longer have to visit him; or the college student who had virtually stopped eating, having lost her appetite not only for food, but for life in general following her younger sister's suicide.

Understanding that a skewed relationship with food is the manifestation of physiological, psychological or interpersonal distress, the therapist's interventions do not directly address the symptomatic issue of food intake. Rather, her attention is focused on the restoration of integrity, which will naturally support disengagement from destructive creative adjustments. Nonetheless, it is important to be mindful when supporting adolescents who are experiencing disordered eating that, whilst working at the symptom level does not address underlying issues, neither does meaning-making equate to recovery, such is the inexorable and potentially life-threatening nature of this presentation. A multi-disciplinary approach is advised, and medical assessment is often necessary. Consequently, parents, if they have not done so prior to contact assessment, are directed to consult with a GP, a dietician and possibly a child and adolescent mental health service as these treatment approaches focus on weight gain and other dietary matters. Parents, however, often bring their child to therapy with the expectation that the therapist will focus her interventions on the problematic eating behaviour, monitoring the adolescent's diet and supporting him to eat in a healthier manner. Whilst this seems a reasonable request, monitoring dietary intake is the responsibility of medically trained professionals, and in much the same manner that one might correct the cancer patient who engages in therapy expecting the therapist to administer chemotherapy treatment in addition to psychological support, the therapist reminds the adolescent and his parents that she is not medically trained, clarifying her position as a professional who supports meaning-making and integrity repair. There are other more suitably qualified professionals to undertake these aspects of the adolescent's recovery. One would never consider administering medical treatment to the cancer patient, and similarly it is imprudent, both in terms of contact and praxis, for the adolescent therapist to undertake a diet and weight management programme with a young client who is struggling with an eating disorder. For the therapist who colludes with this expectation, the outcome is an inevitable power struggle which establishes healthy weight maintenance and a balanced relationship with food as the successful outcomes of therapy. Instead, the therapist becomes interested in the phenomenology of the eating disorder and the adolescent's wider developmental process; otherwise she risks creating an unsafe and alienating therapeutic space for the adolescent by holding to a diet-focused agenda.

Hostility and spontaneity

Many of today's generation of adolescents, whilst not meeting the threshold for diagnosis of anorexia nervosa, nevertheless demonstrate concerning levels of restriction and rigidity regarding food intake. This quasi-anorexic profile is alarmingly common since adolescent girls and boys are under phenomenal pressure to acquire the emaciated-body-beautiful, often striving for unrealistic body shape, thanks to advancements in medicine and graphics. Similarly, an inhibitively organised eating pattern, such as anorexia, may emerge as a creative adjustment in an otherwise impulsively configured lifespace, as in the case of Abbie, a 23-year-old client who experienced anorexia for two years during her earlier adolescence as a creative adjustment to childhood sexual trauma, and who has since been struggling with bulimic impulses and alcohol dependency.

More typically, the presence of rigidity in the adolescent's relationship to food is indicative of a characteristically inhibitive lifespace configuration. The adolescent does not set out to become anorexic; he simply decides to diet. This shame-based decision taken by someone who is characteristically highly disciplined, driven and perfectionist in his approach to tasks, is a dangerous combination. The feeling of empowerment which initially emerges from the satisfaction of weight loss quickly develops into a wholly imbalanced power struggle within every aspect of his lifespace. All too often, his effort to shed a few pounds morphs into a disturbing weight loss obsession which proves fatal for some (Bruch, 2001).

Therapeutic intervention with the adolescent who is struggling with anorexia requires thorough contact assessment and ongoing field intervention work. Typically, the field is inhibitively configured and family culture may support the adolescent to be overly compliant, to worry about what others think, and to suppress his choicefulness and needs. Superficially the adolescent appears to flourish in the world: often excelling academically and in sport, however his accomplishments belie a feeling of not being good enough, as he doubts his capacity to satisfy the stifling sense of expectation he experiences.

The pulsating energy which so frequently characterises the therapeutic space with an impulsive or directional adolescent is notably absent. His voice, as a fundamental gateway to self-expression in the world, is muted – and possibly has always been. The idea of conveying thoughts and feelings may be alien to someone who has become so externally referenced and who has conditioned himself to inhibit these impulses. His lifespace lacks resonance and responsiveness and he may not be sure what he thinks or feels about anything, with the exception of all things food and weight related. His rigid cognition is not congruent with his bodily experience; he does not speak his truth because it has typically been constricted by the conditioning to express what people want to hear or for fear of what others might think. His lifespace becomes overshadowed by a cloud of self-criticism and hostility as he embarks on a relentless drive to improve himself: his grades, his sporting performance, his diet, his body. Expression of this hostility within the therapeutic space fosters the emergence of a useful power struggle, namely, the conflict between the adolescent's *concern* and *denial*. Facilitation of the adolescent's development of a reflexive relationship to this self-directed hostility through visual representation is particularly effective.

One adolescent, Sarah, described how she would rise at 5.00 a.m., tearfully lather her exhausted and emaciated body in muscular pain relief cream and secretly work out in her home gym for an hour each morning before studying for an hour prior to beginning each school day. Concerned for her health, she yearned to rest and stop the relentless regime, yet another part was highly critical of this weak-willed inadequacy. She described herself as 'trapped inside myself' and named this hostile part of herself 'Doof' – food spelled backwards (Figure 8.1). The adolescent spoke of feeling terrified of calories and of fat, and to avoid accumulating either, she moved her body any time she could. Sarah spoke of her frustration that 'Doof', who lived in a cave in her brain, would not permit her to watch

Figure 8.1 Sarah and "Doof"

her favourite TV programmes or have fun any more as these things would make her lazy and fat. The adolescent felt desperately unhappy and pressured by this increasingly hostile aspect of her experience.

She expressed her sadness at having lost her place and her identity within the family, describing her experience as *'they just see me now as someone who needs to be fed'*. She began to feel both sad and compassionate when she reflected on the level of hostility she relentlessly directed towards herself, and the wider repercussions of this hostility and her inhibitive configuration throughout her lifespace. This awareness helped establish the ground conditions for change.

There is an inherent wisdom in the hostile anorexic voice, which sees this normally acquiescent adolescent hold his own in heated verbal exchanges with parents and professionals when he perceives that they are conspiring to make him put on weight. His rageful objections are perhaps the first expression of impulsive responses within his lifespace, and so exploring with him his experience of expressing his dissent and of retaining a position of strength in these challenging situations is a valuable intervention. The therapist's fundamental task is the encouragement of the adolescent's impulsive voice to neutralise his overly developed inhibitive approach to experience. Spontaneity in voice and in contact, initially within the therapeutic space, and latterly extending to more regions of his lifespace, supports the development of a more directional configuration for the adolescent. This is the work of the adolescent psychotherapist, not engagement in a refeeding programme.

Emma

Eighteen-year-old Emma attended the initial contact assessment meeting along with her parents, who had grown increasingly concerned about her state of mind and recent weight loss. As her mother began to describe her urgent concern, I noted Emma's embodied expression of frustration and contempt. My participation in these conversations may possibly translate to the adolescent as collusion in the adult-world project of making her fat and I have learned to quickly park the issue of food and weight during contact assessment, as the adolescent shuts down a little more with every shaming, threatening sentence uttered.

Acknowledging her mother's concern, I indicated the need to involve the family GP, who may make a referral to the appropriate service, explaining that refeeding and weight gain are not the work of adolescent psychotherapy, assuring the parents that there were medically trained experts who attend to these issues much better than I. Offering a rationale that an imbalanced relationship with food and the body is often an indication of deeper unhappiness supports parents to widen their lens and see the value of psychotherapy in attending to these underlying themes in their child's experience. Turning to Emma, I indicated that if she wished to come see me, I would very definitely not be getting interested in this issue and embarking on a refeeding programme. Instead, my interest would be in supporting her wider lifespace experience, finding out about how she experienced the world, her family, friends, school and her future intentions, and hopefully helping her to feel more assured and satisfied in her life. My explicit disengagement from this potential power struggle created the first possibility of ongoing meaningful connection between us. Emma's relief was tangible, as evidenced in her more relaxed breath and body. She lifted her head and made substantial eye contact. Throughout the meeting, whilst verbally she gave very little, posturally she let me know that she was feeling met and was curious about our contact.

As the initial meeting unfolded, some potentially relevant aspects of family life were revealed, including an interruptive episode of heavy drinking by her father, who had been sober now for several years. As her parents tried to figure out the timeline of his drinking, this relatively passive and muted adolescent energetically sat up in her chair, reached towards her parents and somewhat aggressively said, "from I was eight until I was fifteen", after which she sat back, readopting her apparently quiescent poise. Emma was the eldest of three siblings, with twin brothers aged fourteen, and was repeating her final year at secondary school, having missed out on being offered a place to study medicine at university. Her parents described her dream from childhood of becoming a doctor and the family's shock that their academically brilliant daughter had failed her biology exam by one mark. It also emerged that the impetus to seek therapeutic support at this point followed a dramatic self-harming incident in recent weeks where Emma got drunk and slashed both her legs from thigh to ankle with a broken bottle. As the dialogue unfolded, I ensured minimal exposure for Emma, framing her disappointments and challenges sensitively and supporting her parents to reflect on family process. I elected not to invite the adolescent to commit to a further meeting as the session concluded because, whilst contact was subtly deepening between us, my hunch was that commitment to attending may have equated to conceding to parental wishes. And so I invited them all to reflect on our conversation and to get in touch if Emma would like to come back, which I knew she would and which she did.

Our next meeting was a one-to-one session in which we reviewed the initial dialogue. I translated her spontaneous response and precise recall of the duration of her father's years of drinking, as a statement of the significance of this time as a painful chapter in her life, suggesting that she was holding more hurt around the experience than her parents might have imagined. I framed her experience of school as exposing and humiliating, as she was predicted top grades and now was in the potentially shameful position of repeating the year, offering my hunch that she felt like a failure and was holding considerable disappointment at the delay in her dream to become a doctor one day. Emma's voice emerged tentatively in our dialogue as she responded to my reframing of her experience. Therapeutic contact became increasingly relaxed and less remote.

Inhibitively configured adolescents are generally reserved in their expression and reaching, which is partly why I did not push her to decide about a second session at the end of the first, and why she spoke hesitantly and was slow to warm up in our contact. Introducing sideways contact to support and strengthen contact boundaries, I invited Emma to paint during the session, having placed materials by her. The potential of a blank canvas, both literally and metaphorically, creates uncertainty and reticence for the inhibitive adolescent who finds security in living by guidelines and who is largely disconnected from her impulses. Initially she expressed disinterest, though later, as I saw her glance at the paints, I guided her to lift the paintbrush with her non-dominant hand, dip it in the colour which interested her most and make a single mark on the page. Once the initial mark was made, I encouraged Emma to keep going and as she became absorbed in painting, an image emerged of a floating figure whose hair fell over one eye and whose mouth had been sealed with barbed wire (Figure 8.2). I wondered what was hidden from this figure's right-side view. I was also struck by the potency of the clamped mouth and considered how painful it might be to eat or speak – that is, to accept or express anything in the world. I sensed it may be premature and potentially exposing to share my thoughts with the adolescent in these emerging moments of therapeutic contact and trusted that an opportune moment to introduce my reflection would present itself in time.

Figure 8.2 Emma, floating and muted

During the following session, as the adolescent painted another similar image, we explored her experience in the family. Emma recounted two particularly poignant memories associated with her father's drinking – the first when she was 8 years old and excited that her older cousin was coming to babysit as her parents, who rarely went out together, were going for dinner to celebrate their anniversary. She walked to the local shop to buy sweets and choose a movie to watch with her cousin, waiting excitedly all day for her cousin to arrive. She recalled her father arriving home drunk after work, which resulted in the evening being cancelled. Emma described her sorrow that everyone's plans had been ruined by her father and her irritation that neither an apology was issued nor her disappointment acknowledged. Emma also recounted an incident at age 14 when her mother spent a number of weeks in a hospital several hours drive from the family home. It had been organised that her father would take the children to visit their mother one evening after school. As Emma and her siblings got off the school bus, a taxi carrying her intoxicated father arrived at the house. She felt angry, alone and weighed down by the responsibility of having to take care of her younger brothers. Later in the work, during a joint session with her father, Emma was supported to articulate these memories and her experience of his years of drinking, which was a healing and empowering moment for the adolescent, if somewhat difficult for her father to hear.

As we explored the adolescent's relationship with her mother, it emerged that throughout the drinking years, Emma had been her mother's confidante and primary support; however, sobriety had compromised their close connection. During a session in which all three participated, Emma articulated her experience of feeling dislocated, having lost her place in the family now that her mother no longer needed her support. The adolescent's mother conceded that since Emma's father had stopped drinking and was participating more in family life, the couple had become closer and she no longer felt it necessary to seek support from her daughter. As they developed greater insight into the inhibitive family culture which had shaped family relatedness, both parents recognised that failure to acknowledge either the impact of the alcoholism on family life or the change in family dynamics which resulted from her father's sobriety had been difficult for Emma. Meetings became more contactful, and support for Emma's voice meant that she was increasingly comfortable at holding her own in these dialogic encounters with her parents.

As a greater depth of trust and spontaneity emerged within the therapeutic space, during a one-to-one session, Emma spoke of the self-harm incident which happened on a recent night out with friends. She seldom drank and rarely went out, though as her friends were returning from college at Christmas, she felt she ought to make the effort. The thought of seeing her former classmates made her cringe as she felt the humiliation of repeating her final school year and so she decided to get drunk. After smashing a bottle and cutting both her legs, one of her friends called Emma's parents, who drove her to the local A&E department.

During the journey, her parents wondered if they were doing the right thing by taking her to hospital as this would appear on her medical record which may jeopardise her entry into medical school. Instead they phoned their GP who was also a family friend, who instructed them on how to dress the wounds. As we unpacked this experience, Emma described her memory of sitting in the back of the car bleeding, parked outside a hospital and in need of medical attention, whilst her parents made the decision to drive home to protect her dream of becoming a doctor. She tearfully expressed a strong sense of her parents caring more about her career than they did about her, indicating that this dream to be a doctor was in fact theirs. She felt utterly missed by her parents. During our dialogue, the adolescent developed the familiar artistic theme of herself floating and muted. This image included a fire in the foreground which represented her experience of the pressure she felt within her lifespace and said this was what she has been avoiding looking at with her hair draped over her eye in previous artwork (Figure 8.3). The adolescent expressed relief at giving voice to and visually representing her experience.

Emma revealed that her personal ambition was to own a vintage tea and cake shop where she would play alternative music on vinyl and sell art, though she was realistic that having a profession would be a prudent move at this time in her life

Figure 8.3 Emma's avoidance comes into focus

and so she began to explore her possibilities. She loved science and considered studying biomedical science, deciding that working in lab environment would suit her better than being a doctor as she was shy around people, and the research aspect of the work appealed more to her. We scheduled the next session to include Emma and both parents once again to explore the agenda of her studying medicine and this new development regarding choice of study programme. As Emma articulated her experience of feeling that her career mattered more to them that she did, both parents conceded that, whilst Emma had talked about being a doctor as a child, they had driven the idea through her adolescence, influencing her choices because they believed she was so capable. Emma's parents supported her decision to take ownership of this second college application process, albeit with a hint of disappointment that she had chosen biomedical science over medicine. Towards the end of this session, Emma's mother expressed concern that whilst the psychotherapy process was proving beneficial, her daughter continued to lose weight, restrict her food intake and over-exercise despite attending the local Child and Adolescent Mental Health Service where she was under the care of a consultant psychiatrist, dietician and cognitive-behavioural therapist. Mindful of Emma's inclination to become withdrawn and guarded at the mention of food or weight, I suggested that next time she and I might explore her tendency towards rigidity which seemed to emerge in respect of academics and food, to which she was agreeable.

Emma arrived to the next session with a vividly altered physical appearance. Her long, lank brown hair had been cut short and dyed pink. Her baggy clothes had been replaced by a tight-fitting top, fishnet stockings, leather skirt and boots. She exuded a notably increased faith in herself, which I suspected has been mobilised by the exertion of her choicefulness and the parental support she had received for this. Her spontaneous voice had emerged powerfully, and it was now time to create a more challenging concern-denial power struggle for Emma with regards to the anorexia.

With the cultivation of relational ground and the adolescent's trust that the therapist's agenda was not to make her fat, ironically, she began to reveal this otherwise highly defended aspect of her experience. As our exploration was framed through the lens of meaning-making rather than weight management, Emma engaged in a candid dialogue with me about her relationship to her body, food and exercise, disclosing her eating habits and describing her fear of putting on weight. I invited her to express any concern she held with regard to this rigidity, prompting the adolescent to recount a recent reunion with her best friend who had returned home from college for a few days. Emma described feeling anxious that their meeting would involve food as it had been arranged that they would meet in a coffee shop. On the way to meet her friend, Emma was preoccupied with what she should eat – she wanted a wrap but panicked when she arrived and ordered a black coffee, lying that she had already eaten. The next evening, they both decided to order a takeaway and watch movies together at her friend's house. Emma hid her plate under a cushion and worried throughout the evening about how, if discovered, she might explain that she did not eat any food. As she reflected on the experience, the adolescent was saddened to realise that contact with this friend was wholly overshadowed by her preoccupation with food. This insight facilitated the expansion of this theme of restriction and rigidity, and we had a similar dialogue regarding exercise. The adolescent became aware of the extent to which her inhibitive configuration impacted many aspects of her lifespace and developed motivation to challenge her inhibitively configured relationship to food and exercise.

As spontaneity emerged within the adolescent's lifespace – in contact generally and in her relationship to her body, food and exercise specifically – she learned to tolerate uncertainty and adequacy, moving away from her rigid demand for certainty and perfection. In a spirit of curiosity, the adolescent began to experiment with developing a relationship with '*enough*': enough study, enough exercise, good enough, smart enough, thin enough, etc., and as the need for external acceptability loosened its grip, Emma began to appreciate the redundancy of inhibition in her life and moved into a more directional mode of relating within her lifespace.

The impulsively configured adolescent

At the other end of the spectrum is the adolescent, just as pained and shamed about his body as his stick-thin counterpart, and equally for whom enough is never enough. The binge-eating adolescent's relationship with food is strongly impulsive. This creative adjustment appears, in many cases, to mirror a family style of impulsivity (Zerbe, 2008). Appetite is relentlessly awakened and in need of satisfaction. Yearnings are experienced physiologically and are translated into desire for pizza, crisps and chocolate. His inhibitive intentions are overtaken by his impulse to eat which he often experiences as out of control, creating an ongoing sense of distress and humiliation about his body. He tends to be preoccupied with his weight, berating himself for his lack of self-control and recycling through moments of intense self-loathing and great intention to lose weight, all the time battling his urge to satisfy his yearnings by overeating (Lask and Bryant-Waugh, 2013).

The adolescent struggling with bulimia does his best to remain inhibitively configured; however, his strong inclination towards impulsivity draws him into a more sporadic relationship with food as the inevitable impulse overtakes his inhibitive intentions. He experiences a pervasive sense of shame and disgust for his body shape, his binge-purge behaviours and himself generally (Zerbe, 1995). He feels repulsed by himself, making himself sick both literally and metaphorically. The possibility of disclosure about his bulimia is daunting, given the depth of shame he experiences and his expectation that the therapist will reject him on learning about how revolting he really is.

Ciaran

Fifteen-year-old Ciaran's parents discovered that he had been self-harming when he disclosed his behaviour to a friend whose parents informed Ciaran's mother and father. The adolescent's mother was extremely overweight and his father was a heavy drinker. As part of our one-to-one dialogue, we explored Ciaran's relationship to his body. He did not like the way he looked: he felt fat and was urging his parents to permit him to have surgery to remove his 'man boobs'. The adolescent also told me about his rigorous diet consisting mainly of protein which supported his exercise regime as he had a strong desire to become more muscular through weight training.

As we explored the phenomenology of his self-harming behaviours, he described intense self-loathing which had followed him since childhood. Ciaran was an overweight child and easy prey for peer humiliation, being bullied by several boys in his class throughout primary school. He experienced himself as defective and somehow deserving of the intimidation and humiliation, and it was evident that he still felt the shameful impact of this integrity compromise. During one session, as we dialogued, Ciaran created two images as he doodled (Figure 8.4), describing the first as representative of the cutting experience, with the monster's teeth symbolising the blade's incision causing the flow of blood. The second was a character from the Harry Potter series known as a *Dementor* (Rowling and GrandPré, 2003).

Many bulimic adolescents feel disgusting and noting the presence of my uncharacteristic subverbal self-reproach as well as a ravenous hunger for refined sugar prior to Ciaran's appointments, I had a hunch that I was picking up information

Figure 8.4 Ciaran's expressions of self-directed disgust

about my client. I waited for an appropriate moment to introduce the possibility of bulimic behaviour into our dialogue. His artwork offered this space and I tentatively noted how the monster looked like he was vomiting, adding that people who didn't like themselves very much sometimes made themselves sick after they had eaten. Ciaran assured me that this was not the case. During the following session, the adolescent referred to the doodles he made and indicated that he did indeed force himself to throw up sometimes. He admitted that he wanted to tell me from the outset, though he couldn't because he liked me and he was sure I would judge and reject him if he did. This was a plausible assumption and his reticence was understandable given the disgusting nature of the behaviours associated with the bulimic cycle.

Ciaran then revealed how he had two toothbrushes in the bathroom – one for brushing his teeth and the second for pushing down his throat to force himself to vomit. Sometimes he threw up in the toilet, other times in the shower. He also made himself sick in his bedroom whilst playing loud music to conceal the sound, vomiting into plastic bags and hoarding them in wardrobes and under his bed. He kept these as reminders of how disgusting he was, lest he forget. I appreciated his courage in telling me and expressed my gladness that he had allowed me to join him in this isolated and wretched place. Ciaran was both relieved and deeply shamed at his disclosure. It was important that I did not minimise his shame by creating a positive veneer over his disgust. Rather, the seeds of transformation were sown in our joining and acknowledgement. It was healing for Ciaran to experience how I could see beyond these nauseating behaviours, holding no disgust for him. Later in the session, I told him that I had since researched a little about *Dementors* and read aloud the description I had found of them:

> *Dementors are among the foulest creatures that walk this earth. They infest the darkest, filthiest places, they glory in decay and despair, they drain peace, hope, and happiness out of the air around them. . . . Get too near a Dementor and every good feeling, every happy memory will be sucked out of you. If it can, the Dementor will feed on you long enough to reduce you to something like itself . . . soulless and evil. You will be left with nothing but the worst experiences of your life.*
>
> (Harry Potter Wiki, 2018)

I wondered if this resonated at all for Ciaran who responded that "this sounds just like me". As we expanded our dialogue, the adolescent experienced both sadness and relief at being met in the depths of his shame.

As the work progressed, Ciaran spoke of his contempt for his morbidly obese mother whom he was mortified to be seen with. He ensured that she dropped him off some distance away from school in the mornings lest his peers see her and humiliate him. He was resentful that she created an unhealthy childhood diet for her children and was utterly terrified that he would become as fat as she was. The adolescent described a lifespace filled with shame and preoccupation about body shape and food from his earliest memories.

As Ciaran began to appreciate his impulsive configuration, he made meaning of his self-harming and bulimic behaviours as creative adjustments to this preoccupation, to the impulsivity which had characterised family life and to the childhood bullying he had endured. Compassion and insight soon translated into an eagerness to maintain balance within his lifespace. With support he moved into a more directional manner of being, which was challenged for a time when he began experimenting with alcohol. During this episode, impulsivity became problematic within his lifespace, heralding the return of the bulimic and cutting behaviour for several months. The adolescent appreciated his propensity towards impulsivity, though now understood that he could be choiceful, and that choice implied directionality.

References

Bruch, H. (2001). *The Golden Cage*. London: Harvard University Press.

Harry Potter Wiki. (2018). *Dementor*. Available at: http://harrypotter.wikia.com/wiki/Dementor [Accessed 18 Apr. 2018].

Lask, B. and Bryant-Waugh, R., eds. (2013). *Eating Disorders in Childhood and Adolescence* (4th ed.). London: Routledge.

Muris, P., Meesters, C., van de Blom, W. and Mayer, B. (2005). Biological, psychological, and sociocultural correlates of body change strategies and eating problems in adolescent boys and girls. *Eating Behaviors*, 6(1), pp. 11–22.

Rowling, J. and GrandPré, M. (2003). *Harry Potter and the Order of the Phoenix*. New York: Arthur A. Levine Books.

Zerbe, K. (1995). *The Body Betrayed*. Carlsbad, CA: Gürze Books.

Zerbe, K. (2008). *Integrated Treatment of Eating Disorders*. New York: W. W. Norton & Company, Inc.

Chapter 9

Alcohol and drugs

Experimentation with alcohol and drugs forms part of the adolescent experience for most young people. Whilst some use in moderation, many participate in the socially embedded practice of recreational binging. This cultural phenomenon has virtually become the norm in many peer groupings and whilst their overindulgence may be a source of grave concern for adults, the majority manage to avoid getting caught in a world of danger and high risk (Siegel, 2013). Thankfully, for most adolescents, whilst they may engage in regretful and cringeworthy behaviour from time to time when drunk or high, substance use does not adversely obstruct their developmental path (Kegan, 2003). However, life tends to be more problematic for the impulsively configured adolescent whose relationship to alcohol and drugs is centrally located within his lifespace.

The adolescent whose lifespace is generally balanced and supported tends to "enjoy the party", yet has developed a capacity to consider other aspects of his lifespace when negotiating his emerging impulses. He may want to get drunk and smoke cannabis all weekend with his friends, but recognises that he has homework to complete, that his parents will be unimpressed and that, despite the fun he might have, a weekend of substance abuse is not a great idea; so he decides to go home at a reasonable hour. He has developed the capacity to recognise and consider the lifespace implications of his emerging impulses, at least to some degree. In contrast, the adolescent whose relationship to alcohol and drugs is impulsively configured does not organise his experience in this manner. He *feels* like getting drunk or high and this impulse becomes powerfully figural so that other aspects of his lifespace lose their significance. By downplaying his responsibilities, he convinces himself that he does not care about his homework or what his parents think. When he experiences his impulse as particularly potent, he is heavily invested in avoiding the thought of anything other than fulfilling his urge to party.

The inclination to satisfy his impulses without wider lifespace consideration is typical of many younger adolescents. However, impulsivity leading to problematic substance misuse may also emerge in situations where the family field is impulsively configured or as a creative adjustment to the experience of trauma (Van der Kolk, 2015). The capacity to thoughtfully consider his impulses and to act in a directional manner which supports his lifespace integrity is a developmental achievement for the adolescent (McConville, 1995), who, because he has not yet developed the art of regulating his impulses through thoughtful and responsible discernment, tends to be on the receiving end of criticism and reproach from adults who demand that he abstain from this selfish and irresponsible behaviour. He typically experiences contact with adults as shaming due to the discrepancy between their expectations and his developmental capacity. Parents are inclined to reprimand, punish, lecture and nag in a bid to influence him, which typically results in the adolescent becoming artful at avoiding contact with the adult world, often experiencing himself as a disappointment to them, which potentially reinforces his creative adjustment.

Towards directionality

As the issue of problematic alcohol or drug use is identified, the therapist's focus is on supporting the adolescent to develop a more directional manner of relating to his impulses, carefully avoiding power struggles or falling into the therapeutic reactions of urgency and despair. If she finds herself in lecture mode about the hazards of overindulgence, she can be certain that therapeutic contact has become remote and she is wise to stop talking lest she lose the adolescent entirely. Rather, once adequate relational ground has been established, she cultivates a concern-denial power struggle for the adolescent, challenging him to adopt greater ownership of his lifespace experience.

The adolescent whose substance use gives cause for concern tends to focus his interest on the immediate present. Any long-term plans are typically unrealistic given the discrepancy between his current lifestyle and the commitment required for actualising this vision for the future, such is the nature of his impulsive configuration. The adolescent cannot become a choiceful, active organiser of his lifespace experience until he develops the capacity to relate to his impulses and spontaneity in a manner which supports his integrity. Encouraging the adolescent to reflect on both his creative adjustment of substance abuse and on his wider lifespace experience fosters his inhibitive capacity, which is a necessary step towards a more directionally configured lifespace. This process is not so much about behaviour modification as a developmental shift, which often takes time to grow into. As he becomes interested in how he constructs his experience, and how this process often undermines his integrity, the adolescent begins to take himself more seriously and mobilise towards choicefulness.

James

Seventeen-year-old James finally conceded to attending therapy as he had recently been sacked from an apprenticeship placement for failing to arrive at work on a number of occasions, having developed a penchant for extending his weekends to include Fridays and Mondays. His presence at the contact assessment was an attempt to appease his parents who were desperately concerned about his weekend binging on alcohol and methamphetamine. The adolescent was neither concerned for himself nor interested in embarking on a process of psychotherapy: losing his placement was no big deal. He'd simply get another one. He could handle his partying, if only his parents would calm down.

To avoid power struggling by adding my voice to the attempt to convince James that he needed therapy to overcome his problematic and potentially addictive behaviour, I widened the dialogue by inviting the adolescent and his parents to discuss family life and their experience of one another. I heard the description of someone who had been impulsively configured from childhood and whose substance abuse was an extension of his cavalier approach to life. As James' parents were supported to access the yearnings beneath their persistent criticism, they expressed their love and care for their son, and their disappointment that, despite having huge potential, he seemed determined to sabotage his future. They described the impact of the stress and concern they were learning to live with in their lives, including having to hide car keys to ensure that he did not drive whilst drunk or high and having to secure a several thousand pounds bank loan to repay drug debt he had accrued. James's mother engaged well and despite being invested in the process, his father was evidently uncomfortable in a therapist's office, averting his gaze and nervously laughing at times. To support the adolescent, I offered my hunch that all this nagging and criticism must be difficult to tolerate and that he likely felt stressed living at home with his parents. Supporting his mother and father to attune to their son's experience, I invited them to consider family life from James's perspective. This facilitated James, who made contact in the manner one might expect a 12- or 13-year-old to conduct himself, to articulate more of his experience. As each person began to feel supported by me and without directly naming James' alcohol and drug use, I suggested a return visit to support the family during this stressful episode.

During the next session, following a short time with all three together, James and I spent most of the hour talking without his parents present. I made this intervention to meet James in a one-to-one situation to integrate the dialogue thus far and because I sensed that he could tolerate and was yearning for richer contact. I reminded the adolescent that my agenda was not to influence his partying behaviour, but that I was interested in supporting him to feel less stressed in the world, especially within parenting spaces. We reviewed the joint parental dialogue and I reflected on my experience of his father as quite repressed and uncomfortable in himself. James described his father as overly moralistic and unnecessarily panicked about his son's substance use simply because he was a recovering alcoholic and could not tolerate his son enjoying himself. He found his parents insufferable at times and could hardly wait to buy a car and move into his own place as soon as he got a job. The adolescent found the relaxed tone of our dialogue supportive and was agreeable to continuing the work.

The initial stage of psychotherapy with the impulsively configured adolescent requires patient sensitivity and involves supporting the development of insight into his behaviour as creative adjustment to compromised integrity, as well as collaborative dialogue regarding adolescent configuration styles – in short, the therapist attempts to get the adolescent interested in himself. Once this ground has been established, therapeutic dialogue may extend to his substance use. Premature challenge and therapeutic reactions of urgency and despair are avoided to ensure richness of contact.

I suggested that James and his father, Paddy, met with me to discuss their relationship in depth. I learned during the contact assessment that his father had stopped drinking before James was born and continued to attend regular AA meetings. The pair had enjoyed a close, though fairly wordless connection throughout James's childhood and early teenage years, with a shared passion for sport and cars until alcohol and drugs guided the adolescent in a different direction, and his father adopted a posture of intolerance. As they entered my office, James looked decidedly uncomfortable and I sensed tension between them. At the meeting commenced, Paddy articulated that they *'had a bit of a falling out on Saturday night, but I think it's okay now'*. He looked nervously at his son. As I invited them to explore what had happened, James said, *'No, let's go upstairs'*, and was clearly uncomfortable at the idea of joint dialogue. As he and I sat together, the adolescent recounted his experience of Saturday night, describing how he wanted to watch a boxing match at his friend's house. His father did not believe him, assuming that James was planning to go to a birthday party in the next town, and forbade him to go. When Paddy later learned that James had gone out regardless, he contacted his son by telephone and during a heated exchange, told him "not to bother coming home". James, who had gone to watch the boxing match, hung up and refused to answer his phone for the remainder of the evening. The adolescent left his friend's house and went to the local playpark where he had always gone when he needed to be alone. He cried and felt very lonely; he couldn't believe that his father had said what he did. Several hours later, when he could no longer stand the cold, the adolescent reluctantly went home. His father was waiting for him, stood up and said, 'let's forget about it'. They shook hands, though this did not mean anything to James, who felt that his relationship with his father had been irrevocably damaged since this episode.

I suggested that we involve Paddy in the dialogue, indicating that it was important he was made aware of the impact of his words on his son. James agreed when I indicated that he would not be required to speak, if he did not wish to do so. Paddy, who owned a bar in town, described how he had heard earlier on Saturday about this birthday party and assumed that James would make plans to go. Both father and son acknowledged that this was a reasonable assumption, given James's poor track record with regard to being where he said he would be on nights out. I asked Paddy how he thought James might have experienced his words during their telephone conversation, to which he replied, 'sure you say things on the spur of the moment that you regret'. I supported Paddy to offer a more contactful response by inviting him to share how he felt when the phone call ended. He immediately regretted his words and tried to call James back, but his son wouldn't answer his phone, turning it off after a while. Paddy described how worried he became about the impact of his words on James, frightened that his son might 'do something stupid'. He was frantic and very angry at himself. As I indicated that I saw tears in his eyes, Paddy burst into tears and sobbed uncontrollably. James also became tearful. I translated their tears into a statement of care and love for one another. Afterwards I asked James what it was like to see his father cry. He responded by saying that for some time he had doubted his father still loved him but knew now that he did. I remarked at how important it had been to include Paddy in the dialogue, so that James was made aware of what happened for his dad in the phone call.

This dialogic encounter softened the ground for deeper exploration of James' alcohol and drug use. I invited his father to talk about his own adolescent years, his path to becoming sober and his intolerance for James' partying. This was helpful for James to hear and it was possible now to frame Paddy's criticism and tough standpoint on James' behaviour as care and concern. His father's expression of this concern touched his son and James became more contactful in the dialogue. Following this session, contact between father and son grew richer and more relaxed. I involved Paddy in the next few sessions and was careful to translate any criticism and challenge as statements by this father of care and concern for his son. This re-establishment of receptivity within the parenting space created significant support for James as he became more directionally configured.

One important aspect of the work in supporting the impulsively configured adolescent is the subtle creation of discomfort with regard to his impulsivity. James was immersed in a binge culture which promoted heavy drinking and recreational drug taking. Rather than focusing on his impulsivity, which potentially would create a power struggle, James and I initially explored the pay-offs of his party lifestyle. As is typical of many Irish adolescent males, he was not in the least bit concerned about his partying. In fact, he took pride in being able to handle his drink. Being a drinker was a core feature of his identity and because, in his partying world, young men who drink heavily are 'men's men', James found respect, status and belonging within this world. Subsequently, any lecturing about the dangers of the demon drink, whether by his parents or a therapist, would be met with ridicule.

As we explored this aspect of his lifespace, James appreciated how respect, status and belonging had been missing from his life up until now and how he had always craved them. The adolescent described his experience within his family, of growing up with sisters who were well-behaved and smart, and how he was perpetually in trouble and being reprimanded by parents. He spoke of a 'naughty chair' in his house that only he was ever sent to as a child. James then tracked his experience of school through childhood and adolescence, where again, he tended to be the focus of the teacher's admonishments within every class. He learned to become the class clown and not take academics seriously. As the adolescent explored peer friendships, he came to see how he was always the entertainer, though lacked close friendships and would feel sad that he was overlooked for birthday party invitations and sleep overs. As we scratched the surface of this aspect of his lifespace, James reflected on how his behaviour was often outrageous to get laughs, though this behaviour, which was an attempt to connect with peers may actually have served to keep them at arm's length. He felt disappointed by the realisation that peers enjoyed his company for its entertainment quality, though did not consider him a friend. When I suggested that perhaps by not taking himself seriously he was inviting other people to do the same and relate to him similarly, James agreed. This aspect of our dialogue softened the ground for more honest reflection with regard to his current lifespace configuration as I told James that my hunch was that he continued to not take himself seriously in the world.

I indicated to the adolescent that I had no intention of getting him to stop drinking or taking drugs, but that I wanted to support him to have as meaningful a life as he could have, though it seemed to me that his partying was a continuation of his modus operandi as a child and younger adolescent. This subtle expression of my concern was focused on his integrity rather than his partying lifestyle and as such, he could tolerate and accept my concern. He told me that he did not particularly like some of his friends and felt somewhat out of his depth in this new world at times, especially with regard to their drug culture. Some of these new friends were also engaged in other criminal activity and this frightened him a little.

We explored the wisdom of becoming immersed in the world of hard partying as his heavy alcohol and recreational drug use were the criteria for membership to this particular peer group. His new friends all met in one pub and several party flats in town and their binging behaviour created a badge of belonging. This was the first time in James' young life that he had had friends and felt that he belonged. The prospect of ceasing his weekend binging on alcohol and methamphetamine meant the loss of peer friendships which, for James, equated to social suicide. James also conceded the emotional spinoff from getting high was to forget about what a disappointment he felt in the world.

Directionality was the next focus of our dialogue as I became curious about how James saw himself in the future. His principal yearning was to have a girlfriend. He also wanted a sports car and would like to emigrate to the United States or Australia. We explored each of these in turn, and I gently and subtly supported James to see for himself the discrepancies between his impulsivity and these things which he felt would make his life more satisfying. The adolescent began to identify how much of his present lifestyle was creating obstacles for him, which mobilised more of his concern. Being identified as a 'druggie' around town made him unattractive to the type of girl he would like to be with; spending all his money and accruing debt on partying, added to the potential of losing his work placement, made the prospect of being able to afford a bicycle, never mind a top of the range sports car, intangible; an occasional foray into selling drugs and his tendency to drive whilst high heightened the risk for him procuring a criminal record which may jeopardise any plans to live abroad. James slowly recognised that whilst his party lifestyle was momentarily satisfying, his impulsive configuration was keeping him caught in this cycle of behaviour. In time, he became increasingly invested in inhibiting his impulses and moving towards directionality as he took himself more seriously. The art, for the therapist, is to remain disengaged from power struggles and support the adolescent's emerging integrity.

Cannabis: 'It's actually good for you'

The adolescent who is a habitual user of cannabis is often keen to offer a rationale as to why this drug is of benefit to him: it helps with his anxiety symptoms, keeps him calm and stress free, is way better than alcohol, tobacco or other drugs, and is not addictive. In fact, it is so good for people that there is a call to legalise marijuana and it is already legal in some countries. (He and his friends are usually hatching plans to take a summer trip to Amsterdam.)

This was precisely Dan's posture when we first met just before he left home to study medicine at college. His parents brought him to see me because he seemed down following a relationship breakup and because it had been discovered that he was smoking cannabis. Dan was clearly disinterested in engaging, which I did not challenge. Instead I created a power struggle between him and his parents with regard to attendance at therapy. Dan persevered somewhat ambivalently for several months, expressing mild reluctance at the thought of attending, despite enjoying sessions and engaging well when we were together. We explored various aspects of his lifespace experience including parenting spaces, the relationship with his ex-girlfriend, peer connections, his interests and his approaching move away from home to attend college in England. However, in general, Dan did not see any particular need for therapy and remained firmly defended with regard to cannabis smoking. The principal intervention I made in relation to cannabis use was to tell him that in my experience (which comes from many conversations with boys his age who also smoke cannabis) whilst it may not be overtly addictive or destructive, cannabis was likely to diminish his motivation and create an increasing propensity towards avoidance of stressful situations in his life. Habitual users appeared to me to live their lives in a fog, as it were. I suggested that he continued to use cannabis in more choiceful awareness of these factors. He was not that bothered and was sure this did not pertain to him.

At the end of his second year I received a telephone call from Dan's mother saying that he had returned home from college for the summer and had requested to see me. The adolescent admitted that he was in difficulty with non-attendance at lectures and clinical placement and was finding it difficult to motivate himself. He shared a house with other students and while the others might smoke a joint in the evenings after lectures, his friends were fully engaging in student life. Dan, on the other hand, was not. He lived next door to a pet shop and had spent a considerable amount of his student loan and parental contribution on cannabis, fish tanks and tropical fish, and had accrued some debt because of unpaid rent. He experienced anxiety, especially in the mornings, and found that getting stoned whilst gazing at the fish soothed him and diminished this anxiety. Dan had created a safe, avoidant space for himself in a bid to regulate his anxiety levels; however, cocooning himself in this peaceful, oceanic world was creating increasing difficulty for him in many aspects of his life outside the security of his student accommodation. Parallel dialogue was a useful intervention here for the adolescent who, at birth, was induced on his tenth day overdue, empathising with him for feeling forced out of the space he yearned to inhabit.

Dan became invested in reducing his cannabis habit, though still felt that he would like to smoke recreationally to unwind in the evenings and weekends. I did not challenge this posture, though I trusted that as he became increasingly directional, the draw towards cannabis would be less appealing and he would eventually see neither place nor need for it in his life. I suggested that, whilst he was at home living with his parents for the summer months, he might consider stopping altogether until he returned to college. The adolescent agreed that this was a good idea as he did not want to get into any more trouble with his parents, to whom he had admitted his cannabis habit. It did not take long before clarity and motivation returned regarding his studies and college life, and as we explored the anxiety, Dan described feeling lost and ill-prepared to navigate college life and the wider world of adulthood which was oppressively approaching.

Dan felt pressure to be successful and described a 'suffocating' work ethic which infused his family culture. He explored his passive relationship to his lifespace and how fear of failure and of disappointing others often rendered him frozen. As clarity and motivation emerged, Dan moved in the direction of becoming increasingly directional. He was studying medicine as it seemed like a good career choice with his grades and because he knew his parents would be proud of him, however he began to question whether he wanted to continue on this study path. On reflection, he decided to return to study medicine on his own terms, made much easier by the absence of cannabis from his life. During our work together, Dan came out and expressed his fear that his father would be disappointed and unaccepting of his sexual orientation. Joint parental sessions were both supportive and affirming of Dan in many aspects of his life, including his sexual orientation. By the end of the summer break he was tentatively ready, with ongoing support, to return to college and re-engage in his life as an emerging adult.

Dan lacked faith in himself and this void was filled by good grades, sporting achievement, a girlfriend and latterly by cannabis. Therapeutic work encouraged the adolescent to stand in reflective ownership of his emerging and expanding lifespace once he was willing to hold the power struggle between concern and denial. In the end, he saw through the fog and realised that his habit was obstructing his developmental path.

References

Kegan, R. (2003). *In Over Our Heads*. Cambridge, MA: Harvard University Press.

McConville, M. (1995). *Adolescence: Psychotherapy and the Emergent Self.* San Francisco: Jossey-Bass Inc.

Siegel, D. (2013). *Brainstorm*. New York: Jeremy P. Tarcher/Penguin Books.

Van der Kolk, B. (2015). *The Body Keeps the Score*. New York: Penguin Books.

Chapter 10

Sexuality and gender

Emerging identity and boundary development

Expansion of the adolescent's lifespace includes ownership and integration of his sexual orientation and gender experience. These parts of his self-experience are to be embraced and supported if he is to live with full integrity in his world. Exploration of his feeling, thought and behavioural creative adjustments to these aspects of his identity is an important dimension of therapeutic work with the adolescent, as the therapist affords him support to accept and make meaning of who he is in terms of sexual orientation and gender experience. The therapist is often called upon to attempt to create additional environmental support and validation for his authentic self-expression where necessary, neutralising the shame of rejection and prejudice.

The developmental task of managing sexual experience and expression in a directional manner, irrespective of how he defines himself with regard to orientation and gender, presents a difficult challenge for many adolescents. Burgeoning sexual impulse is influenced by the adolescent's developmental immaturity, his yearnings for acceptance within the peer landscape, as well as his capacity to navigate social media with integrity, and his use of alcohol and drugs. Heightened feelings of sexual arousal happen within an expanding lifespace whose context may also include hostile parenting, sexual trauma, an impulsive configuration style and digital addiction. These factors may make it difficult for him to manage his sexual impulses appropriately, resulting, for some, in sexually abusive behaviour towards others. The important issue of sexual integrity is addressed with each adolescent to support him towards achieving a safe, empowered and respectful relationship to sexuality and sexual expression within his lifespace.

Choiceful sexual expression

Today's adolescent, irrespective of orientation or gender identity, is presented with a confusing dilemma. On the one hand, he is supported to conduct his sex life responsibly and respectfully through exposure to informative sex education programmes and having parents who are more willing than ever before to engage in open dialogue with their adolescent children; whilst conversely, the wider world promotes a boundaryless and highly sexualised culture of indulgence and desensitisation, where impulse satisfaction equals empowerment (Damour, 2017). Information, however, does not overcome impulse; and risky, potentially compromising sexual expression is commonplace (Saleh, Grudzinskas and Judge, 2014). It is evident that something is still amiss in how adults address the need to support adolescents to think and behave with integrity regarding sexual matters.

The developmental task of this enthralling new dimension of contact is to bridge the discrepancy between the adolescent's conceptual posture regarding his sex life, how the modern world shapes his relationship to sexuality, and his behavioural response to the allure of sexual arousal. This is especially the case for today's generation of adolescents whose hyperconnection to cyberspace has become a major influence in how they perceive sexuality and engage in sexual relationships (Saleh, Grudzinskas and Judge, 2014). The disparity between moral reasoning, cultural conditioning and sexual arousal is pronounced for some adolescents, and so, despite widespread access to information, the adolescent commonly finds himself, either intentionally or inadvertently, in sexually compromising situations as he attempts to navigate this aspect of his expanding lifespace. Emerging sexuality is a complex and potentially exquisite aspect of adolescence though sadly, for many, compromised integrity defines the experience. An important dimension of psychotherapy is support for the adolescent's emerging sexual feelings and identity to foster the development of an empowered and relationally respectful sexual integrity. Addressing this sensitive issue in therapy offers the adolescent the possibility of standing in relationally attuned and choiceful ownership of his body and sexuality. The art is to present the adolescent with a tangible framework for negotiating this developmental gap, weaving the subject of sex into therapeutic dialogue in a manner which supports the growth of physiological, psychological and interpersonal sexual integrity.

Rarely does an adolescent initiate conversation about sexual matters unless his experience is problematic, for example, in the aftermath of sexual boundary violation, or as the result of a sexual encounter which has resulted in unplanned pregnancy or contraction of an STI. Adolescents typically do not wish to speak about the subject because of embarrassment and for fear of exposure, though this is not always the case. With this in mind, once relational ground is well established, the therapist indicates that having a discussion about sex might be useful. The therapist's task is to introduce and frame the dialogue in a manner which assures minimal discomfort and exposure for the young person. This typically creates an awkward withdrawal moment for the adolescent who senses exposure. The therapist quickly reassures him that she is not interested in his sexual exploits and does not even necessarily want him to join her in the dialogue. The therapist's interest, she informs him, is in supporting him to make choiceful decisions regarding sex. From the outset, she communicates to him her perspective that how he wishes to conduct himself sexually is really his business, however, in the therapist's experience, adolescents are sometimes not very artful at making these decisions, so she wants to help him think more clearly and in a more considered manner about sex. In saying this, she has put him at ease with regard to expectation for participation and disclosure within their dialogue, and has articulated to him that she wishes to support the development of his *relationship* to sexual expression. This introduction tends to create both relief and curiosity. Sexual arousal is then framed as an impulse, which like any other of the adolescent's impulses, if left uninhibited, is likely to lead away from directionality and get him into some kind of trouble. The therapist indicates that she hopes to spark the adolescent's interest in becoming directionally configured with regards to sex.

The box of chocolates metaphor

As adolescents respond well to both visual and metaphorical cues, this bridge between sexual yearning and responsibility is addressed through the metaphorical conceptualising of *desire* and *choice*. The therapist does this by paralleling the adolescent's sexuality to a box of chocolates, and in a casual manner, weaves all aspects of adolescent sexuality into their dialogue. She begins by saying that if someone were to gift a chocolate lover with a box of his favourite chocolates, his natural impulse may be to open the box immediately and eat its entire contents – because upon tasting, all one wants is *more*. And whilst this may momentarily be an immensely pleasurable experience, it is likely that he will regret his overindulgence. He may dislike the physical feeling of having eaten too much; may feel shame and become concerned about such things as his unhealthy diet and putting on weight. Eventually, if he continues to eat chocolate in such an impulsive manner, he increases his risk of diabetes and other significant compromises to his health. However, if he decides, *prior to tasting* the chocolates, precisely how many he will eat in this moment, he is much more likely to hold to his decision. So, for example, he decides that he will take only two sweets now and eat more later, eventually finishing the box over the period of several days and without the regret of impulsive overindulgence. He has much more likelihood of holding to the two sweets because of having made the decision *before experiencing the taste*. Similarly, if beforehand, he decides to eat all the chocolates, then he does so with conscious awareness of the potential implications of his decision.

The therapist suggests that sexual behaviour seems to work in much a similar manner for adolescents who, if they have not figured out how much sexual exploration they are comfortable to engage in prior to becoming sexually aroused, are likely to make decisions fuelled *by sexual arousal*. The therapist adds her hunch that decisions made in sexual arousal may not always hold integrity for either the adolescent himself or those with whom he experiences sexual contact. She proposes that they explore some aspects of sexuality in a generic manner, assuring the adolescent that the therapist does not intend to impose her value system on him and neither should he feel obliged to adopt any other person's or institution's value system with regard to his body and his sexuality. Use of this metaphorical dialogue is effective at several levels: it offers the therapist and client an indirect way of giving voice to potentially embarrassing and intensely private experience, creating a mode of *sideways contact*. At the same time, it supports the adolescent to deepen his relationship to his emerging sexuality whilst modelling a directional mode of decision-making regarding his sex life. Symbolic use of the box of chocolates is effective in exploring such issues as arousal, responsibility, consent, danger, victimisation, contraceptive use, pornography and the implications of alcohol and drug use in making decisions regarding sexual expression. It also gives the adolescent a conceptual framework to bring to mind during sexual encounter – and many report its usefulness.

There are some exceptions when this dialogue is not therapeutically appropriate, as in the case of the adolescent who appears fearfully uncomfortable and frozen at the mention of sex. It is advisable to divert the dialogue away from the issue of choiceful sexual expression as it is possible that the therapist has unwittingly stepped on a landmine of sexual trauma. Similarly, the idea of sexual feelings and identity as part of the adolescent landscape is wholly unthinkable for others. This may be a statement of wider developmental stalling which requires field intervention and attendance to other more pressing aspects of lifespace constriction before the issue of sexuality is addressed. However, in most cases, it is useful to introduce this dialogic thread into the therapeutic space for the adolescent. For the therapist who holds concern that this discussion may be premature for the younger adolescent, I am reminded of a 12-year-old girl who, as we spoke in the metaphorical language of chocolates as a mode of empowering her sense of choice and ownership, expressed regret that she had not realised that she could say 'no' and wished she had been told earlier that 'you don't have to do what the boy wants'. Waiting until after sexual experimentation has begun is often too late for the young adolescent whose emerging sexuality is already compromised.

Metaphorical dialogue encourages embodiment of directionality as opposed to impulsively configured sexual expression, promoting an empowered voice and choiceful ownership of aspects of emerging sexual expression such as online sexual activity, sexual progression when dating and contraceptive use. This capacity for choiceful, meaningful decision-making with regard to sexual matters is a developmental achievement and can be effectively supported within the therapeutic space, so long as the therapist does not power struggle through urgency, becoming prohibitive or promoting abstinence – this will create remoteness and passivity within the therapeutic space and is not a developmentally sound posture to model to a young person one is attempting to empower. The therapist's posture is always one of supporting choicefulness, promoting the adolescent's experience of respectful mutuality, and creating dilemmas for the impulsively configured adolescent.

Sexually maladaptive behaviour

The lifespace of an adolescent who perpetrates sexual abuse may include a personal experience of having been sexually abused, overexposure to sexually explicit material and the inhabiting of hostile parenting spaces (Keogh, 2018). As this context is met with a strengthening sexual impulse during puberty, the adolescent begins to compromise the integrity of others in the pursuit of impulse satisfaction and empowerment, through sexual contact which lacks integrity and mutuality. The adolescent shapes his contact around opportunities to be sexual and abuses his victim's vulnerability.

Multi-disciplinary contact is an essential component of therapeutic intervention in these situations. Working in isolation with an adolescent sex offender is unethical, as risk assessment is an important aspect of the work and this is not undertaken by an adolescent psychotherapist alone. Clearly setting the ground rules of therapy with both the adolescent and any adults involved is an important boundary to establish at the outset of therapeutic work. It is important not to power struggle with the adolescent who has been accused of sexual boundary violation, attempting, with urgency, to help him see the error of his ways. Rather, the therapist's task is to assess the adolescent's capacity for and openness to contact, and to convey her experience of this to other professionals involved in the case. Assessment includes an exploration of the adolescent's quality of contact within the therapeutic space and in all aspects of his lifespace experience, especially his willingness to engage in reflective dialogue regarding the offending behaviour. Interventions aimed at educating the adolescent in maintaining appropriate sexual boundaries and supporting him to appreciate the consequences of his actions on both himself and his victims will likely fall like a lead balloon if his contact is remote and furtive. Refusal to make meaningful therapeutic contact is communicated to other adults involved in the case, with a clear indication that the therapist continues to hold concern regarding ongoing interpersonal contact within the adolescent's wider lifespace, given his intransigence within the therapeutic space. The therapist may decide to terminate psychotherapy at this point if she determines that the work has reached an impasse, advising child protection professionals as to the context of her decision. A strongly worded, heavily circulated report containing solid recommendations is advisable if the therapist believes that the adolescent is failing to take therapeutic work seriously, as failure to take ownership of and reflect on his sexually maladaptive behaviour may point to his propensity to continue abusing children and adolescents.

If the young person chooses to engage, therapeutic work focuses on his impulsive configuration with regard to interpersonal contact in general and sexual arousal in particular. The therapist becomes most curious about the abusive reaching out and precisely how the adolescent came to translate sexual impulse into traumatising behaviour. As therapeutic trust deepens, the adolescent is supported to explore the dynamics surrounding his maladaptive behaviour including his sense of responsibility for the abuse; premeditative intent; implications for himself; and impact on his victims. Over time, the lifespace context of the adolescent's abusive behaviour is also attended to as meaning is made of the pain and trauma in his own formative experience. This aspect of the work often creates a more profound experience of empathy for the adolescent's victims as well as moving him into a more directionally configured lifespace experience. Long-term work with adolescents who transgress sexual boundaries is necessary, as appropriate interpersonal and sexual contact boundaries are a developmental achievement established over time.

Working with parents is also an important intervention as they come to terms with the trauma of parenting a child who has sexually violated another young person, which can be particularly complex if the abuse involves siblings or other young family relatives. Parenting strategy work is vital as parents play an important role in supporting the adolescent with regard to boundary development in such areas as proximity to children, monitoring screen use and general impulse management through holding the adolescent accountable for his behaviour.

Daniel

Thirteen-year-old Daniel's mother sought therapy for her son following disclosure by an 8-year-old cousin that he had sexually abused her. Parental involvement involved only the mother, as the parents separated when Daniel was three years old and Daniel's father had no contact with his son since then. He had been physically abusive to his partner, emotionally and verbally abusive to Daniel and was alcoholic. A multi-disciplinary approach to treatment included engagement with the juvenile justice system and social services. Daniel's mother struggled to believe that her son was capable of such a serious violation, though did not protest his innocence. She expressed both concern at the impact of the sexual trauma on her young niece and distress at the rupture of important family connections in the aftermath of disclosure. Daniel neither admitted nor denied the allegations, maintaining silence when confronted by his mother and other professionals.

The adolescent's developmental and social immaturity became apparent as his mother described his struggle to relate to same-age peers, though was 'brilliant' with younger children, whom he oriented towards. His best friend was a 9-year-old boy, and the adolescent had frequently been left unsupervised to care for younger neighbours and family members until disclosure. He struggled academically and attendance at school was poor as he often refused to go. Daniel's mother had indulged her son throughout his childhood and now appeared to lack any capacity to influence him. Since separating from Daniel's father, she had been in several relationships, which involved new partners moving in and out the family home on several occasions. She worked as an assistant in a local primary school and in her spare time wrote erotic novels.

Joint parent-adolescent work was the sole intervention during the early stage of psychotherapy. Daniel's initial lack of willingness to engage in therapeutic work, as evidenced through passive disinterest and silence, gradually gave way to some degree of openness in our dialogue. We explored the mother-son relationship and the adolescent reflected on his mother's inclination towards emotional inconsistency, which confused him. She would often become frustrated and shout at him, which would invariably end in her becoming tearful, demanding an apology for his behaviour and requiring a hug from him. Parenting strategy work supported this mother to re-establish some boundaries and influence as she began holding her son accountable for his behaviour to some degree. As we spoke of the potential impact of the paternal parenting space, Daniel expressed contempt for his father and was supported in making meaning of the implications of this hostile parenting space in his wider lifespace experience.

During a session where Daniel and his mother spoke of his close and loving relationship with his aunt whom he had not seen since her daughter had made the allegations of sexual abuse, the adolescent began to sob. He described how he missed her and how his life 'was hell now'. At this point, as Daniel became more reachable and amenable to support, the one-to-one work commenced. The adolescent engaged in some potentially meaningful and influential therapeutic work with regards to developing insight into and integrating many difficult aspects of his lifespace experience, in addition to exploring appropriate boundary development. However, despite becoming increasingly contactful, Daniel continued to strenuously deny the allegations of sexual abuse, maintaining his innocence and failing to take responsibility for his behaviour, which was communicated to the appropriate agencies. Daniel's mother terminated the work when they relocated to another area.

Sexual orientation and gender experience

People experience a felt sense of orientation and gender from early childhood, though defining, making meaning of and giving deeper expression to this experience generally begins in earnest during adolescence. Emerging sexual orientation and gender identity is an organic lifespace phenomenon which, if supported, brings rich and vivid lifespace integrity. For the young person who defines himself as heterosexual and feels no discrepancy between his physiological and psychological gender experience, there is no issue with self-definition as his sexual and gender identity position him as 'typical' within our society. The adolescent, on the other hand, who is located outside of these social norms may be defined as 'different'. He is not different; he is simply expressing his felt sense of orientation and gender. The shame potential here is enormous, however, as it is not his expression of orientation or gender which creates shame, but rather the environment's relationship to his positioning as not 'typical'. Communicating this to the adolescent is crucial so that he does not internalise environmental hostility as a statement about the self as somehow defective.

It is important that the therapist does not make assumptions with regard to orientation and gender with any young person as this creates shame and therapeutic isolation for the adolescent who is attempting to define and make meaning of his experience. Avoiding assumption communicates openness and space for the adolescent to introduce these aspects of self-experience into the dialogue. As the conversation begins, the therapist's validating reception of the adolescent informs him that he can count on her for support. Regardless of how the adolescent defines himself, it is important that the therapist does not treat his revelation as an 'issue' because it is not one. Rather, as a first intervention, the therapist meets the young person's statement about his identity by exploring the *process* of telling as opposed to the *content*. In doing so, the therapist ensures that the therapeutic space remains contactful and free from shame. She might say, "*I'm glad that you were able to bring this important part of your identity into our dialogue. I'm wondering what it was like to tell me?*"

Following this exchange, it is useful to enquire if the adolescent is *certain* or *questioning*, as he may have clear definition of his sexual orientation and gender identity or may be engaged in a process of curiosity and exploration. With certainty, the therapist supports the exploration of both the adolescent's phenomenological experience of his emerging identity and the level of lifespace support available to him. When the adolescent's response is that he is questioning, then it is helpful to support him to do so freely, mindful that some adolescents feel the need to definitively label their sexual orientation and gender experience as a matter of urgency. Each adolescent's emerging sexual expression unfolds *relationally*, and so, creating support for him to trust this emerging experience and to tolerate the uncertainty of not having a clearly defined sexual orientation is important for him to arrive at a place of knowing with integrity and clarity.

As we become a more progressive and inclusive society, principally because of the efforts of the LGBTQi community to be acknowledged and validated as people of integrity, growing acceptance of diversity regarding sexual orientation is making a difference in the lives of adolescents who identify as lesbian, gay or bisexual (Singer, 2001). Regrettably, there is less support for those young people for whom gender identity emerges as figural in their lives. For the adolescent who experiences discrepancy between the physiological, interpersonal and psychological aspects of his gender experience, social shaming of his atypical gender expression can be pronounced, which gives context to his disproportionately high level of internalised shame and vulnerability (Reisner et al., 2016). Here, the therapist's support is a powerful antidote to the shame of discrimination and marginalisation which potentially pervades the young person's lifespace as he embraces his transgendered experience.

Roisin

Roisin, a 14-year-old adolescent, was referred for therapy as she had been self-harming and seemed subdued of late. Previously she had appeared happy both at home and school, enjoyed peer friendships and was an interested student. Roisin's parents were concerned that she had started to hate school and had become isolated within her year group. During one-to-one work, as trust was growing, Roisin nervously said to me, "I have something to tell you . . . I'm pretty sure I'm not straight". I welcomed her telling me and we explored the process of disclosure. The adolescent had been 'bursting' to tell me. However, Roisin feared that I would tell her parents immediately (a commonly held concern for younger adolescents regarding disclosure of sexual orientation to a therapist). My response indicated a receptive posture: I expressed confusion as to why I might feel the need to tell her parents, adding that it would be most peculiar if she had just told me that she was heterosexual and I immediately felt the urge to tell her parents that she was attracted to boys. This explanation of the absurdity in making her sexual orientation an issue assured Roisin that shame would not be present in any dialogue regarding her emerging sexual identity. I also pointed out that knowing what she *wasn't* was a good beginning, rather than needing to know what she *was*, and supporting her to tolerate her uncertainty and embrace her curiosity as she began to trust her emergent relational sexuality.

I wondered if Roisin had told anyone else and discovered that she had confided in her best friend, who had betrayed her trust by telling other peers, which resulted in the entire year group knowing. This was humiliating for the adolescent who resented the fact that her sexual orientation was public knowledge. Soon afterwards, she and another student started to date, which ended painfully for her. Subsequently, she found it increasingly difficult to have to attend the same classes as the other girl who did her best to alienate Roisin. My young client creatively adjusted by engaging in self-harming behaviour in response to the distress of having had her sexual orientation exposed in such a dramatic manner, of having to tolerate being rejected by her 'first love' and of having to endure ongoing contact with her in school. As we attended to the shame she had experienced, Roisin felt more assured. The peer landscape became less hostile for her, as she found her place again. In time Roisin defined herself as lesbian, initially questioning bisexuality. Having support to trust her emergent experience minimised Roisin's anxiety regarding this process and after several further sessions, she chose to tell her parents. The adolescent felt empowered and my task was then to create optimum lifespace support for her experience, which included offering support to her parents, who quickly became accepting of her sexual orientation.

Amy

Seventeen-year-old Niall was referred to therapy by his parents because he seemed depressed. He arrived at the initial meeting dressed completely in black, wearing eyeliner and mascara. Niall sat passively at the beginning of the conversation, though became increasingly engaged as he sensed support and the absence of a pathologising culture in our contact. His parents described a vibrant, creative child who had become progressively subdued and withdrawn throughout his adolescent years. We spoke about many aspects of the family lifespace, focusing especially on life through Niall's lens, and it was obvious that these parents loved their son very much. His mother expressed a sense that her son was struggling with sexuality issues, recalling his declaration to her, when he was thirteen years of age, that he was bisexual. Curious about how this interaction unfolded, I learned that Niall's mother responded to this disclosure with silence and a hope that it was merely a 'phase' he was going through. I invited the adolescent to speak, if he wished, at this point. Niall articulated that he was not bisexual but was transgendered.

Each family member, and especially Niall, required support at this point in our dialogue. I welcomed his courage and honesty, affirming the risk he had just taken and offering my hunch that he was possibly feeling a mixture of relief and trepidation having just expressed such an important aspect of his experience. The adolescent was surprised that he had said what he did and spoke of feeling fearful that his parents would dismiss his gender experience. As each parent spoke, neither was entirely shocked at the revelation, nor were they accepting of it. His mother felt that her son was merely confused; his father avoided responding directly, instead he spoke of the urgent need to get his son 'back on track' and wondered how long the therapy might take. I acknowledged to all present how the parents were likely feeling overwhelmed and at a loss as to know how to respond and how to support their son. I suggested that I would like to meet next with Niall himself and that it would be useful to meet with both parents together also, as I was mindful that his parents' support would be an immense gift to this adolescent.

In situations where sexual orientation or gender experience are central for the adolescent, intervening with parents, where possible and appropriate, to support their acceptance of these aspects of their child's identity can be significant. Supportive parents make all the difference in the world for the transgendered adolescent whose experience of harassment and discrimination in his wider lifespace may be commonplace. And so I supported Niall's parents, without their son present, to express their scepticism and sadness as they hoped this was all simply a passing phase and that he was being influenced by friends or some social media phenomenon. I informed his parents that I would support Niall to explore his experience of gender identity, together with all aspects of his lifespace identity, and that if he felt clear that he was transgendered, then it would be important for his parents to be supportive, as the road ahead may be much more difficult and isolating for him without their validation. Over time, his parents were afforded space to grieve the son they loved, experiencing the loss of Niall as akin to a death, and accepting the newly emerging identity which fitted with his self-experience. We addressed their embarrassment about this sensational news filtering throughout their community and wider family circle; their grave concern for the backlash Niall and they might receive; the threat to belonging which their son might now experience within his family, his home town, his school and wider society; and their sense of powerlessness at being unable to protect him from potential vulnerability and harm, as a cost of giving expression to his gender experience. Throughout regular parental sessions, his parents gradually adjusted their focus and moved from a posture of shame to one of support for Niall, who had now begun to identify and express herself as Amy. This was at times a painful and challenging journey for the parents who had no frame of reference for this aspect of their parenting or family lifespace. Their developmental task, as parents, was much like Amy's – integration of her gender identity and expression into an overall lifespace experience. Parents whose relationship to gender expression is either non-receptive or hostile, create an additional layer of rejection and isolation for the adolescent whose journey is already likely to be fraught with shame and bias.

During one-to-one work with Niall, we tracked the evolution of his gender identity from a felt sense throughout childhood, to a pervasive experience of body dysphoria during puberty which coincided with pervasive bullying and humiliation by some peers (both of which he creatively adjusted to through self-harm, anxiety and suicidal feelings at times), towards a burgeoning need to name, make meaning of and give expression to his experience. Treating the adolescent's gender experience with integrity includes inviting the adolescent to direct the languaging of his gender experience so that validating pronouns form part of the therapeutic dialogue. Niall was *certain* with regards to his experience of being transgendered and so, early in the therapeutic work, we established comfortable identity markers for the adolescent, including my addressing Niall now as Amy. This mirroring and support for his phenomenology of gender is immensely validating for the adolescent who is *certain*, as he can begin to experiment with a relational experience of his gender expression. The therapist ought to be mindful that it is prudent to stall on support for any aspect of transitioning until a grounded and embodied certainty emerges for the adolescent. In many cases, this is present prior to the commencement of therapy.

The therapist supports the adolescent's expression of desire for social and medical transition, engaging with parents, where appropriate, to create optimum lifespace support and empowerment for the transgendered adolescent. And so, as Amy explored the possibility of gender transitioning interventions, supported by her parents, she accessed medical support, resenting the need to be labelled as 'disordered' to do so. Social transition has been more difficult as she has encountered adversity from some people. However, validation of her gender identity and support for its expression has been rich within her expanding lifespace and has largely counteracted the shame she has met. Therapeutic work with Amy is ongoing as she and her parents continue to integrate her gender integrity into an overall experience of lifespace integrity.

For each young person, the therapist creates support for *safe* integration of sexual orientation and gender integrity within wider lifespace experience, ensuring that the adolescent's experience does not become fixated at the level of identification as lesbian, gay, bisexual, asexual or transgendered, but is part of the young person's overall lifespace identity. Her role is to support each adolescent to fully and unashamedly embrace and express with integrity his experience of sexuality, orientation and gender. Nevertheless, I have met a considerable number of adolescent clients who have experienced homophobic and transphobic prejudice with previous therapists, many being told that 'it's just a phase that many teenagers go through'. *Please do not work with adolescent clients if you discriminate on the basis of sexual orientation and gender as this does untold harm both to the adolescent and to the profession of psychotherapy.*

References

Damour, L. (2017). *Untangled*. London: Atlantic Books.
Keogh, T. (2018). *The Internal World of the Juvenile Sex Offender* (2nd ed.). Oxon: Routledge.

Reisner, S., Poteat, T., Keatley, J., Cabral, M., Mothopeng, T., Dunham, E., Holland, C., Max, R. and Baral, S. (2016). Global health burden and needs of transgender populations: A review. *The Lancet*, 388(10042), pp. 412–436.

Saleh, F., Grudzinskas, A. and Judge, A. (2014). *Adolescent Sexual Behavior in the Digital Age*. New York: Oxford University Press.

Singer, A. (2001). Coming out of the shadows: Supporting the development of our gay, lesbian, and bisexual adolescents. In M. McConville and G. Wheeler, ed., *The Heart of Development: Gestalt Approaches to Working with Children, Adolescents and Their Worlds Volume 2: Adolescence*. Cambridge, MA: Gestalt Press, pp. 172–192.

Chapter 11

Sexual trauma

Adolescence is a fascinating and remarkably complex developmental process. Each young person, whether having inhabited a receptive or hostile childhood world, is faced with the challenge of extending beyond this familiar landscape, entering the proverbial forest and returning with the holy grail of being situated in a sufficiently functional and personally meaningful adult lifespace. Throughout adolescence, each unfolding situation holds the potential for lively expansion or shaming constriction of self-experience, depending on the level of support and challenge available to the young person. When sexual trauma forms part of his lifespace experience, life in general, and self-experience in particular, can feel like a bewildering and disappointing morass.

Every sexually traumatised adolescent who presents for therapy emerges from a unique lifespace, which is a coalescence of all aspects of his experience of being in the world up to this point. Each adolescent will have a uniquely individual experience of both having been sexually violated and its legacy within the lifespace. It is reasonable to assume, therefore, that whilst there will be many common features and themes, there are likely to be many more distinctly nuanced differences. In supporting the adolescent who reveals that he has been sexually traumatised, the therapist must bear in mind the circumstances and nature of the sexual boundary violation itself, as well as the wider context and implications of this trauma-within the adolescent's lifespace, as these elements of his experience will influence the developmental and therapeutic process. For example, Mary and Jane are 15-year-olds who have both recently disclosed sexual abuse to the therapist following a suicide attempt. Mary is growing up in a loving, supportive family, has a group of good friends and is fairly self-assured. She recently attended a house party and hooked up with an 18-year-old boy. They went off to one of the bedrooms, where he forced her to have sex. Mary is devastated and after several months of struggling to contain her distress has begun to self-destruct. Jane's world is darker: her father was an aggressive man. She has vivid memories of him regularly kicking over the kitchen table and tossing everyone's dinner to the floor after stressful days at work. He drank and was prone to being violent with his wife during these episodes. He died in a work-related accident eighteen months ago, and Jane reveals that her father had sexually abused her throughout her childhood.

Both girls are naturally and equally devastated, yet the interpersonal implications of her experience will create an added layer of complexity for Jane as she struggles to come to terms with her ordeal.

Context of the violation

The adolescent may describe the sexual attacker as a stranger who remains watchful for an opportune moment to launch his assault, as in the case of 12-year-old Katie, who went swimming with her friends and was molested by a man whom she did not know. The perpetrator digitally penetrated the adolescent and one of her friends whilst they were in the pool, devastating Katie's integrity as a result. Eminently more common, however, is the account of being sexually abused by someone who is known to the adolescent (Van der Kolk, 2015). Extended family members, peers, neighbours, family friends and other adults within the adolescent's lifespace who are entrusted with responsibility such as teachers, sports coaches and clergy, often portray a benevolent and caring persona which belies a more sadistic, sexually exploitative nature. This charm seduces not only the adolescent but also the adults in his world who tend to view the offender's contact as innocuous, given his observable presentation and status. The sexual predator often capitalises on his power and relational proximity by establishing a grooming process, which has a tranquilising and desensitising effect on the adolescent. His sinister and self-serving modus operandi ensures an aura of quasi-mutuality to facilitate the initiation of sexual contact with the duped and muted child or adolescent (Van Dam, 2013).

The complexity and extent of the traumatic imprint experienced in the case of intrafamilial sexual abuse, where the perpetrator is a parenting adult or sibling, is catastrophic and potentially more common than people care to admit or imagine (Herman, 2000). In these situations, the degree of bewilderment, isolation and lack of safety in the adolescent's world is extensive as he tolerates an ongoing menacing experience of family life whilst creatively adjusting to a shattered integrity.

And of course, sexual trauma for many adolescents involves multiple perpetrators with varying degrees of relational connection within his lifespace over the course of his childhood and adolescence.

The dilemma of disclosure

There are a number of impediments to disclosure, and although some adolescents reveal their trauma, many more do not (McElvaney, 2013). It is highly likely that a therapist will meet numerous adolescents whose creative adjustments are the symptomatic manifestations of this trauma, though who do not disclose sexual abuse for reasons related to shame, safety and exposure.

The most obvious reasons for maintaining secrecy are threat of harm befalling the adolescent, his loved ones, or the perpetrator following disclosure, as well as the fear of not being believed. In situations where the sexual predator is a member of the family field, the adolescent's reluctance to be responsible for family breakdown also ensures that he is intimidated into silence. He knows that if disclosure is believed and taken seriously, this will mean partial or complete family reconfiguration, with all the ensuing dislocation, isolation and insecurity.

The sexually traumatised adolescent has a propensity to bear the shame of having been abused by holding himself accountable (Herman, 1992), particularly if he sees himself as having been a willing participant, and even more so if he experienced any sexual arousal during contact. The adolescent erroneously experiences his silence as collusion, misinterpreting his apparent compliance and any sexual pleasure or advancement on his part as evidence of guilty collaboration rather than as a statement of the sexual predator's artful capacity to exploit and dominate the young person in a skilled grooming process. It is my experience that the degree of quasi-mutuality created is commensurate with the depth of the perpetrator's adroit capacity for manipulative enchantment. His prowess in priming and relationally seducing his victim supports the adolescent to conclude that what happened could not possibly be constituted as sexual abuse. The young person does not yet appreciate that sexualised contact with a minor *cannot ever* be consensual and is *always* an abusive and criminal act, regardless of the young person's quality of involvement.

In addition to shame's stipulation of silence, recent neuroscientific research has substantiated the therapist's clinical experience that traumatic shame renders the adolescent aphasic – with the discovery that trauma directly impacts the Broca's area of the brain – a mechanism which facilitates the expression of one's feelings and thoughts through speech. This aspect of brain functioning is similarly impaired when a person suffers a stroke, causing temporary or permanent damage to speech (Van der Kolk, 2015). Neither the stroke patient nor the sexually violated adolescent is wilfully silent.

Elucidation of the fact that his physiological inertia during the sexual assault is a freeze response also gives meaning to trauma-induced paralysis which he is prone to translate as a statement of willingness as opposed to stupefaction (Herman, 1992). I am reminded of Eimear who, when she was 12 years old, whilst spending a weekend at her aunt's house, was raped by her uncle, who entered her bedroom in the middle of the night. The adolescent subsequently spent years berating herself for not physically resisting or screaming for help, perplexed at her shamefully passive response to the traumatic experience. The adolescent who eventually discloses childhood sexual abuse typically persecutes himself for not having resisted or told someone sooner, and so, the sharing with him of these scientific research findings goes some way to validating his bewildering lack of protest and the aphasic quality of his "secrecy".

Disclosure brings relief and healing to many adolescents who are met with concern and validation from supportive adults. Regretfully, however, the process of disclosure is very often experienced as a parallel trauma for the adolescent who finds the courage to expose the abuse – particularly if the relational status of the perpetrator is family member, close family friend or other trusted and respected citizen. The implications of disclosure for those within the adolescent's lifespace can feel calamitous and so his revelation may be met with strong ambivalence, disbelief and coercion never to mention this outrageous untruth again. In Eimear's case, once she had risked disclosing the sexual assault to her family, she was lambasted by her aunt who described her as an attention-seeking liar. The aunt added that in the unlikely event of the allegations being true, Eimear had always been a flirtatious child and had likely seduced her poor uncle. This further betrayal reinforces the adolescent's already immense shame and isolation.

Hesitancy in exposing the sexual violation may also relate to the thought of professional agency involvement following disclosure, such as social services, police and legal personnel. This process can engender much anxiety and unease in the adolescent whose fantasy often includes immediate removal from the family home and placement in a residential care facility, followed by national media exposure. In the wake of disclosure, the adolescent may experience contact with investigative professionals as extremely respectful and mindful of the adolescent's sensibilities, or as an appalling and shameful interaction. Commonly, the adolescent also reports feeling disconcerted when he is not readily believed by involved agencies, feeling that he is being treated with scepticism. I recall an adolescent once say that he understood the word *alleged* to mean *this boy is making it up*.

Confrontation of the perpetrator following disclosure, whether by the adolescent, family or professional agencies, customarily results in categorical denial (Herman, 2000). In instances where the abuser accepts culpability (sometimes motivated more by the potential of lighter sentencing than genuine remorse), he may protest the absurdity that sexual contact occurred in a spirit of mutuality and willingness, justifying his actions through the downplaying of the violation's impact (Van Dam, 2011).

Finally, given the adult world's reticence with regard to addressing the issue of sexual boundary violation with our young people and consequently denying this as a potential reality in the adolescent's life, it is surprising that so many of them choose to disclose at all.

Developmental impact

The insult of sexual abuse creates violation at the physiological, psychological and interpersonal realms of experience, leaving a traumatic imprint of diminished integrity as its legacy. The compromise of body integrity and affront of relational deception, together with the isolation of aphasic silence which inhibits the potential of healing and support, creates pronounced psychological dissonance within the lifespace. The adolescent is often plagued with a feeling of inadequacy which is experienced at all three levels of integrity. His complex shame is concealed by feeling and behaviour-level creative adjustments as the adolescent typically adopts an impulsive or inhibitive mode of relating within his lifespace. Even if the adolescent holds no conscious cognitive memory of being sexually traumatised, he is imprinted (Van der Kolk, 2015) and will creatively adjust accordingly. In such instances, it is likely that he will be disposed to feeling anxious, given that anxiety is an assumed consequence of distressing aspects of the lifespace being relegated to the shadows (Porges, 2011).

The adolescent becomes artful at hiding his shame, and this leads to creative adjustments which may belie or at other times be an obvious statement of his devastated yearnings for integrity. In the same manner we now accept the perpetrator to just as likely be the sophisticated, educated and well-regarded member of society as a creepy stranger lurking on the street corner, it is erroneous to stereotype the abused adolescent as an impulsive, troublesome and suicidally preoccupied individual. An infinite spectrum of creative adjustments ranging from addiction, promiscuity, eating disorders and self-harm through to academic brilliance, high-achieving perfectionism, popularity and leadership are exhibited by sexually violated adolescents.

For the adolescent whose experience of sexual trauma happens within the context of an otherwise consistently supportive lifespace experience, he has possibly developed sufficient faith in himself and his world to become directionally configured. Sadly, in many instances, he lives his life as a painful statement of broken integrity and experiences the physiological, psychological and interpersonal worlds as dangerous, unpredictable and hostile landscapes. His traumatic arousal and chronically dysregulated affective state mean that he perpetually feels lost, unlovable and loathsome, as the experience of the *self-as-defective* becomes entrenched. His bewilderment at what has happened is translated into a self-directed accountability and hostility, creating a pervasive sense of despair and devastation. For many who have been sexually violated, the path through adolescence is more about survival than development.

Therapeutic intervention

For the adolescent who has suffered sexual violation, whether or not he chooses to disclose, any anxiety about the experience of entering into a relationally intimate encounter with a therapist is hopefully eclipsed by the rich humanity and sense of belonging cultivated within the therapeutic space. How the therapist receives disclosure of sexual violation sets the tenor for the healing work that is to follow. It is important that she compassionately acknowledges both the courage in telling, in addition to communicating the impact of hearing about the young person's ordeal. There is a tremendous healing synergy generated through the experience of having someone, who is not indifferent to his pain (Orange, 2011), bear witness to the adolescent's story. The relational sustenance in knowing that he and his suffering matter to someone is a great antidote to the cruelty and humiliation endured through interpersonal trauma. This trauma-sensitive therapeutic space supports the neutralising of the experience of hostility and devaluation he may have come to expect from interpersonal contact, contributing to the restoration of integrity.

Intervention is focused at the interlacing levels of physiological, psychological and interpersonal integrity compromise. The adolescent typically finds it difficult, if not impossible, to clearly articulate his experience due to the aphasic quality of the trauma, coupled with the presence of considerable shame. He is mortified, not only about what happened, but also cringes at the idea of uttering the words which describe body parts and sexual contact. Despite its challenge, moving out of aphasic silence is a very healing stage in the transcendence of the trauma of sexual abuse (Kepner, 1996).

The therapist gently supports disclosure of detail by first reminding the adolescent that their work is therapeutic, *not investigative*, and that she does not have an agenda of full disclosure of the abuse. The therapist's wish is to support the young person to make meaning of what happened to him in the context of his wider lifespace experience and to review with him any creative adjustments stemming from the trauma which do not have his integrity at heart, if he so wishes. Making clear her intention not to push for disclosure of detail creates safety. In time, through the process of meaning-making, the adolescent is likely to conclude that an important next step for him is to describe precisely what happened. If his decision is not to disclose detail, the therapist does not challenge the adolescent's position and attempt to procure it regardless. *The therapist must always be mindful that this young person was coerced by another to do something he did not want to do through exploitation of their power differential. She must be careful not to support a replaying of the abuse dynamics within the therapeutic space.*

As the adolescent explores and appreciates the legacy of sexual trauma-within his lifespace, the therapist supports this process by reframing the shame of accountability and complicity. As he finds his voice, the need to have someone bear witness to the precise detail of his ordeal emerges and he becomes choiceful about sharing the detail of what happened. These are gruelling moments for the adolescent and active empathy is vital. The neutralising of shame is a slow and complex process, involving expression and validation of the adolescent's phenomenological experience of the abuse and realistic reframing of the sexual violation which clarifies the adolescent's involvement as traumatic exploitation. This also involves attending to any transmarginal despair engendered by his lost possibilities and innocence. In addition, the therapist supports the adolescent to appreciate his feeling and behaviour responses as creative adjustments to the devastation he has experienced, supporting him to transcend rigid and unhelpful contact boundaries and move towards a more directional manner of relating within his lifespace.

Evelyn

Evelyn was 17 years old and had recently disclosed sexual abuse to her friend, resulting in adults discovering the situation and mobilising a multi-agency response. The contact assessment involved both Evelyn and her parents and when I was informed of the sexual trauma, I assured the adolescent that our dialogue would not be exposing for Evelyn.

I expressed my regret both to Evelyn and to her parents that she had endured such trauma and sensed the adolescent's ambivalence in this micro-episode of contact. I supported the parents to express something of their sadness and anger that a family friend had abused his position of trust and devastated their daughter's life, quickly shifting the focus onto wider family-field dynamics as I was conscious that Evelyn might find this focus both exposing and overwhelming in the opening moments of our contact. I shaped the dialogue towards other lifespace dynamics: I was curious as to how her parents experienced Evelyn throughout her childhood and prior to the sexual trauma, whether they sensed something was troubling their daughter during the two years of her sexual abuse, and I invited them to reflect on the parenting spaces. Her father admitted that he drinks heavily at times, her mother presented as a passive woman and family life was generally described as chaotic.

In one-to-one dialogue during subsequent sessions, Evelyn described how she found information online which defined what had happened to her as 'sexual abuse'. Prior to reading the information, she had thought of her experience as 'having had an affair with a married man' as their contact appeared fully mutual and consensual to her, despite having felt very shamed and sometimes suicidal in the aftermath. Evelyn expressed the typical confusion associated with the grooming process – bewildered and shamed by her apparently compliant participation, and at the same time, perplexed by the devastation she had felt. The desensitising nature of the sexual predator's persuasive contact inhibited the adolescent's capacity to feel concern, seek support or have a voice. Over time, the stupefying effect of the grooming process gave way to a grim reality of feeling physiologically, psychologically and interpersonally violated. Validation of this experience of having been traumatised is difficult until the adolescent begins to fully appreciate the grooming dynamics which she has been subject to. Evelyn revealed that the sexual trauma took place from approximately ages 12 to 14 years. The perpetrator was in his early 40s at the time. Soon the adolescent began to appreciate that this was far from an affair, rather it was an artfully manipulated traumatic exploitation.

Our primary focus was to contextualise the sexual trauma-within her wider lifespace and attend to shame dynamics. The therapeutic space became a safe, trusting space in which Evelyn began to make meaning of her experience. Over time, she identified the need to describe what happened within the two years that she was sexually abused by this family friend. She became more and more conscious that keeping the details secretive was burdensome and inhibitive for her.

As Evelyn detailed a typical grooming process, she reflected on her susceptibility to the perpetrator's attentive and supportive nature, identifying this as the quality of contact she yearned for within parenting spaces. She felt heard, understood, treated like a grown-up and loved by this man, and became upset that lack of receptivity within parenting spaces rendered her vulnerable to exploitation of this nature. The adolescent gradually and painfully tracked the evolution of contact with the perpetrator from apparently innocuous and fun-filled rapport, towards a subtle blurring of physical boundaries, moving to progressively sexualised contact and culminating in penetrative sex. Evelyn remembered feeling out of her depth in the transition to sexual contact, both repelled and mesmerised by what was happening.

The adolescent described several poignant incidences which occurred during this time. She recalled visiting this family friend's house to play with his young children. The man was drunk at the time and repeatedly requested her to kiss him. The adolescent felt torn between wanting to and not wanting to; she had never kissed anyone before. As Evelyn was leaving the house she kissed him briefly, feeling that she somehow could not leave without fulfilling his request, although there was no overt coercion. The adolescent described how, after leaving the house and walking home, she felt 'very grown up'. Sexual contact grew more intense until one evening she was babysitting for this man and his wife. The perpetrator arrived home early and kissed Evelyn, directing her to follow him into the bathroom where he partially undressed and sat on the side of the bath. The adolescent was frightened when she was asked to remove clothing and straddle this man, though she felt she had no alternative. Evelyn described experiencing a more sinister edge to the man's contact for the first time and of feeling choiceless and isolated. She tearfully recounted the physical pain she experienced, her traumatic realisation that she had just lost her virginity and the degradation she felt at being told to "clean herself up, get dressed and go on home". The adolescent received an additional £10 for her babysitting that evening and walked home "feeling like a prostitute". She described a veil of numbness which enveloped her by the time she had walked the short distance home where she behaved with her parents as if nothing had happened, got into bed and tried not to think about what had just happened. Evelyn spoke of her sadness that this apparently benevolent man had such a calamitous agenda for her and began to acknowledge the extent of its imprint within her lifespace. As the adolescent voiced her memories, we reframed her experience so that any accountability she held was repositioned firmly with the sexual predator.

Evelyn described herself as having become an increasingly melancholy teenager who began self-harming, smoking and getting drunk. She thought at one point that she might be pregnant and, having heard that it was possible to perform an abortion by inserting a knitting needle into one's vagina whilst having a very hot bath, she tried this. During our work together, the adolescent felt profound grief and compassion for the lonely and bewildered image of herself in the bath. The abuse finally ended when the offender directed the adolescent to lie about going on a school trip and arranged to spend the day with her. It was discovered that the adolescent had skipped the event, lying to both her parents and the school. Evelyn was suspended for several days and, when confronted, said she had gone to the next town for the day. However, Evelyn felt so disappointed about getting into trouble, missing the trip and lying to her friends that she resolved to refuse any further advances, avoiding one-to-one contact with the man. Whilst she felt relieved that the sexual abuse had stopped, the adolescent felt increasingly angry and disgusted at what had happened, with condemnation apportioned to both the perpetrator and herself in equal measure. For the next few years, Evelyn struggled with impulsivity and made regular suicide attempts until she found the courage to confide in her friend. As the adolescent developed an appreciation of the context of sexual contact and understood the dynamics of grooming, she came to realise that the perpetrator's agenda was violation – initially of her relational and psychological integrity in order to abuse her body integrity. Over time, Evelyn's depth of shame diminished so that she felt mostly liberated from the trauma. Integrity was repaired and expanded.

Maria

Maria attended several psychotherapy sessions with me when she was aged 14, having been identified as depressed by her school principal. I met with the adolescent and both parents for the contact assessment and experienced an apparently cooperative, though frozen quality to our relatedness, which I understood as an indication of the presence of secrets. Everyone, including Maria herself, was bewildered as to the possible cause of the pervasive sadness and withdrawal she experienced. The adolescent was popular and smart, though she could not understand why people liked her and derived no satisfaction from academic success, recounting how she hated her life and could not remember ever enjoying anything, including birthdays and Christmas. Maria presented with an inhibitive configuration style: restrictive, rigid and high-achieving in her relationship to most aspects of her lifespace and perpetually finding herself lacking. Her mother expressed passive concern. Her father portrayed a bright and positive outlook, putting this low feeling down to his daughter simply being a teenager and was not particularly worried. After three appointments, I received a phone call from Maria's mother to say that her exams were approaching, and they had all decided that she needed to focus on her study and would not be attending further sessions.

Maria decided to re-engage in therapy with me aged 23, having recently graduated from college. She was now living and working in a nearby city and was struggling with anxiety and vivid nightmares. As we explored her lifespace, distance from her family afforded the adolescent greater space to make meaning of her experience within the family field, describing a fraught and loveless parental relationship which created ongoing tension within the home and which she felt implicitly forbidden to discuss with me some years earlier. Maria had two older brothers, with a gap of almost a decade between her and her nearest sibling; she was described within her family as 'the wee mistake'. Her father was alcoholic – a weekend binger. Drinking episodes inevitably created upheaval, with the associated family drama, including late night rows, crashed cars and financial debt. When sober, he was often pleasant and generous within the family, though the absence of sincerity and authenticity in his contact meant that his gestures never quite reached his children. Both lack of unwillingness to acknowledge the impact of his drinking on family life and lack of commitment to getting sober, coupled with the familiar silent hysterical despair which children of alcoholic parents often learn to live with, created the familiar gradual emergence of contempt. Their mother, a passive woman, who had almost no sense of herself and certainly no voice in the world, was subtly and artfully controlled by her husband. As a child and young adolescent, Maria begged her to leave at times, even offering to pack the suitcases herself.

Maria spoke of hating her father all through her childhood and the relief she felt that she lived her life essentially in avoidance of any contact with him now. As this exploration advanced, the adolescent described feeling both relieved and anxious at reflecting on family process. We also worked with her dreams which had a terrifying and oppressive quality to them. One afternoon Maria arrived at the session clearly unwell. We discussed her lack of willingness to cancel the appointment which prompted a dialogue about how unsafe she felt as a child if she was forced to miss school due to illness. I was curious about the unsafety aspect and the adolescent described how she would be alone for the day with her father, who farmed at home. Maria appeared agitated and I offered my hunch that she may be feeling exposed following this statement. The adolescent expressed ambivalent feelings of relief and disquiet at trusting me.

During the following session, Maria disclosed that her father sexually abused her throughout her childhood and adolescence until around the time she first attended psychotherapy with me. He molested her in her bedroom and in his van whenever he had the opportunity, sometimes forcing her to drink a foul-tasting concoction which made her sleepy. If she refused, he would force the liquid into her mouth and rub her throat to stimulate swallowing, in the same way Maria watched him do with lambs that required medication.

Frequently during subsequent sessions, the adolescent recounted memories of the trauma. She recalled lying in bed each night with bedclothes wrapped tightly around her, fearing that her father would enter her bedroom. On the nights that he did, her father pulled the bedclothes off Maria, removed her clothing, tethered both her wrists and one ankle with the cord of her dressing gown and raped her. She dissociated as much as possible during these sexual assaults, floating to the ceiling and looking on as if she was watching this happen to someone else; or she would revise academic work in her head. Maria added that the worst aspects of the abuse throughout the years were never knowing when it would happen next and the shame she felt at having to wipe her father's semen off her body. Her father, an active member of the local Catholic parish, had threatened to kill himself if she told anyone and assured Maria that it would be all her fault and she would burn in the fires of hell for eternity, adding that God was already mad at her for making him do these things to his daughter.

One afternoon while she was off school through illness a neighbour came into the house and, realising she was home alone, raped Maria. This incident led her to the realisation that 'bad people did these things' and she determined that her father must be 'bad'. The next time he entered her bedroom, she fought back and ran out of the room, threatening to tell. He never touched her again. Maria became depressed and withdrawn following these occurrences which resulted in her referral to psychotherapy with me several months later when she was 14 years old. Maria confided that whilst she desperately yearned to tell me, she was too terrified to disclose the sexual trauma during our initial episode of therapeutic contact as she still feared her father would kill himself or harm her. Following disclosure to me and the subsequent reporting to the relevant authorities (*see* Chapter 13 *for detailed discussion*), Maria's father categorically denied the allegations. Her mother adopted the passive and wholly absurd stance of believing them both, which further distressed the adolescent who felt it necessary to disconnect entirely from her family.

Psychotherapeutic work with Maria involved supporting her to de-shame and make meaning of multiple dimensions of her experience including coming to terms with having been sexually traumatised, tolerating the investigative and legal processes, and reframing hostile parenting spaces. Below is an image she created (Figure 11.1) and some of Maria's journal excerpts:

> *Something inside hurts really badly but I can't soothe it. I look to others to make it go away – but no one can make it leave. It's a pain that I have to live with. When I accept that it's there and realise it will neither go away nor kill me I can begin to focus on other things. . . . There are days when it is all I think about but on other days now I can let it go. Thoughts feel unmanageable at times and painful to think in the first place. Sometimes my thoughts take on a life of their own – I feel almost separate from them but they are*

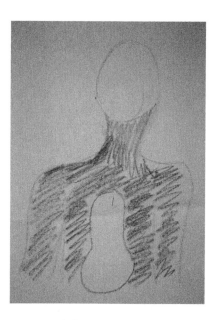

Figure 11.1 "I have a space inside."

so real and so strong that I feel like I'm living in a nightmare. I cannot control these thoughts; I can't silence them and they really affect life. These are physical thoughts too. My body remembers things my head has managed to hide. Sometimes my body just has a bad day. Sometimes the memories are so horrible I wish I could stop them – physically on days like these banging my head off a wall seems like a good idea.

I'm neither male nor female; I don't have a gender or sexuality. I don't exist below the waist. I'm essentially pointless and dead. I don't feel much anymore. I don't fit with the category of 'female' because I don't fit the definition in my mind – I'm not very feminine. At the same time I'm not masculine. It's like I'm stuck at an age before puberty and adolescence . . . like I'm a child walking around in an adult world and that is scary because I spent too much time in a bad part of the adult world when I was a child. I have a space inside – it's empty because someone got inside and damaged it. I don't have a face because I don't really know who I am – other people have eroded that.

I was the person my dad needed me to be, I protected him and kept his secret – even though it's not what I wanted, I was afraid of him, I believed what he said to me, I thought I deserved to be treated the way he treated me. I thought I was bad and that I had brought it about myself. I was pretty disgusted with myself. I did my best to isolate myself because I really couldn't take any more pain and in my mind everyone was causing me pain. Had I not met you I know I would have continued to get quieter and quieter and would have eventually ended my life.

As Maria reflected on her lifespace experience, she appreciated her inhibitive proclivity and creative adjustments as attempts to both counterbalance and distract from the trauma. Gradually, and with a great deal of support, Maria recognised that she was not at fault. This vindication liberated her from entrenched shame, and in time, the adolescent's lifespace was no longer defined by the trauma and loss she had endured. Maria developed sufficient faith in herself to feel that she deserved to live with integrity which supported her to tentatively expand her lifespace and begin becoming choiceful and directional. Today she has a life worth living.

References

Herman, J. (1992). *Trauma and Recovery*. New York: Basic Books.

Herman, J. (2000). *Father-Daughter Incest* (2nd ed.). Cambridge, MA: Harvard University Press.

Kepner, J. (1996). *Healing Tasks: Psychotherapy with Adult Survivors of Childhood Abuse*. NJ: The Analytic Press.

McElvaney, R. (2013). Disclosure of child sexual abuse: Delays, non-disclosure and partial disclosure. What the research tells us and implications for practice. *Child Abuse Review*, 24(3), pp. 159–169.

Orange, D. (2011). *The Suffering Stranger*. New York: Routledge/Taylor & Francis Group.
Porges, S. (2011). *The Polyvagal Theory*. New York: W. W. Norton Company, Inc.
Van Dam, C. (2011). *Identifying Child Molesters* (2nd ed.). New York: Routledge.
Van Dam, C. (2013). *The Socially Skilled Child Molester* (2nd ed.). New York: Routledge.
Van der Kolk, B. (2015). *The Body Keeps the Score*. New York: Penguin Books.

Chapter 12

The diagnosed adolescent

Many adolescents who are referred for psychotherapy have been previously labelled with a neurodevelopmental disorder such as autism or ADHD, or with a psychiatric disorder such as schizophrenia, bipolar disorder or borderline personality disorder. A compromised capacity for contact is the fundamental essence of each of these presentations (Francesetti, Gecele and Roubal, 2013). The adolescent commonly feels either overwhelmed or underwhelmed at the sensory, psychological and relational levels of experience, and as aspects of his lifespace become more amplified or tapered than those of his more typical counterparts, this creates intensity in the modulation of his experience. His sensibility to physiological, psychological and interpersonal stimuli manifests in impaired contact process.

Diagnosis follows analysis of the adolescent's psychological presentation and expressive behaviour patterns. For example, he may be dangerously impulsive, display extreme mood reactivity, be prone to paranoia and dissociation, experience pronounced anxiety, feel depressed, or make repeated attempts to end his life. The diagnosing professional identifies the label based on the number and extent of presenting symptoms which fit within a specific diagnostic category. Medication may be prescribed, in the hope that it will inhibit certain symptoms (American Psychiatric Association, 2013).

Enduring lifespace limitation

Clinical diagnosis may create relief and understanding for some, though it also runs the risk of further isolating and pathologising the adolescent. Diagnosis has implications for the adolescent's self-experience. Regrettably, it can often imply enduring lifespace limitation, engendering a sense of powerlessness and resignation, almost as if he has been handed a life sentence. Some are prone to identify closely with the diagnosis, which in many cases continues into adulthood as a significant identity marker. A diagnostic label can also shape how others around him think about and interact with him, including parenting adults and wider family members, educators, peers and professionals. Frequently the adolescent describes an experience of interpersonal contact in which he is consistently found to be lacking, and which validates his experience of the *self-as-defective*. The diagnosis may become a rigidly held, defining aspect of his identity, which is tremendously debilitating to the developing adolescent. De-shaming and supporting the adolescent to step into greater ownership of his experience are important therapeutic considerations to ensure that the central definition of his lifespace is not some diagnosis or other.

Whilst genetic and biological factors may be causative (Charney et al., 2013), for the adolescent who has received a diagnosis of neurodevelopmental or psychiatric disorder, the presence of significant physiological, psychological and/or interpersonal stress somewhere from the wombspace onwards is very often revealed during the assessment stage of psychotherapy. It would appear that the impact of this transmarginal stress is such that the capacity to mitigate this extreme pressure and restore equilibrium is impaired, thus creating an unstable lifespace experience. The imprint of this traumatic stress and its manifestation as symptoms of a diagnosable disorder may be, to some extent, immutable; however, there is an immense difference between *living with* and *being defined by* a diagnosis. Enduring lifespace limitation need not be an inevitability.

Expectation and sensibility

An experience of ongoing therapeutic intervention throughout adolescence may be sought for the young person, however it is more likely that a presenting symptom issue such as the adolescent's oppositional, risky or unmotivated behaviour, or his experience of, say, anxiety or an eating disorder is the reason for referral. The diagnosis is named as a context, and very often these creative adjustments are in response to and an expected outgrowth of his anomalous modes of contact. Increasingly rich lifespace contact is the goal of adolescent psychotherapy, however, therapeutic expectation can be high, with parents and adolescents hoping for psychological miracles that are not always possible. It is not unusual for referral to come with expectation not only to quickly solve the problem of maladaptive behaviour, but to entirely eradicate the diagnosis. Therefore, at the outset of the work, it is prudent to establish realistic parameters with regard to the focus, limitations and ongoing need for therapy. The therapist who works to ameliorate symptoms without addressing the wider dynamics of the adolescent's lifespace structure can expect to experience frustration and pressure.

Oftentimes, therapy cannot erase the symptoms upon which the diagnosis was based, yet ongoing therapeutic intervention throughout adolescence can still offer valuable phenomenological support to the young person even if there is minimal observable difference in his presentation. For example, an adolescent who has been diagnosed with high functioning autism may still display all of the characteristics that he did on first engaging in therapy. At first glance, one may conclude that psychotherapy has been ineffective. Yet, he may have developed a capacity to understand and appreciate his experience in a non-shaming manner, his anxiety may be less pronounced and his lifespace may be extended in ways which have created for him a less isolating and more meaningful existence. He remains autistic *and* has a life worth living. On the other hand, in cases where therapeutic intervention attends to the imprint of distress that is shaping the adolescent's contact functions, there are times when symptoms vanish and the diagnosis is rendered redundant.

On meeting her client, the therapist may clearly see symptomatic evidence of the diagnosis. Conversely, she may suspect misdiagnosis, knowing that traumatic experience and developmental process may be mistaken for and diagnosed as psychopathology (Van der Kolk, 2015) in adolescence. Yet again, she may meet an adolescent whose presentation warrants diagnosis and may initiate a referral process. The presence of a diagnosis may be useful to the therapist with regards to the formulation of a broad therapeutic plan and, in some cases, the likely prognosis for the adolescent. However, she must remain attuned, first and foremost, to the young person's humanity and phenomenology, and not see him principally through the lens of a diagnosis, for in doing so, she will most certainly compromise the adolescent and the therapeutic space.

Attunement to the adolescent's phenomenology supports him to develop an empowered relationship to the diagnosis, exploring the meaning of its presence within his lifespace and how it shapes contact. Therapy offers a nurturing and affirming experience for the adolescent where he is supported to become optimally directional and where his emerging sense of self is depathologised. It is likely that the therapist will also be required to attend to case management matters during the course of therapy with an adolescent who has received a diagnosis *(see* Chapter 13 *for detailed discussion)*.

Aisling

For 14-year-old Aisling, much of her life created great distress. She was the eldest of three children, and hers was an unplanned pregnancy for her parents. Aisling understood, erroneously, that she was not wanted (mistaking unplanned for unwanted is a common misperception for adolescents) and that it would have been better for everyone if she had never been born. Her mother developed ulcerative colitis during the pregnancy, and Aisling endured a torturous birth, with a 24-hour labour, ingestion of opioid pain medication and vacuum extraction. Throughout her childhood and early adolescence, Aisling struggled with sensory, psychological and interpersonal aspects of her experience. She had been diagnosed with high-functioning autism six months prior to commencing therapy, which was sought due to ongoing school refusal issues. At school, the adolescent was top of her class in most subjects, though anxiety and peer isolation made it difficult for her to attend.

Aisling found sanctuary in screen time, fascinated by computer games and anime, a style of Japanese animation ("Anime", 2018). She spent most of her time in her bedroom, including mealtimes, eating alone as she could not tolerate the sound of family members chewing their food. Sleep disturbance meant that she was often using her laptop in the middle of the night, which suited as she could interact with other adolescent anime fans from various time zones around the world. For the past two years, Aisling had a best friend in whom she confided much of her experience and who had been diagnosed with autism since childhood. This friend lived in the United States and they communicated every day via audio, though never visually as this felt too intense for them both. Face-to-face encounters were arduous for the adolescent unless she was attending a comic book convention, dressed in her favourite anime character, where she felt a confidence and connection as she related to others. As we explored her interests, Aisling acknowledged that she found the intensity of human contact overwhelming, favouring indirect contact, via screens or dressed as an anime character. She felt ill-equipped and flummoxed in direct contact with others, including herself. Aisling described herself as *more humanoid than human*, preferring 'humanoid people' – such as anime characters, online acquaintances and those whom she met at conventions.

The adolescent was supported through a multi-disciplinary approach, including occupational therapy. Intervention was supplemented with medication. It was important that Aisling would neither experience therapy as a pathologising nor intensely human experience. It was evident that she was already living with tremendous pressure, so the therapeutic space must not increase this pressure. Initially the focus was on acknowledgement of the adolescent's phenomenology of life during childhood and early adolescence as well as her experience of the diagnostic process. Sideways contact was always at the heart of the unfolding of any therapeutic dialogue, lest our contact become overwhelming for the adolescent. Aisling sketched and painted, and I sculpted aspects of her lifespace with three-dimensional figures, as we sat across from each other at the art table. This triangulation of contact facilitated ever richer moments of joining.

Gradually the dilemma of living in a manner as to avoid intensity of direct contact (which meant confining herself to her bedroom and cyberspace) and wanting to be an actor (which meant completing her education and negotiating the interpersonal world) emerged more poignantly for Aisling. The art was to amplify this dilemma in such a manner as to avoid power struggling or creating pressure, by sensitively highlighting discrepancies between her aspirations and how she was presently living her life. Once Aisling became determined not to become a victim of the diagnosis, her tenacity emerged, and she became increasingly motivated to improve her executive functioning, attend school with the help of a classroom assistant, complete homework and take ownership of personal hygiene matters. The adolescent found a rationale for decreasing her screen time, appreciating that it ultimately exacerbated her difficulties. Acknowledging her wish to belong within the peer landscape, she also became curious about how to interact with others socially, acquiring some basic relational cues and learning ways to manage her overwhelm. The pain of peer isolation has been the most difficult aspect of living with autism for Aisling and is an ongoing struggle for her. The adolescent continues to attend therapy, and three years later is continuing to bridge the chasm between her desire to live life on her terms, which means avoidance of direct contact to create optimum comfort, and honouring her yearning to live a rich and personally meaningful life, necessitating lifespace expansion. She describes herself as journeying 'from the humanoid to the human realm'.

Rosie

I first met Rosie when she was 5 years old, soon after she was diagnosed with autism and dyspraxia. Sleep had been a challenge from birth and she had difficulty processing sensory information, with a notable intolerance to touch. She had never spoken a word in her five years and appeared disinterested in interpersonal engagement, with the exception of her mother. Since starting school, she had been having outbursts most mornings and evenings before and after school. These outbursts included screaming, banging her head, biting, punching and kicking out at herself and her mother, to whom she was very attached. When she was in the classroom situation, she presented as timid, preferring to work and play alone.

The child endured violence in the wombspace from her father when he was drunk, who was also verbally abusive and psychologically controlling of Rosie's mother throughout the pregnancy. Following a relatively uncomplicated birth process, Rosie's mother described how her daughter fed constantly and was attached to the breast almost continually. Her mother recounted incidents of physical aggression, which included her being punched in the face whilst breastfeeding Rosie. The father was also inclined to be rough and threatening with his daughter. During the first two years of the child's life, neither mother nor daughter, who lay in the same bed, slept much at night. They 'clung on to each other' petrified. Violence continued within the parental relationship until separation when Rosie was two years old. One particular evening, her mother locked Rosie in the car to keep her safe from her drunk and violent father. The child's mother was beaten outside the car, sustaining a broken arm, as the child looked on in terror. Following this incident, Rosie's mother sought support and ended the relationship.

By the end of the third session of therapy, Rosie had begun to speak. Features of her play inevitably included a 'bad man' attempting to hurt her and her mother, who were desperately trying to flee from the harm. As we processed the trauma, and the world became safer for her, Rosie became more trusting within her lifespace, warming up to people and to her school experience.

Seven years later, in her first year of secondary school, Rosie was referred again for therapy as she was depressed and anxious, becoming increasingly agitated and was self-harming. It was assumed that the transition from primary to secondary school had been stressful for the adolescent. As we reconnected, Rosie disclosed that, when she spent time with her father, as agreed through the courts following separation, he had sexually abused her for several years until she was 6 years old. He had subsequently moved overseas and she had rarely seen him since. Rosie's agitation was, in fact, in response to flashbacks which had begun since she had started menstruating some time before. School refusal was more a statement about being frightened of experiencing flashbacks in unfamiliar surroundings than the anxiety of having to tolerate social exclusion. The adolescent's ambivalence towards her father was strong, and she also felt overlooked by her mother, who had since remarried and had two more children.

Rosie felt that dying would make all her pain go away, such was the integrity compromise and overwhelm she had endured in her young life. As we attended to the complex experience and legacy of being sexual traumatised by her father, Rosie again found safety and expansion within her lifespace. Over time, as healing and trust emerged, the symptoms of the diagnosis abated. For this adolescent, the imprint of trauma resembled autism, the symptoms of which receded with the restoration of integrity. Rosie came to understand her childhood presentation more as an expression of trauma than a specific neurodevelopmental disorder. I still see her from time to time, and at 17 years of age she is living a personally meaningful life and beginning to flourish psychologically and interpersonally.

Dylan

I received a call from Dylan's mother to say that he had been diagnosed with emerging psychosis and had been prescribed medication. Since he was 15, she was reluctant to medicate her son and wanted a second opinion. Dylan's presentation included withdrawal, agitation, erratic and unusual dialogue and behaviour and extreme anxiety. This episode of psychosis had occurred some weeks ago, when he had been overseas on a school trip, away from the familiarity and containment of his typical lifespace experience. Since arriving home, the adolescent had rarely spoken and spent most of the time in his room, rocking back and forth on a chair.

The adolescent's anxiety and agitation meant that a contact assessment would prove too intense for him, so I worked separately with both Dylan and with his parents until such times as he could tolerate joint parental work. He had older twin sisters, with a gap of eight years between himself and his siblings. He was described by his parents as 'our baby', and I was surprised at Dylan's slight physical frame, given the tall and robust physique of both his parents. At 15, Dylan had not yet reached puberty and sang soprano in the local church choir. Making contact with him resembled therapeutic contact with a 10-year-old child initially. Before too long he had settled well and had become interested in himself. After several sessions, we began to tentatively explore his experience on the school trip. Towards the end of this meeting, I left him to finish some artwork while I organised the next appointment with his parents. After they had gone, I returned to the room to find that Dylan had left me a note which read, "*I know I need to talk about what happened but I don't know how. One of the group their parent was told they had cancer. This affected me because the story was so intense. Also I recently found out that my uncle had cancer. This is why I hid in the cupboard*".

During the following session, as space emerged, we talked about the note. The adolescent expressed regret that his uncle was so ill and spoke of his general fear of death. I suggested that it might be useful to involve his parents in the dialogue, as they were still bewildered about their son's presentation and it would benefit them to learn the context of Dylan's distress. In the intervening weeks since therapy had commenced, the adolescent's agitation had faded had he had found his voice to some degree. This was the first time we had all sat together and as we spoke, his parents expressed confusion that Dylan should be so affected by his uncle's condition, as they were not particularly close. Still curious as to the context of the adolescent's distress, I invited them to explore the experience of death in their family and felt a sudden shift, as if terror was in the air. Dylan's mother began to sob and revealed that their first son, also named Dylan, had died aged three weeks as the result of a congenital heart defect. She resolved that the only way she could heal was to 'hold another baby in her arms' and became pregnant as quickly as possible. Some years later, as her daughters had started school and were beginning to grow up, the pain of losing her first child began to re-emerge and she felt it necessary to conceive once more. At this point, Dylan interjected with some aggression, protesting that he hated having been christened the same name as his dead brother.

As the dialogue progressed, it became apparent that, prior to the overseas trip, his parents had been unconsciously invested in Dylan not growing up, because to move out of childhood would mean that the grief of losing 'dead Dylan' (as the adolescent referred to him) would begin to be deeply felt. I learned that Dylan's favourite pastime was sitting on his father's knee, sucking his thumb and watching cartoons which they loved. His mother dropped him off and collected him from school each day, despite them living very near the train station, on which most other students would travel to and from school. She also told him what to wear each day and dissuaded him from spending time with friends. The school trip was Dylan's first experience of life away from the familiarity of his inhibitive lifespace, presenting him with an opportunity to experience himself outside the family for the first time. It would seem that this situation created space for the emergence of the developmental impulse to adolescence, which had been a threat to parental happiness, and had subsequently been repressed for some time. Following some field intervention work which included supporting the parents to grieve the loss of their infant son, I suggested that we meet again in eight weeks to see how the situation had progressed.

When I met Dylan at the door of my office, he had notably grown in height, the beginnings of facial hair were visible, he had started travelling to school by train and had stayed over after school with friends on occasion. His voice had broken, and he had been moved into another vocal section of the choir, which he was considering leaving now as he no longer believed in God. Any evidence of psychosis and anxiety had disappeared as his parents were supported to embrace and move beyond their grief. Dylan's developmental impulse no longer posed a threat to family lifespace integrity and, as a result, began to emerge more and more vividly.

This phenomenon is not uncommon in adolescence, though it resembles and may be mistaken for anxiety or first-episode psychosis. Fortunately, for Dylan, his parents refused the medication and he was not compelled to adopt the label assigned to him.

Michaela

Nineteen-year-old Michaela had been diagnosed with and medicated for depression in early adolescence, losing interest in peer friendships and academics, and finding it difficult to sleep. Over the past two years she had experienced some psychotic episodes and felt paranoid much of the time. The adolescent had been hospitalised twice for several months at a time and had been diagnosed with paranoid schizophrenia. She suspected that her symptoms were triggered by drug use. However, her older brother and two uncles had also been diagnosed with the disorder. Michaela felt broken and debilitated by the anxiety, paranoia and psychotic episodes. She was compelled to withdraw from her college application process and was unable to move out of home, feeling deeply shamed at letting her parents down.

She talked about her experience of psychosis, describing her attendance at a family wedding where she feared terrorists were attacking the guests. She was the Messiah and spent most of the day in her hotel room in talks with the prime minister, who was communicating with her through screens and a newspaper. She recalled feeling very distressed and tearful that she could not stop the unfolding carnage at the wedding reception. During another psychotic episode, Michaela experienced somatic hallucinations where aliens were sexually violating her, causing her to orgasm up to one hundred times a day. The antipsychotic medication prescribed for her left the adolescent feeling tired and heavy, also causing her to gain weight. She struggled to take it on a continual basis as it caused her to stop menstruating and she was convinced that unshed blood was gathering in her stomach and would eventually lead to her death. Michaela also wondered if her doctor, a Protestant, was principally concerned with curbing the Catholic population, and had surreptitiously prescribed the medication to prevent her conceiving.

Since commencing therapy some six years ago, Michaela's paranoia has diminished somewhat. She has experienced several further psychotic episodes. Michaela oscillates between feeling safe with and finding it difficult to trust me. The principal consideration and starting point for each session is the quality of her contact and groundedness. Therapy with the adolescent has included supporting contact boundary development and maintenance of physiological, psychological and interpersonal balance within her lifespace as much as possible. There are times when she flourishes, living life in a manner which respects but does not permit the diagnosis to define her lifespace. At other times Michaela struggles to accept her diagnosis, feeling shamed and restricted, convinced that others are contriving to render her powerless.

Hugh

Sixteen-year-old Hugh, diagnosed with ADHD in childhood and more recently with bipolar disorder, was referred for therapy due to escalating impulsivity and aggressive outbursts, interspersed with depressive episodes, in which he was filled with dread and anxiety. He regularly self-harmed and had begun to experiment heavily with alcohol and drugs. The adolescent felt close to and had great respect for his father, although sensed that he disappointed his dad, who was a placid, hardworking man. Hugh yearned to be a strong, powerful, masculine figure like his father and feared being called a 'wimp'. He placed great emphasis on improving and displaying his physical strength, though wished he could find ways to do this without becoming aggressive. Exploring his anger, the adolescent described entering 'a blind rage' at times and felt out of control in these situations.

Hugh's symptoms certainly matched the criteria for diagnosis of bipolar disorder. However, his adoptive status had neither been considered nor attended to at the time of assessment. As we explored this major aspect of his identity and he integrated the experience into his overall lifespace experience, Hugh found greater balance, evolving into a more directional and choiceful emerging adult. Developmental momentum was established and his proclivity to impulsivity and depression reduced considerably, over time.

Shannon

The youngest of two girls, 17-year-old Shannon attended therapy following a diagnosis of borderline personality disorder. She had lived with suicidal ideation since 11 years of age and had experienced pervasive self-loathing. The adolescent was also convinced that others judged and ridiculed her, and felt bewildered when people wanted to be her friend. Mood swings had escalated since she began drinking excessively and both she and her parents feared how she would manage a fast-approaching college life, without the structure and relative containment that had been afforded her to date. Hypersensitivity and intensity defined her relationships with family members, such that she felt small, needy and vulnerable at times, wholly dependent on her loved ones. At other times she felt unwanted and abandoned by her family, whom she was sure despised her. Shannon described *knowing* that she was loved by her family, but not being able to *feel* or *trust* the love.

Shannon's postnatal experience helped shed light on her struggles: Following an arduous birth process, Shannon was placed skin-to-skin on her mother's body. She began breastfeeding, and they spent several hours in direct contact, gazing at and exploring one another. A mild breathing difficulty was identified in the middle of the night, and the child was moved to the neonatal unit within the hospital. Shannon spent three days and nights in an incubator. During this time her mother, who was encouraged to get a full night's sleep each night, visited and breastfed the child at intervals.

We tracked the imagined phenomenology of Shannon's experience of being born, her first few hours in the world and the sudden, prolonged and bewildering separation from her mother's safety, love, holding and familiarity. The adolescent began to appreciate the potential imprint this distressing experience might have had for her as a newborn, despite her having no conscious recollection of this. Shannon described how her present lifespace experience mirrored almost identically her earliest moments in the world: She often sat in her bedroom, listening to her parents and younger sister relate to one another and engage in family life. Shannon described feeling desperately alone during these times, knowing that she could simply go downstairs and join them, but feeling incapable of doing so. She felt it necessary for her mother to come get her, though that rarely happened, and if it did, Shannon would experience herself as both relieved and resistant, spurning her mother's care and affection – loving and resenting her in equal measure.

Shannon began to refer to her bedroom as her 'incubator' and to understand how fears of being unloved and abandoned by others shaped her creative adjustments at the feeling, thought and behaviour levels. The adolescent frequently self-harmed and made repeated suicide attempts to tolerate the pain and isolation she felt in the world. Parallel dialogue was a core intervention in the work with this adolescent, who began to make new and more integrity-rich meaning within her lifespace. Eventually she exited the metaphorical incubator and opened herself to more satisfying interpersonal connection – experiencing her lifespace as receptive and herself as worthy of belonging. Supporting her through the college process and beyond was important to facilitate the development of her configuration style from impulsive towards an increasingly directional way of being. Symptoms associated with borderline personality disorder receded as Shannon gradually stepped into greater ownership of her experience.

Therapeutic perspective

Adolescents are increasingly being diagnosed with and medicated for various neurodevelopmental and psychiatric disorders, which is of great concern (van der Kolk, 2005). (At any given time in my practice, at least one third of the adolescents I meet will have received a diagnosis.) Whilst diagnosis is both useful and even empowering for some, living with a label can be an immense shame for others, perpetuating the myth of the *self-as-defective*.

It is important that the therapist remains mindful of the possibility that developmental contexts may be shaping the adolescent's presentation. Her starting point is *always* the conceptualisation of creative adjustments in non-pathological terms. Therapeutic intervention ought not be primarily concerned with symptom management but should support the adolescent to access his humanity beyond the diagnosis, so that his lifespace does not become defined by a label. In those situations where diagnosis has been made, it may also be necessary that the therapist communicates with other professionals if she is part of a multi-disciplinary response.

It is my strong conviction that many diagnoses are reversible, with sufficient support for the adolescent. However, this requires ongoing commitment from the young person, which is neither always a therapeutic nor organisational possibility. It may take several years of therapeutic intervention for the adolescent to grow into a more directional way of being. Sadly, this is a 'luxury' many are not afforded.

Even with a lasting diagnosis, it is entirely possible for a person to live with optimal meaning and directionality. However, the reality is that countless adolescents needlessly live medicated lives, enduring lifespace limitations due to a diagnosis received. We can do better than this.

References

American Psychiatric Association. (2013). *Diagnostic and Statistical Manual of Mental Disorders* (5th ed.). Arlington, VA: American Psychiatric Association.

Anime. (2018). *En.wikipedia.org*. Available at: https://en.wikipedia.org/wiki/Anime [Accessed 28 Apr. 2018].

Charney, D., Sklar, P., Buxbaum, J. and Nestler, E. (2013). *Neurobiology of Mental Illness* (4th ed.). New York: Oxford University Press.

Francesetti, G., Gecele, M. and Roubal, J. (2013). *Gestalt Therapy in Clinical Practice: From Psychopathology to the Aesthetics of Contact*. Milan: Franco Angeli.

Van der Kolk, B. (2005). Developmental Trauma Disorder: Toward a rational diagnosis for children with complex trauma histories. *Psychiatric Annals*, 35(5), 401–408.

Van der Kolk, B. (2015). *The Body Keeps the Score*. New York: Penguin Books.

Chapter 13

Case management

It is the therapist's responsibility to develop proficiency in navigating the various dimensions of case management associated with adolescent psychotherapy. In many instances the work proceeds without complexity: the only people the therapist encounters are parenting adults and the adolescent himself, and note keeping is all that is required. However, in some situations it is necessary to act upon child protection matters, liaise with other professionals, provide written reports and attend court proceedings. Addressing case management issues creates considerable stress and anxiety for many adolescent therapists. However, in my experience, much of this trepidation has to do with lack of training and experience. Consequently, the therapist may be prone to adopting a professionally defensive posture, which is unhelpful to everyone concerned, most especially her adolescent client.

Child protection

Child protection issues may have been identified prior to the commencement of therapy. Similarly, the therapist may initiate child protection procedures if disclosure of abuse or neglect is made, or if she holds reasonable concern that this may be the case (Dept of Children and Youth Affairs, 2017). It is the therapist's responsibility to take action to protect an adolescent, and others who have been or may be at risk of harm or exploitation, by informing the appropriate agencies, such as social services or police. It is incumbent upon the therapist to have comprehensive knowledge of relevant child protection procedures as well as contact details to hand for the related agencies.

If disclosure is made to the therapist it is important to keep a clear record of the reporting process, including names of those professionals with whom she has been in contact and copies of any written submissions, such as reporting forms and professional reports. If the therapist is working within an organisation, she will communicate with designated child protection personnel who will possibly initiate and remain involved throughout the process. It is always advisable to ensure that others within the organisation have followed up on the necessary protocol and have communicated all relevant information to the therapist. She should not take this for granted.

The interprofessional context

If therapeutic work is situated within an interprofessional context, it is both necessary and professionally courteous for the therapist to introduce herself to key
members of any multi-disciplinary team. These may include the psychiatrist, GP
and appointed social worker. Collaborative contact with other professionals may
involve attendance at meetings to establish a coordinated and optimally effective
response to the adolescent's situation. It may be useful to research the remit of
other professionals involved, so that the therapist has some idea as to the role each
plays within the multi-disciplinary forum. It is possible that these will include
social workers, psychiatrists, general practitioners, paediatricians, educational
psychologists, guardians ad litem, police officers, family support workers, school
personnel and representatives from services such as probation or addiction services, among others.

When therapeutic intervention takes place within a wider multi-disciplinary
context, often the therapist is the professional with whom the adolescent has the
closest relationship and whom he trusts most. Accordingly, it is likely that the
therapist holds significant information which may be of benefit to other professionals who are involved in the adolescent's care. Supervision can be helpful in
supporting her to discern how to balance the honouring of her ethical obligations
with protecting the privacy of the therapeutic process from unnecessary intrusion.

The therapist is required to offer any relevant information which arises in relation to the adolescent's welfare, always ensuring that any child protection concerns are communicated clearly and promptly to a duty (general) or designated
(assigned specifically to the case) social worker (Dept of Children and Youth
Affairs, 2017). In all interprofessional contact, it is important that the therapist's
role remains therapeutic and not investigative, as the introduction of such agendas
will compromise the therapeutic space. Once an adolescent discloses details of
abuse or neglect, the therapist must notify social services (and the police service if she considers the client to be at immediate risk of harm) of the details
of disclosure. However, it is not the therapist's task to pursue the adolescent for
further information. It is the responsibility of other professionals, such as social
workers and police officers, to investigate and seek clarification. Instead, she
acknowledges and supports the adolescent's phenomenological experience of
being involved in such a process and continues to attend to the cultivation of trust
and integrity within the therapeutic space. Her position as guardian of therapeutic
space integrity will likely increase the adolescent's psychological readiness, not
only to provide further detail of the trauma, but also to process the experience of
abuse or neglect he has endured.

There may also be times when the adolescent therapist finds herself appealing
for greater involvement from other professionals. Sometimes her concerns do not
reach the threshold for initiation of child protection procedures and she continues
to offer support to a vulnerable adolescent whom she feels is inadequately protected. These situations can be stressful for the therapist whose challenge is to

care without risking burnout. In many instances, when social services and health service professionals are involved and the therapist experiences delays in significant multi-disciplinary process, shortcomings are more likely to be a reflection of overwhelmed and under-resourced systems as opposed to a statement about the competence of well-meaning individuals. Irrespective of how others undertake their professional obligations, the therapist must always maintain a standard of professional excellence, holding the adolescent's wellbeing at the heart of any interprofessional contact and stating her position in a clear, respectful and dispassionate manner.

Report writing

There are times when the therapist may decide, or be requested to provide information in the form of a written report. Circulation of a report can be a useful mode of communicating concerns and relevant therapeutic progress to other professionals. It can also act as an effective catalyst for renewed intervention from other agencies. Reports may be sought for the purposes of psychological assessment and diagnosis, to support the adolescent's experience in school (for example, to verify extenuating circumstances in advance of examinations), or when requested by a solicitor. Reports can also provide a useful alternative in cases where solicitors demand that the therapist forward notes pertaining to the case. In situations where notes are subpoenaed, the therapist should forward her original records.

When considering writing a report, it is important that neither anxiety nor urgency influences the therapist's judgement. Any communication, written or verbal, should be reviewed carefully to ensure that only relevant information is shared. Supervision can be a helpful forum in which to identify an appropriate way forward. Reports should be written on stationery containing a letterhead. The initial section of the report should include practical information such as the client's name, address and date of birth, referral source, presenting symptom issue, number and dates of sessions. The more substantial section of the report will include an outline of the development of therapy, which may be more clearly understood if it is organised around themes which have emerged, as opposed to a blow-by-blow account of each session. It is important that the therapist holds the focus of the report in mind throughout and refrains from using therapeutic jargon, as this will only create confusion for other professionals reading it.

Court work

The thought of appearing in court typically fills the therapist with anxiety and dread, however, it is important that she clarifies for herself the purpose of the case and her role as a witness. The therapist is not being called on to defend her client, but is being asked to give an impartial account of the psychotherapeutic work which has been undertaken in order for dynamics of the case to be further illuminated. Thorough knowledge of the particular therapeutic process, and a capacity to articulate this clearly and succinctly is advisable. Whilst she may be asked her professional opinion about certain points, it is also prudent for the therapist to avoid commenting on matters outside her field of expertise. A dispassionate posture is required for appearance as a professional witness in court. Whilst the therapist may have strong feelings with regard to the case, the outcome of court proceedings are not her business in this moment.

Onward referral

In some situations the therapist may decide to refer a client to another therapist or agency. She may initiate onward referral in cases where the adolescent has received a specific diagnosis which she feels is outside her area of competence, such as referral to a clinic which specialises in eating disorders or the treatment of neurodevelopmental disorders. In these instances, it is appropriate to forward a letter to the adolescent's GP (and psychiatrist if involved) informing them of her recommendation. Referral to other agencies may also happen if the therapist feels unsafe or uncomfortable within the therapeutic setting, for example, when working with a sex offending, violent or actively psychotic adolescent. Here, the therapist communicates her concerns to the relevant professionals, requesting appropriate support and intervention for the adolescent in question. The therapist is not compelled to work in situations where her own integrity may be compromised or when she feels that another supportive context would be more beneficial to the adolescent.

Preserving therapeutic integrity

Comprehensive training in these aspects of case management, which have been only broadly outlined above, is necessary and indispensable – both to enhance the therapist's level of competence and ethical professionalism, and to support the reduction of her anxiety with regard to these features of the work as an adolescent psychotherapist. Failure to do so may result in the therapist being disposed to avoidance or over-reaching as case management issues arise – where breaching her duty of care to the adolescent by failing to act to protect him, or embarking on a crusade marked with urgency are the possible consequences. Moreover, it is important for the therapist not to become so absorbed with case management issues that she loses sight of the therapeutic space. The art is to attend to these matters whilst continuing to foster rich contact with the adolescent. It is very possible to do both.

Terminating the work

With short-term psychotherapy, in which sessions may be limited due to organisational parameters, both therapist and client are aware from the outset that the work will terminate at a given point. This enforced ending may be well-timed or premature, and if it is the latter, onward referral is recommended. Yet again, the adolescent or parenting adults may choose to terminate the work before it reaches a natural conclusion. This may occur if they have little faith in the therapist, when family expectations about the client's progress are not being met or as a result of the drama of parental acrimony. Premature ending may also happen when the adolescent is expressly disinterested in continuing, when the therapist has allowed the therapeutic process to become too intense for him or when the therapist shames her client. These experiences can be a dissatisfying and disempowering, as well as effective, if painful, learning for the therapist. Similarly, the therapist herself may be forced to bring the work to an early conclusion due to her own personal circumstances.

When natural momentum and fluency have been present within the therapeutic process, the frequency of sessions organically lessens as integrity is restored within the adolescent's lifespace and there is evidence of developmental momentum. A mutual decision moves the fortnightly or three-weekly sessions to a more spontaneous arrangement, where the therapist invites the adolescent or his parents to make an appointment when it feels appropriate to do so. At this point, it is important to validate the adolescent's progress and reiterate that whilst he is most welcome to return as soon and as regularly as he wishes, the therapist imagines that he may not need to do this particularly often – and it is likely that she will not see much of him again. This is an important statement, as any residual dependency on the therapist, on the part of the adolescent, will hopefully morph into faith in himself.

As therapy tapers off, the therapist indicates that, should he feel in need of support in the future, she will be there for him. This 'leaving the door open' rather than firm closure of the therapeutic process lessens the intensity of ending for the client. This flexibility also acknowledges both that new situations may emerge in the days ahead for the adolescent which may require her support, and that whilst he has processed and made meaning of lifespace experiences in so far as he is developmentally capable, a growing developmental sophistication may mean that he will feel compelled to revisit aspects of his experience as he moves through adolescence and emerging adulthood. This open invitation to return also ensures an ongoing experience of the therapist's supportive hand at his back, which makes a difference for many on their onward journey through these fascinating years.

Reference

Dept of Children and Youth Affairs. (2017). *Children First National Guidance for the Protection and Welfare of Children.* Dublin: Government Publications.

Index